Praise for *Beneath and Between*

"If you have let the world lock God into a dark box, this is a book for you. If you have let the world lock *you*—your faith, your wonderings, your soaring love—into a dark box, this radiant book is also for you. It will lead you straight to a wild, uncontained God whose lavish love can be found not just *beneath* and *between* but *within*, *among*, *beyond*, and in every other place love can reach. Which is to say, everywhere."

—**Margaret Renkl**, author of *The Comfort of Crows*

"If we accept the ancient recognition that 'God is love,' then relationship (and relationality) is at the heart of divine being. With that in mind, I'm surprised no one has entered the mystery of God through prepositions until now, but what a joy that Varina Buntin Willse has done so. *Beneath and Between* is both broad in its scope and deep in its exploration, and every chapter hums with insight and invitation. Read it and let your soul be nurtured."

—**Carl McColman**, author of *The New Big Book of Christian Mysticism* and *Read the Bible Like a Mystic*

"Where faith might have the tendency to become rote in word and in concept, Varina Buntin Willse offers an enlivening creativity that transforms the most humble slivers of our theological language—prepositions—into vessels of profound, fresh truths. Willse's warm curiosity invites readers to consider how paying careful attention to God's manifestations, whether *within*, *throughout*, or *among* us, leads us to a fuller understanding of God's presence. This work of 'outsider theology' is a blessing to all of us who long to experience a living, breathing, multidimensional God who cannot be contained in a box and who shows up in the most surprising places."

—**Kristin T. Lee**, author of *We Mend with Gold: An Immigrant Daughter's Reckoning with American Christianity*

"In gorgeous prose reminiscent of Annie Dillard, Varina Buntin Willse takes us by the hand and whispers this secret in our ear: *The smallest, humblest words are actually portals to the infinite.* Through reflections, theology, and prayers, Willse invites readers to linger in these portals, where every *beneath*, *before*, and *beyond* is right there waiting to offer an encounter with mystery. *Beneath and Between* is a beautiful and wise book for anyone seeking a view of God that is enveloping, expansive, and electric."

—**Bonnie Smith Whitehouse**, PhD, author of *In Our Hands* and *Seasons of Wonder*

"God talk can be such a loaded, tricky Gordian knot, but with her humble prepositions, Varina Buntin Willse effectively slices the knot. Her central insight about prepositions works as a narrative vehicle and organizer, while her personal stories of childhood and mothering take readers into the ripe territory of spiritual autobiography, a challenging genre to pull off but one that Willse executes beautifully. The way she weaves interspiritual voices, telling biblical references, and the sheer fun of playing with words is altogether fresh. Like Barbara Brown Taylor, Varina Buntin Willse is capacious in mind and heart. With so much revelation to encounter in every chapter and so much beauty to digest in the writing, you will likely want a pen handy when you read this book. It goes that tender and that deep."

—**Gordon Peerman**, DMin, author of *Blessed Relief: What Christians Can Learn from Buddhists about Suffering*

"Varina Buntin Willse has written a *book of hope*. My greatest compliment is to say that, after reading this book, I have fallen deeper in love with God. In this upside-down world, our lives find their true meaning—and hope—when we connect with a loving God who lives *above*, *beneath*, *among*, and especially *within* us. Hallelujah! I received Willse's writing as a balm to my soul. We can never know enough about God—so thank you to Willse for inviting us on a beautiful adventure."

—**Farrell Mason**, author of *Soulfull*, *The Pocket Cathedral*, and *Alma Gloria and the Olive Tree*

Beneath and Between

VARINA BUNTIN WILLSE

beneath and between

and other overlooked words that illuminate God

BROADLEAF BOOKS
MINNEAPOLIS

BENEATH AND BETWEEN
And Other Overlooked Words That Illuminate God

31 30 29 28 27 26 1 2 3 4 5 6 7 8 9

Library of Congress Control Number: 2026935486

Cover image: Rawpixel//CC/Public Domain: Cloud Study (Early Evening) by Simon Denis; sunset over horizon by Joel Henry on Unsplash
Cover design: John Calmeyer

Print ISBN: 979-8-3419-0193-3
eBook ISBN: 979-8-3419-0194-0

Printed in India

Contents

Introduction

On one of those early nights of spring when the air is just starting to warm, my husband and I were relaxing on the porch swing. He had made us a lovely dinner and cleaned the dishes. The kids were all in bed, and we were having one last sip of wine. It's in moments like these that dreams are shared and hopes revealed, and so it was that I tiptoed toward a treasure of my own.

I hesitated and then ventured to say, "So, you know how I have always loved prepositions?"

In my mind, the conversation was to unfold something like this: I ask this question, and he responds, "Yes, honey. I do. You've always been intrigued by prepositions. Let me guess: You are writing a book about how they can help us reimagine and experience God in new ways."

And I say, "How did you *know*? I love you so much."

Sixteen years into marriage, I remain delusional. His actual response? Guffawing. As in hearty, I'm-not-even-trying-to-stifle-what-I-think laughter.

He must have seen me retreat into my shell. "What?" he asked, baffled but lovingly. "You can't be serious. I don't even know what a preposition is."

In response to my continued silence, he said, "V. Seriously. What is a preposition?"

You may be wondering the same thing, and why it even matters.

Prepositions, seemingly insignificant as they are, inform our place in the world. They are the part of speech that dictates relationship, precisely how things are in relation to other things. The easiest definition of a preposition is likely the one you learned in elementary school. You take an object—say, a box—and you put something else in relation to that box. *I* tends to work nicely. Then you explore the way the meaning shifts when you swap out differing prepositions. Here's how it goes:

I am *near* the box.
I am *beside* the box.
I am *in* the box.

Change the preposition, and you change the scenario entirely. There are about 150 prepositions in the English language to choose from when you play this game. *Over, under, around, against*—you get the picture. So many ways to commune with a box.

As to why it matters? Well, that's a longer story.

GOD AND THE BOX

Several years ago, I was listening to a book recorded by contemporary poet and philosopher David Whyte in which he shares his poem "Sweet Darkness." Having read its closing lines, which profess that "anything or anyone that does not bring you alive is too small for you," Whyte poses an unexpected question of his audience. "How did you let it get too small for you?" he demands, challenging us to reflect on the ways in which we have been complicit in limiting, even shrinking, vital aspects of our lives.

I recognized the import of this question long before I could discern its implications. By so many accounts, my life was characterized by fullness. My heart was full. My home was full. My cup was full. And yet something nevertheless felt small.

There's no shortage of ready explanations for why that might have been the case. The sphere of my daily life was contained in a roughly fifteen-mile radius in which I drove to and from activities, nearly all of which belonged to my children. Though I dreamed of getting away, travel was too costly and the kids' schedules too challenging. Any ideas I might have had for a spontaneous local excursion were typically smote by exhaustion when it came time to actually doing them. Plus there sat endless piles of laundry that needed folding and a sink that somehow repopulated every single time I turned my back. Meanwhile, projects at work stymied any wholeness that writing might have brought me. And my marriage, though solid, was chafing against old skins.

I might easily have been fooled into thinking that any one of these things was to blame for the smallness I felt. I might easily have pointed my finger in some direction, any direction, and said: *That. That is what is suffocating me.* And yet none of this was to blame. Something else, something much further out of reach, was not bringing me alive. To ascertain what it was, I had to go on a deep inward journey.

For a long time, my relationship with God had been intensely personal, and I liked it that way. I was not into Bible studies nor was I interested in small groups at church. I have some theories about why. Some of it was rooted in my Episcopalian upbringing. We Episcopalians aren't exactly known for our evangelism. Some of it was rooted in my forays into youth groups. During high school, I joined a club for Christian athletes and was very taken by it—until I discovered that our leaders were from a conservative sect of Christianity that believed fervently in the importance of being born again. "Jesus is the way, the truth, and the life," they quoted, less an invitation than a threat. A dear friend told me through tears that, yes, he believed I was going to hell because I refused to put limits on God's love. It's no wonder I retreated into a faith bunker. I would keep what was between God and me strictly between God and me.

In that private space, my faith flourished. It was so holy and safe in there. I could ask hard questions or space out. I could be mad or be awed. I could boldly or blithely doubt. Keeping my relationship with God private felt like a way to keep it sacred. But then I started thinking that if I was going to call myself a Christian, I had probably better have read the Bible. Like all of it. (We Episcopalians aren't too obsessive about Scripture either.)

So I enrolled in a yearlong discipleship class at a Presbyterian church in town. It was everything I had told myself I would never do: read the Bible and then talk about it in a small group. But I did it, and I learned a lot, and I formed lasting friendships. I signed up for the next class in the series and then again the following year. When our group had run through all the available curricula, we started in on a new series.

Meanwhile I had made vows to God to cherish another human, no matter the circumstances that might befall us. Soon I carried new life inside me and brought that life—two lives at one time, no less!—into this world. On Sunday mornings, my girls and my husband and I would assume our regular spot in the side pews of Christ Church Cathedral in downtown Nashville, where I had worshipped as a child and where generations of my family on both sides had worshipped for hundreds of years before me. We knelt on the long velvet prayer cushion and talked to God. We came to the altar and held up our palms for the sacred wafer. We sang, and we shook hands with our neighbors, passing them the peace. God was there in the rituals and symbols and hymns. God was there, alive in the faith and hope and love expressed by Scripture and collective prayer, alive in the stories Jesus shared, indeed alive in the story of Jesus himself. I continued to attend worship, becoming a more active parishioner. I took to the lectern on Sundays and read from Genesis, from Acts, from Paul's many letters. I accepted leadership positions. This felt right to me.

And yet something was shifting within me on a cellular level. Even as I struggled with the banality of motherhood—diapers and bottles and spills and burps—I was undergoing some kind of transfiguration. When I knelt at the altar rail for Holy Communion, I was no longer receiving the bread and the wine; I felt like I had *become* the bread and wine. Those bodies over there were separate from my body and yet were not. This was true, at first, of only my children. And then, slowly, it became true of all people and not only all people but all things. I felt myself expanding, like the universe of God's making.

In turn, my spiritual cravings intensified. I began practicing meditation and adding stacks of spiritual nonfiction to my reading list. I was finding more wisdom in the prophets of our time—Thich Nhat Hanh and Mary Oliver and Richard Rohr—than in the prophets of the Old Testament. I was delving into coursework on archetypes, greeting the Innocent, the Witch, the Sage within. I was reading about goddess mythology and undergoing vivid journeys during meditation. Daily I was discovering what felt like signs from God: owl sightings, feathers, synchronicities.

Depending on who you are, this might all sound weird and scary. But entering the hallowed portals of silence, of stillness, of imagination, of openness, I was encountering God—a Divine at once wild and intimate, wise and fertile—in a way that I had not previously experienced, except perhaps when I was a child exploring the woodsides of my country home. The church doesn't much like this kind of behavior, certainly not historically. Many women have been penalized, even killed, for this kind of expansive spiritual thinking. Yet it registered for me as profoundly rich and true.

And so I felt like I was keeping secrets. I did not know how to account for the stark disconnect between me, the junior warden at church, and me, the spiritual seeker waking early to burn palo santo and align my chakras. These two worlds had not overtly clashed—that would come soon enough—but they did feel increasingly misaligned.

What I loved most about church had always been the liturgy, specifically Rite II from *The Book of Common Prayer* beginning on the well-worn page 367. As a girl, I was enchanted by the lyricism and the mystery of its words, both spoken and sung each Sunday morning. They captured the essence of the God I felt when roaming fields, gathering feathers. As an adult, I found the consistency and familiarity of the liturgy comforting.

Until cracks started to form.

Following along, dutifully giving the cued responses, I began to hear with new ears. And what I heard were nouns, so many masculine nouns: *Lord God, Heavenly Father, Father Almighty, King of Kings.* The more I heard them, the more I felt I could not utter them. The Nicene Creed, which I had recited almost weekly for four decades, fell dead on my tongue. Codified by a council of bishops under the rule of Roman Emperor Constantine I in 325, the creed would not be how I characterized my core beliefs. At all.

Where did that leave me? What was I chafing against? Was it the liturgy? Was it our church or our denomination? Was it Christianity itself? How many other people in those pews wanted to purge God of thrones and Jesus of lordship? How many others felt stifled? Felt that God *Godself* was being stifled?

And there it was: *God Godself was being stifled.* The thing that had become too small for me was the biggest, deepest, mightiest thing of all. It was God.

The truth had been emerging slowly, the way moss grows—an ancient, unhurried greening. The truth was not that I had let my marriage get too small for me, or motherhood. It wasn't domestic life or work life. It wasn't the radius in which I was traveling. It was God. All expertly labeled and sealed up in a box, God had gotten too small.

This disruptive yet fertile discovery happens to many of us, often in middle age. "My perception of the Divine had proved rigid, inadequate," writes Sue Monk Kidd in her revolutionary book *The Dance of the Dissident Daughter.* She published that book in 1996, one year after I graduated from high school. It would be nearly four decades before Kidd's book found me, its pronouncements upending the establishment I had relied on, its sentences ringing both terrifyingly and liberatingly true. "Western Christian patriarchal boxes could not hold it in," she boldly proclaims.

There it was again: God and the box.

If we change the subject of the sentence in our little preposition lesson from *I* to *God*, we encounter these statements:

God is *near* the box.
God is *beside* the box.
God is *in* the box.

So much religious dogma seems to operate, if inadvertently, from the vantage point of that last statement: God is in the box. This book is about freeing God from the box.

THE CLASH WITH NOUNS

With three kids and a husband, I get asked *Where* questions all the time. Where are my socks? Where is the peanut butter? Where is practice? Where is Dad? (Good question!) Moms typically have answers for these questions. Occasionally, though, we get a *Where* question that rocks us. There we are at the bathroom sink one evening—so near the finish line of the day we are—when our child looks at us intently and asks, *Mommy, where is God?*

It's a perfectly reasonable question that produces baffling, often contradictory answers. One adult might respond that God is up in heaven. Another might say that God is within the child's heart. Yet another might answer that God is everywhere. If the child persists in her line of inquiry, she might ask how God can be in two or three places at one time. This question is even more challenging than the first. The easiest answer, and likely the truest, is: *Because God is God.* We can speak this answer with reverence, or we can speak it with irritation. It can be a source of awe, something for us to share with our children and marvel over, or it can be aimed at ending the litany of questions and checking the box of bedtime.

Pondering the where of God is an ongoing inquiry in the life of a spiritual seeker. The more we ponder it, the more we understand that God's location becomes inextricably linked to God's nature. The question *Where is God?* marries with the question *What is God?* which in turn marries with the question *Who is God?* All the answers tangle up together and fatigue sets in. Better to be asked for the fiftieth time where the peanut butter is than to grapple with all that.

When we do answer the questions *Where is God?, What is God?,* and *Who is God?* we tend to do so exclusively with nouns. We have *named* god God. Father. Lord. King. And we have located God in specific places: Heaven. Throne. Temple. Altar.

Nouns are an obvious choice for an impossible task. How does one take an unknowable mystery—*the* Unknowable Mystery—and try to make it knowable? By naming it. And furthermore, by personifying it. By likening it to us. This makes perfect sense, and yet what we have as a result is so many nouns weighing us down. So many masculine nouns.

This did not arrest me—until the day it did. That day the slow resistance that had been swelling inside me—the steady sense that our weekly recitation in church was limited and limiting—suddenly made itself known.

It was at our breakfast table. The pandemic had hit, and I had insisted that our family continue to attend church via Zoom. Sunday mornings, around plates of pancakes, we tuned in as the clergy at our church performed the Eucharist to an empty nave. I listened to the words I had been hearing all my life until I could do so no longer. Mid-worship, I pressed pause, turned to my daughters, and said: "You know God isn't a man, don't you?"

They didn't. They did not know that God is not a man. Of course they didn't. How could they?

I felt both angry and sad. Here I was—a woman who retreated to a meditation room in the basement in order to convene with God/Ultimate Reality/The Divine—and yet my three daughters had no idea that God isn't a man.

I have always been one to raise my hand and share what's on my mind, a quality that is equal parts blessing and curse. I decided to write an email to the rector at our church, who is a close friend.

With absolute respect and a heart for effecting change, I expressed my frustration—correction: my great misgivings—over the patriarchal language used exclusively in our liturgical tradition. He called me to discuss, and during the course of that conversation he implored me to consider the way we teach children to cross a street. At first, we make them hold our hand. This keeps them safe. But our ultimate goal is not for them to learn to hold a hand; it is for them to eventually cross the street alone, without a hand. My rector's parable was meant to prove the merits of calling God "Father Almighty" until the more spiritually mature soul can access God without need of such a name. Until she can cross into something more elusive and more inclusive (say, when she is forty-three and totally disillusioned).

This argument—that we need to make theology simple for children and do so by characterizing God as only a Father, and Jesus as mostly a Lord, or occasionally a Shepherd—doesn't square with my experience of being a child. As a child, I revered wildness, magic, and holy intricacies. I understood that God superseded names. Putting only nouns to God—and a select *few* nouns at that—had the reverse effect of reducing the Divine for me.

Which is how I found myself, a faithful and active parishioner, desperately seeking to liberate God from the box. What that would mean and what that would entail, I did not yet know.

At this point I was unsure whether I was even a "real Christian" anymore. The faith tradition that I inherited has a problematic history. Since its inception, Christianity has been misinterpreted, misunderstood, twisted, and abused. In its name, great sweeping wrongs have been done. In its name, slow-leaking insidious harms have been done. It continues to be weaponized in ways that are profoundly lethal. Sitting in virtual church that day, feeling that the God I knew and the God I wanted my daughters to know was missing, was a moment when I might have walked out. It is the exact kind of moment that has prompted many to quit church. The God they *experience* is far more vast and yet more personal, far more inclusive and yet elusive than the church expresses. So they opt for Spirituality instead of Christianity. They opt for something they call "meditation" over something they call "prayer." The word *Jesus* begins to have complex connotations for them, many of which are not good. They become what the ever-wise author Cynthia Bourgeault calls "heartbroken Christians."

This is a critical moment. This is a moment when people who have difficulty with the God of Nouns just might maintain faith if something were different: If the words were different, or if the ways we articulated the Divine were more nuanced, more *animating*. If our language about Jesus did not confine both him and us.

HIDING IN PLAIN SIGHT

I have been a heartbroken Christian, but I am not a retired one. While the expression of Christianity has been alienating and in some ways forsaking, the essence of it is, I maintain, whole and good and true. That I can even make that statement with conviction has been one of the revelations and blessings of writing this book.

What I now understand, which before I took for granted, is that I know nothing of God without the Christian context. I know nothing of God's nature, nothing of God's desires, nothing of God's love, and nothing of God's existence without the framework provided by Christian belief, Scripture, and practice. To be sure, that knowledge has been supplemented and enhanced by the explorations I have undertaken into other spiritual modalities, formal and otherwise. But, for me, the center holds. I am a Christian because, at its essence, this is a faith tradition that characterizes the Divine as singular and yet polymorphic. And not only polymorphic but *multirelational*: capable of being, desiring of being, and actively choosing to be in relationship with itself and all else in myriad ways.

Nouns—masculine or otherwise—feel too fixed, too static to convey the fluidity, relationality, and ultimate mystery of the Divine. The same is true of adjectives, which are often used to attribute to God certain indelible characteristics, whether wrathful or merciful. We need something new: a fresh vocabulary of faith.

That's where prepositions come in.

This part of speech, which includes words dictating 150 different kinds of relationship, proves better suited to the task of exploring the multidimensional aliveness of God than nouns do. At a time of spiritual crisis, prepositions helped me bridge the gap between the mystical encounters I was experiencing and the organized religion I espoused. Yet for all the complexity they reveal, they are themselves astonishingly simple.

When we get rid of the box altogether, this is what we discover:

God is near us.
God is beside us.
God is in us.

Do you feel what I feel, reading that, hearing that, absorbing that? It is a seismic shift as a result of some rather innocuous words. God becomes proximate. God becomes accessible. God assumes a vibrant multilocality.

Wouldn't it be just like God to do that? Wouldn't it make sense for God, who consistently turns everything on its head—making the lowly high and the high lowly, making the weak strong and the strong weak—to ally with the humblest part of speech, the seemingly least consequential and celebrated words of all? The preposition may well be the verbal equivalent of the baby in the manger.

Likewise, wouldn't it be fitting for us humans that a set of mundane words we use pretty much all the time without ever noticing them would be useful tools for helping us access the God we have so desperately been trying to find? Wouldn't it be just like us to miss God hiding in plain sight? God is, after all, right here, everywhere, abundantly beautiful, true, available.

Once I started thinking about them, prepositions seemed to pop up everywhere. I opened my morning reading from the Center for

Action and Contemplation to find Father Richard Rohr writing from an exact shared consciousness, using the prepositions God *for* us, God *alongside* us, and God *within* us, to replace the traditional Trinity (Father, Son, Holy Spirit). I opened my evening reading of Tallu Schuyler Quinn's beautiful memoir, *What We Wish Were True*, to find the next chapter titled "In You and Among You," referencing a verse from the noncanonical Gospel of Thomas. I opened my phone to find the quote of the day emphasizing God not out there but *within*.

Over and over again this happened. With deep gratitude and hope, I felt it happening in church, too, in the very liturgy that had reared its ugly head at me. Among all the Fathers and the Lords and the Kings, I heard familiar phrases anew:

> God *from* God, Light *from* Light.
>
> *Through* him all things were made.
>
> Peace be *with* you. And also *with* you.
>
> *By* him, and *with* him, and *in* him, in the unity of the Holy Spirit . . .

In the Prayers of the People on what our church calls Trinity Sunday, I heard anew the words of this collective prayer: *We bind ourselves, O God, to the strong name of the Trinity. Be with us, within us, behind us, before us, now and always. We call upon you: Three in One, One in Three.* There they were: prepositions, like golden nuggets.

And of course, Saint Patrick, the fifth-century cleric and missionary of Ireland (whose life we perhaps oddly celebrate annually in March by drinking beer and wearing green) famously penned this prayer, which many of us know:

> Christ *with* me,
> Christ *before* me,
> Christ *behind* me,
> Christ *in* me,
> Christ *beneath* me,

Christ *above* me,
Christ *on* my right,
Christ *on* my left . . .

Yes. Yes. Yes. It moves me to think that a full 1,600 years ago, a spiritual seeker and church leader followed the very thread we are following: Christ, or more largely the Divine, through the use of prepositions. It moves me to think that Richard Rohr, sitting with his dog by a window in New Mexico, has been pondering the same linguistic adaptations that I have, sitting with my dog by a window in Tennessee. Like Father Richard, I, too, had been swapping nouns for prepositions in the framework of the Trinity. In my iteration, I replaced God the Father, God the Son, and God the Holy Spirit with God For, God Among, and God Throughout. But for me, three was not enough.

One day, on the white wall of the nook of my desk where I jot ideas, I drew a triangle and started adding prepositions. I kept adding more prepositions, more points, more arrows. A new portrait of the Divine was arising, characterized by rampant dynamism. God *Above*. God *Beneath*. God *Near*. God *Through*. God *Into*. God *Within*. God *Among*. God *Throughout*. . . . On went the arrows and the possibilities.

As this happened, a portrait of God began emerging on my very wall, one that was mysterious, inescapable, and animated in the very way that I had been yearning for it to be. In many ways, it was a blueprint more than anything, or perhaps a map: a guide to the myriad locations, relations, and directions of the Divine. No longer a fixed person, place, or thing, no longer trapped in a triangle, God appeared truly omnipresent and truly omnipotent, with freedom and power emerging not from being on a throne but in creative relationship.

This was no longer a top-down situation. This wasn't even two footprints on the sand. In this scenario, the Divine accesses us, and we access the Divine, in myriad, astonishing ways. Nouns can't help us one bit. When we're getting close to the holy, the ineffable, the sublime, we are now in the terrain of prepositions.

PREPOSITIONAL TRUTH

I have hesitated to write about God, given the fact that I have not attended seminary or studied theology. I am not ordained, and I am not a religious studies professor. Without proper training, by what authority would I share my impressions? Would anything I say about God be valid? I found an answer on the walls of my parents' home, of all places.

My mother collects what is known in the art world as "outsider art." These are works—sculptures, paintings, drawings—by artists who have never formally studied their craft. The proportions may be off, the figures simplistic, the materials salvaged. "Crude" as they might seem to a certain eye, these works of outsider art ring profoundly true. With art school either not accessible or not desired, these artists forge ahead anyway, giving of their talent and their belief boldly, from a place outside academia.

Maybe that's what this book is: outsider theology. I come to God from perhaps the same place as you do: not the pulpit but the pew—or the meditation cushion, or the woods, or wherever you sense a living God. Just as I am no ordained priest, no expert on my own chosen religion, I am certainly no expert on other major religions. I am, though, curious about and quickened by the insights I glean from other traditions, really by anything that illuminates a pervasive and relational God. There is so much I don't know.

Eager to engage with this humble part of speech, I wonder: What aspects of God have we been missing all these years by overlooking prepositions? What dimensions of the Divine have we not sensed because we have not noticed these little words, throughout Scripture and songs and prayers of the church, hiding in plain sight?

So much of Christianity is propped up by *propositional truth*, dependent as it is on declarative statements to impart meaning. This dualistic model, which claims this over here true and that over there false, is how many Christians have been schooled in faith. It makes sense: Bold assertions offer a solid start. But used exclusively, propositional truth fails to convey the essential paradox and mystery of a triune God, the three-in-one. That's where *prepositional truth* comes in.

This book explores one preposition per chapter, fifteen in all. The sequence of prepositions across chapters progresses systematically. It reflects a movement of increasing proximity—the suprapersonal becoming the interpersonal becoming the intrapersonal—and then back out again, to the transpersonal. You might think of it like an hourglass. It begins at a high level (literally) and then moves closer, and closer still, until it indwells, at which point it opens back up again in an all-encompassing way.

You can read the chapters sequentially to get a sense of this flow, or you can open to a random chapter and dig in. Feel free to circle back or skip ahead, to finish and then revisit. Different prepositions might strike you differently as you age and evolve. How lovely. My hope is that this book will be evergreen and always inspiring for you.

You will find that each chapter closes with a prayer. These prayers offer moments of pause, like mini-Sabbaths, and invite us to make the shift from thinking about God to talking to God. Pray them silently or aloud as you go. Tuck them away for times when they feel particularly poignant, sharing them when the Spirit moves you. If you savor a specific line or verse, repeat it as a mantra to keep you tethered to the sacred. The invitation here is one of engagement.

God's connection with you is already and always so deep and dynamic. These prepositions are simply a way to activate your awareness of that connection. Be on the lookout for them in your reading and in your conversations. Mine for them, like gold. Let them alter where you imagine God to be and how you imagine God relates to you, in any given moment on any given day.

A note on word choices: I cannot write this book without using pronouns, and pronouns usher in the topic of gender. I would prefer not to refer to God as *he* or *she*, but the other options prove, for me, more problematic. The pronoun *it* works in some places but generally falls short of conveying the deeply personal relationship that is God and ours. The pronoun *they* can also prove helpful; however, it contradicts the importance of the oneness of God. As a solution, I use *it* and *they* sparingly; I use *she* in reference to God in some chapters, while in others, I use *he*. My choices of when to use *she* and when to use *he*, which are based on a certain feel-tone that seems befitting a particular preposition, may well be criticized as gender stereotyping. I accept that criticism as legitimate. My aim is to elucidate the attributes of God that are commonly associated with the divine feminine and also commonly associated with the divine masculine, because all are critical in illuminating a multifaceted One. For Beneath, I use *she*. For Above, I use *he*. This does not mean that the masculine divine is not our roots, nor does it mean that the feminine divine is not our ruler. The polydimensionality is the point of emphasis: both/and/and/and/and/and . . .

A word on why all this thinking—which may be overthinking—matters. We are all members of communities, nations, collectives. How we act and how we vote, what opinions we form and what values we champion, all derive from the foundations of our spirituality. What we believe, or don't believe, about God informs all that we are and do. Scripture asserts that we are made in the image of God, but historically the church has made *God* in the image of *us*. And the image of "us" has reflected only the image of the ones in power, the ones writing the liturgies and the creeds, the ones speaking from the pulpits. Lacking diversity, lacking wholeness, lacking spaciousness, God has been reduced. We, in turn, have been reduced. The consequences of this small-making have been felt in all corners of society.

If we want to better the world, we would do well to better understand the Divine: not doubling down on what we already think but rather exploring that which we have not considered. In this way, theology would not be contained in the walls of universities but would be available to outsiders like us, as I believe God very much intends it to be. And prepositions would reveal themselves to be right there in sacred text, where they have waiting for us all along.

Any theology I present is a byproduct of my soul's own "higher education." It is unsanctioned but nevertheless sanctified. While it is true that thinking about God in terms of prepositions rather than solely in nouns has had the power (rather unexpectedly) to revive Christianity for me, Christianity is not the point. *God is.* The goal of religion is not to lay claim to God anyway. The Divine is way too wild—way too beautifully and boldly and unabashedly big—for that. There is no box massive enough to hold it. No doctrine. No code. No claim. Certainly no gender.

What we discover, amid all this valiant searching, is the most obvious truth of all: God was never in a box; only we were.

Let's do the good work of getting out, together.

CHAPTER ONE

Above

Yours, O Lord, are the greatness, the power, the glory,
the victory, and the majesty,
for all that is in the heavens and on the earth is yours;
yours is the kingdom, O Lord, and you are
exalted as head above all.

1 Chronicles 29:11

He is Allah—there is no god except Him:
the King, the Most Holy, the All-Perfect, the Source
of Serenity, the Watcher "of all,"
the Almighty, the Supreme in Might, the Majestic.
Glorified is Allah far above what they associate
with Him "in worship"!

Al-Hashr 59:23

A friend told me a story recently about her boys, ages five and seven. They were standing at the mailbox, waiting for the school bus to pick them up, and the conversation turned to God. "Where do you think God is?" my friend asked her two sons.

The youngest spoke up immediately. "God is up in the sky above the clouds, above where the airplanes fly, but before you get to outer space with the moon and the stars," he said confidently. "He's not that far out; he's right above where the jets go," he added, demonstrating with his hands the various layers of sky, including the one allocated to God.

His older brother, standing behind him, opened his eyes wide with a look that said his little brother was getting it all wrong. "Okay, so where do *you* think God is?" my friend asked her oldest son, who clearly had a different opinion.

"Everywhere," he stated succinctly. "God is everywhere."

At this, the younger brother piped up again. "Well, yeah, God is everywhere. But when you get out of the bouncy house, he's up in the sky."

When you get out of the bouncy house, God is up in the sky. That statement is sheer delight. It relays significant insights but with the unpredictable, highly imaginative spin of a kid. We do tend to think God lives somewhere up in the sky. It's an idea instilled in us from early childhood, when we learn that God is a "Father who art in heaven," with heaven being some vague but distinctly separate place, presumably where clouds break open and rays of light pour through. It makes perfectly good sense. If Earth is *down here*, then heaven is *up there*. Plus, God watches over us, and so God has to be higher than us. If God is anywhere, we think, he is most certainly *above*.

"Above" is a logical place to begin a journey of prepositional truth. It is the most obvious, the most expected of all prepositions. Asked to point to where we think God is, many of us will likely angle our finger upward.

We don't have to look far in Scripture to understand how God assumed this default locality. In the very first chapter of the very first book of the Bible, God does a critical thing in the act of creation: *divide*. First God divides light and darkness. Then God divides the waters, and when he does so, it's on the horizontal. As the King James Version explains it, God "divided the waters which were under the firmament from the waters which were above the firmament: and it was so" (Genesis 1:7). The immediate effect of a horizontal divide is the creation of an Above and an Under. Two key prepositions right there, under our noses.

Before there are nouns or names of any kind, there are prepositions. At the very outset God is, in effect, creating relationality. Light exists in relation to dark. Morning exists in relation to evening. Under exists in relation to Above. One needs the other to have any existence at all. The origin story of Genesis tells us that relationality is the original and prevailing context for existence.

Only after creating these two distinct firmaments—one above and one under, and thus a relationality between the two—is God said to have given each a name: what we know as heaven and earth. Earth is for all the beasts of the fields and the creepy crawly things and everything that grows. It is the terrain of the physical. Heaven is for God and angels. It is the terrain of the spiritual.

We have been taught to consider heaven the higher of the two, literally and metaphorically. But it wasn't always that way.

GOAT

For thousands of years before the birth of Christ, people in the Fertile Crescent and across Asia Minor gave highest praise to matter. As an agrarian society, their work—and in turn their faith—was rooted in the bounty of the earth, which they recognized as closely linked to the female body. Both are cyclical; both are generative. Their god was a goddess. Like the earth itself, she was responsible for producing life and also for reconsuming it after death, only to reproduce it again. The pattern of life, death, and resurrection, which later becomes the central message of Christianity, was likewise esteemed. But for them, God was beneath, in the soil, as opposed to above, in the sky. She was accessed through the *hands* as opposed to through the *head*. Theology, as it were, comes later.

This notion of a Feminine Divine, earthly and cyclical, was subsumed by nomadic tribes who survived by wandering, herding sheep and cattle, and often ravaging the other tribes they encountered.

Their source of survival was no longer rooted in the earth beneath them. As American professor of mythology Joseph Campbell notes, "What we suddenly find intruding into the earlier Goddess cults in these areas is the mythology of a warrior people whose main deity, whether named Zeus or Indra, is a thunderbolt-hurler. This is no different from Yahweh," Campbell emphasizes. The Divine, whether Greek, Hindu, or Hebrew, shifts from richly beneath (*chthonic*) to powerfully above (*ouranic*).

In very broad strokes, what happens next is that humans discern a sense of cosmic order. In 3000 BCE, the Sumerians noted and were able to calculate planetary orbits. By that point, they had already started writing. Ancient clay tablets display both mathematical exercises and script. These were people no longer living in isolated villages or in nomadic tribes but in the world's first cities. When large groups of people live together, differentiation of tasks and concerns occurs. Out of this differentiation comes ranking. Hierarchies were established and, over time, solidified.

It was into this world that Jesus was born, and it was in this world that the authors of the Bible were writing and Christianity was spreading and developing. The Divine was no longer the fertile hidden Earth. The Divine was a mastermind: capable of dividing, naming, and ordering. A Creator but also a supreme Ruler over the order she—or as the people of their time and the majority ever since have considered it, *he*—had established. This order was everything, and it was given a name: the Great Chain of Being.

I remember first learning about the Great Chain of Being in tenth-grade English class. To grasp the medieval texts that we were studying, we needed to understand the worldview held by the authors and audiences of the day. The worldview, it seems, was one of uncompromising order, with everything given a set place. Our teacher, Ms. Renkl, drew the links in the chain crisply on the whiteboard. On the bottom were the minerals. Above the minerals were the plants. Above the plants were the animals. Above the animals were the humans. Above the humans were the angels. Within these categories, further rankings were asserted. The angels topped out with seraphim, the minerals with diamonds. The universe comprised ladders of power tucked within ladders of power. At the very top was God. God makes everything. God rules over everything. God can destroy everything. In this hierarchical structure, which was a construct of Christians, God is the ultimate Above.

Several hundred years later, we still live in a world that values rank order and sees things through the lens of hierarchies. We rank just about everything. Athletes are ranked. Military personnel are ranked. Students, companies, retirement homes, school districts, songs, and even clergy are ranked. The ones that top the list are the most revered.

And God? Well, he's the GOAT. He's the one with all the power and all the might and all the glory, a claim that is espoused often in Scripture, especially in the Psalms. "O Lord, our Sovereign, how majestic is your name in all the earth, You have set your glory above the heavens" (Psalm 8:1). "For the Lord is a great God, and a great King above all gods" (Psalm 95:3). "Let them praise the name of the Lord, for his name alone is exalted; his glory is above earth and heaven" (Psalm 148:13). Every single one of these passages (and countless others) uses the word "above." God is characterized not only as *above* us and *above* the earth but also as *above* all gods and even as *above* the heavens themselves. God just keeps getting more and more lofty. We can't seem to get him high enough.

Indeed, God's primacy, God's power, is one of his defining characteristics. The Hebrew name for God used in the Old Testament, *Adonai*, underscores this point. Meaning "master" or "lord," it was used to refer to a person of a higher ranking and then came to be used to refer to God. Unlike the name YHWH, which was more breath than word, more presence than power, the name Adonai emphasizes God's sovereignty.

Most people who believe in God believe that God's power is primary. To convey this belief, we speak of God as *King of Kings* and *Lord of Lords*, as *Almighty Father* and *Ruler of All Things*, and

Christians emphasize it every single time they wrap up the Lord's Prayer: "For the kingdom and the power and the glory are yours now and forever. Amen."

I remember the first time the magnitude of God's sovereignty started to sink in for me. I was in middle school, and I was facing my first-ever exam. I was a nervous wreck. I studied for days if not weeks in advance, went to extra help sessions, and met up with my friends to quiz one another. Still, I was fraught with anxiety. The day before the exam, my friend Sarah gave me a little slip of paper on which she had written in neat middle-school-girl block letters: *I can do all things through him that strengthens me. Philippians 4:13.*

I was totally floored. I hadn't ever been given a Bible verse before. I hadn't ever been told to turn to Scripture for solace before. (I was an Episcopalian, but Sarah—Sarah was Presbyterian!) I hadn't ever considered the very personal impact of God's much-touted almightiness. Holding that little slip of paper in my hand, rereading it and letting its message sink in, fortified me in a way that no amount of further cramming could do. God is indeed all-powerful. God is indeed the Ruler of All Things, Lord of Lords, King of Kings. The Greatest of All Time.

EL SHADDAI

This does not mean, however, that God is sitting on a distant throne looking down on us, as we are so often led to believe. He is not way up high somewhere, far away from the action, speaking decrees. That distant sovereign—the one who speaks in diktats and imposes his will on humans from a place far removed from their pain—is the source of angst for so many disillusioned and devastated Christians. The true God Above is something different.

Before God divides the firmaments, before he even delineates light, he takes another action. In describing the creation of the heavens and the earth, Scripture says that God "hovers over" the deep, or in other translations God "moves upon" it. The Hebrew word for this inaugural action is *rachaph*. Its meaning is hard to pinpoint. It evokes a sense of hovering, moving, brooding, fluttering, and even relaxing. The image of God as a mother hen is not hard to miss.

But whatever fascinating meaning might best suit the verb, the preposition that goes along with it is just as interesting. In the act of *rachaph*, God is in some way "over" or "upon" the deep as God is creating it. God *is* the deep, and God is also *above* the deep—closely so. It is as Gerard Manley Hopkins so eloquently articulates in his poem "God's Grandeur": "The Holy Ghost over the bent / World broods with warm breast and with ah! bright wings."

This aboveness reveals so much about the nature of the Divine from the very outset. God's position is of both authority and accessibility, of both power and proximity, of both protection and cultivation. I cherish this portrait of the Divine. God is moving above creation like a chef over a potée, an artist over a canvas, a healer over a tincture, a robin over a clutch of eggs. It is only from this position so closely above that the Divine can conduct life: can effectively, mysteriously, and powerfully *animate*.

The term *Shaddai*, a name associated with God some forty-eight times in the Bible, reinforces this maternal image of God. Typically translated as *God Almighty*, which for many of us connotes hypermasculinity, it actually derives from the Hebrew word *shad*, which means breast or teat. Here again, God is presented as a nursing female who hovers over, rather than lords over, her creation.

Another equally revealing image is also hidden in this phrase. As with the Teton Range in Wyoming, breasts and mountains tend to be linked linguistically. In the ancient Semitic language of Akkad, the word *shadu* meant mountain, and so El Shaddai also means God of the mountain.

The Bible gives an estimated five hundred references to mountains and names ten specific ones. Many people know about Abraham saddling up his donkey to climb Mount Moriah to sacrifice his son, Isaac, and about Moses receiving the Ten Commandments atop Mount Sinai, and about Jesus's Sermon on the Mount (Eremos, to be specific). There is also Mount Ararat, a dormant volcano in eastern

Turkey, presumed to be the high ground where Noah's ark beached after the great floods, and the Mount of Olives near Jerusalem's Old City where Jesus went to pray and teach, including on the night before he was handed over to death, among numerous others.

Mountains play an important role in Islam as well, especially Mount Arafat and Jabal al-Nour, where the Prophet Muhammad received his first revelation of the Qur'an. Likewise in Hinduism: Mount Kailash is believed to be the dwelling of the deity Shiva, and the mythical Mount Meru is upheld as the central axis of the cosmos. In Chinese Buddhism, four specific mountains are deemed sacred: Mount Putuo, Mount Jiuhua, Mount Emei, and Mount Wutai. The Shinto worship at the base of Mount Fuji. Taoists venerate mountains, especially those in sacred groupings that represent the four cardinal points.

People of various indigenous populations cherish mountains too. The Māori of New Zealand view Mount Taranaki as a sacred ancestor. Aboriginal Australians ascribe great spiritual significance to the monolith, Uluru, in the Northern Territory of Australia. The Navajo in the western United States revere four peaks as holy, assigning each a color and a direction.

Nor can we forget the ancient myths of Greece and Rome. Mount Olympus, the highest mountain peak in Greece, was home to the Greek gods.

You get the picture. Throughout disparate times, places, cultures, and religions, people have upheld the mountaintop—the highest geographical locale known to us—as both symbol and abode of the Divine. It is home to the "secret Strength of things," writes Percy Bysshe Shelley in his poem "Mont Blanc": "The power is there, / The still and solemn power of many sights, / And many sounds, and much of life and death."

And therein lies an essential truth. From this unique place above—a place only the Divine can fully claim—God possesses the still and solemn power of many sights. In other words, he *beholds*. His way of looking is not so much down *on* us as it is down *at* us, which is altogether different. He can see all the individual pieces of his kingdom, including each of us, but he can also see the kingdom as a whole spreading out in space and time. God beholds not only what is right now but also what is infinity, reading not only text but also context: where we come from, where we are going, who and what surrounds us, both closely and rippling out. God's infinite viewshed heralds infinite wisdom because the view from above is whole. God sees the big picture. God knows the whole story.

Perhaps God *is* the big picture, the whole story.

It is for this reason that God can say, "For my thoughts are not your thoughts, neither are your ways my ways. . . . As the heavens are higher than the earth, so are my ways higher than your ways and my thoughts than your thoughts" (Isaiah 55:8–9). God's way of thinking and being is infinitely above ours. We humans repeatedly pervert the notion of power, understanding it to be a means of selfish gain rather than an opportunity to exercise wisdom. We think that rising is about achievement and being *above* is about being *better.*

Proverbs 15:24 (KJV) has something intriguing and elusive to say about a truer way. "The way of life is above to the wise." There is no object of the preposition *above.* The writer doesn't tell us what exactly the way of life is above. It's just: *above.* Reading it, we might feel obtuse, shut out of its meaning. Or else we might think it's a typo—that there's a word missing.

But the proverb's strange construction invites us to fill in the implied blanks for ourselves. We might say: The way of life is above egoism to the wise. The way of life is above consumerism to the wise. The way of life is above grievances to the wise. Above self-pity. Above excuses. Above irritability. Above reproach. The way of wisdom is above any and all of our intrinsically banal natures. Therein lies its genuine power. It is simply *above.*

To reach this way of life, we are called to "set [our] minds on the things that are above, not on the things that are on earth" (Colossians 3:2). Setting our hearts on things *above,* we relinquish the desire to be in control, which is, in essence, the desire to play God.

The invitation here—you might even say the imperative here—is to surrender (or as the Episcopalian tradition articulates it: to "put all things in subjection under Christ").

FREEDOM OF WILL

I don't know about you, but I get a solid D when it comes to surrender. I beat my head against the wall of wanting to control daily. I want to control whether my kids make the basketball team or get a certain grade or get into a certain college. I want to control how my husband reprimands them when they eat with their mouths open or leave their backpacks in the middle of the floor. I want to control my clients' responses to the work I have submitted. I want to control the health of everyone I know and love. I want to control the present moment. And the future, near and kind of far, too, if I'm honest. I even want to control the weather.

It's crazy and it's futile and it's exhausting, and yet somehow I start in on it just about every single day. And every single day I try to recognize myself doing this and—with intention, faith, patience, grace, and trust—stop myself. I suspect I'm not the only one who has experienced this particular brand of self-imposed mad fatigue. It makes no sense, but could it be true that something in us resists the nature of God as above, even though God as above is also our greatest source of comfort? We want God, or the Universe, or Someone Else, to be in control, but we also can't help but try to do the job ourselves.

Why does God even give us this option anyway? Why not be stingy with all this power? In the same way that we don't raise our kids to keep them captive at home their whole lives, God doesn't raise us to keep us captive either. God so loves us that he gives us the capacity to love also. This is how we are made in God's image.

But the capacity to love necessitates a capacity to *will*. And to will, as we experience it, is invariably to angle (against our better judgment) for aboveness, for power, for selfish gain. Jesus knew this and tried to warn us against it. In his most famous sermon, he preached the Beatitudes, inverting hierarchies by elevating the lowest and the least to a position of favor. Blessed are the poor. The mournful. The meek. Those folks might seem like they are below everybody else, but they're not, Jesus insists. They have a direct line to God. It's those of us who set ourselves above other people—or somewhere in the back of our minds *think* we are above other people—who experience trouble.

I am wary of the word *sin* because it is so often misdefined and misdirected. But is it possible to think of it as the gap between God's aboveness and our belowness? Is sin the space where we come up short, where we miss the point of our own free will, using it to jockey for power instead of to extend love?

God does not lord this space over us, though some doctrines would have us believe he does. On the contrary, God wants us to lift our hearts and minds toward him. God wants us to rise above that which separates us. God wants us to ascend into holiness—not upon the occasion of our death but in this very moment.

In this way, God Above isn't so much *Lord* as *Love*: constant, sovereign, generous, knowing, and inviting. Bestowing us with a will of our own, and the freedom to act upon it, was a radical act of love. Sometimes I think the merciful thing might have been for God *not* to grant us free will at all. If it weren't for free will, we would be ambling around Eden in the evening air, blissfully naked with flowers in our hair. We would be lying on our backs looking up at the tips of trees and marveling. And yet we wouldn't be there by our own volition. We wouldn't be there because of any authentic *relationship*, which was the basis for—and nature of—all creation.

Autocracy may be God's privilege, but it is not God's pleasure. Ever wise, God finds pleasure in something altogether different. The Greatest of All Time rules not with an iron fist but with a secret strength, a long view, and an all-encompassing will to love. God is not an old man on a throne but a sovereign so sublime that the kingdom and the power and glory that are his, he freely and fully bestows on us. All we have to do is rise to receive them.

CONVERGENCE

I think we rise every time we take the extra few minutes to listen to someone else's story. We rise every time we say, *That's okay. I forgive you.* We rise every time we sink to our knees and try to talk to God, every time we tell a hard truth with compassion, every time we speak up about an injustice, however small. The longer I make this list, the more I understand that every moment of every day is an opportunity to rise and therefore to receive "every good and perfect gift," which "is from above, coming down from the Father of the heavenly lights, who does not change like shifting shadows" (James 1:17 NIV).

That might be worth repeating. Every good and perfect gift is from *above*.

As a former high school English teacher, I once worked with my students on Flannery O'Connor's story "Everything That Rises Must Converge." If nothing else (and there was so much else), I was drawn to the title. I knew it was true before I knew what it meant, and so I often pondered it, turning that phrase over in my head like a lovely stone. *Everything that rises must converge. Everything that rises must converge. Rises. Converge. Must. Everything.* Each time I contemplated its meaning, I came to a deeper understanding.

Rising is ultimately an act of convergence. It is the place, or state, or experience, where we reunite with God and with all. This convergence, which is our deepest desire and truest promise, is available in perpetuity, including *now.* That which rises—that which passes from life into eternal life but also that which uplifts rather than denigrates, that which soars rather than sours, that which perseveres rather than calls it quits—is engaging in a process of unification. And this process leaves nothing, not one thing, out. It can't leave anything out because it is a divine process, coming from above and calling us above.

God is undoubtedly on high. When we get out of the bouncy house, God is up there where the clouds part and the angels sing.

Omnipotence is God's. So is omniscience. All those omnis belong to God. It would make sense to fear this God, but given all the blessings he has bestowed on us, all the glory he has given us, all the mercy he has shown us, all the love he has made available to us, awe and praise will likely do: awe, and praise, and an attempt to surrender, and maybe an effort to rise above our egos and unite. Those will likely be the wings we need to meet *El Shaddai*, God Above, whose kingdom is not so much a territory under rule as a place of true and total convergence.

A PRAYER TO GOD ABOVE

God Almighty, Most High,
your thoughts are not our thoughts,
your ways are not our ways.

May we learn to bow humbly and joyfully before you.
May we learn to set our hearts on things above.
May we learn to trust in your expansive wisdom.
May we behold your glory and be awed.

God Above, rule over us.
God Above, watch over us.
God Above, behold us
and help us rise,

That we may all be one
On earth as it is in heaven.

Amen.

CHAPTER TWO

Beneath

And as soon as we had heard these things, our hearts did melt,
neither did there remain any more courage in
any man, because of you:
for the Lord your God, he is God in heaven above,
and in earth beneath.

Joshua 2:11 (KJV)

Gaia / mother of all / foundation of all / the oldest one . . . /
She feeds everything / that is in the world / Whoever you are /
whether you live upon her sacred ground / or whether you
live along / the paths of the sea / you that fly / It is she who
nourishes you / from her treasure-store.

Homeric Hymn 30

Four years ago, our family moved into what can best be described as a mid-century modern tree house. Built in 1970, the house sits on a hillside among mature cedar trees and the occasional sycamore. Its defining feature is its roof—massive and steep atop the home's three slim stories, which sink successively into the downslope. On the top floor is my office, where I sit eye level with the leaves. Our youngest daughter's bedroom is up there also. On the top bunk of the top floor, she is higher even than the perched owls outside. On the middle floor are our primary living areas and bedroom. And on the lowest floor, which sits on bedrock, are our two oldest daughters' rooms and a utility room lined with cinder blocks.

Tucked behind the utility room, past the hot water heater and the water filters, past the furnace and the cleaning supplies, beneath the stairs was—when we bought the house—a small extra space, barely worthy of being called a room. Into that area we shoved an ancient standing freezer, an assortment of junk, and more than one mousetrap. On my way to grab frozen biscuits one morning, I found a snakeskin in there, which struck me as both terrifying and prophetic.

For the first two years living in the house, I spent nearly all my time in high areas. I went to the bottom floor only to say prayers with my oldest girls at bedtime and to serve as their alarm clock come morning. Also to haul clothes out of the dryer and shove dirty ones into the washer. That was it. It was cold and empty down there. In fact, the entire energy of the house seemed stunted midway. No blood flow was getting to the root.

The same thing was happening inside me, it turns out. It took my friend Molly, who is trained in energy work and feng shui, to guide me to this discovery. Because I had invited Molly to collaborate with me on several spiritual retreats, as a kindness she offered to help me clear and align my chakras in return. Chakras are energy centers in the body, first identified in the Vedas, which are ancient Indian texts dating back thousands of years before Jesus was born. Mainstream understanding reveals seven main chakras that run along the spine, from root to crown. When they are clear, energy flows abundantly and freely through them.

Once we had taken our seats on the porch swing to begin the session, Molly invited me to settle into the moment and into my body. She then asked me to focus my awareness on my root chakra, also called the *Muladhara*, which sits at the base of the spine. She explained that the root chakra is associated with the color red and its element is earth. "It is our grounding place, our source of stability and strength. Our fruits are a direct result of our roots. If our roots are too shallow or too thin, they will not send up the nourishment we need to live full and productive lives. If the root chakra is blocked, we are likely to feel apathetic, depleted, and anxious."

Precisely what I had been feeling.

When Molly asked if I saw or felt anything in particular when focusing on this root region, my answer was an immediate yes. A boulder, I told her. What I saw and felt was a massive rock lodged at the base of my spine, weighing me down and blocking the flow of energy. In the months prior, my contemplative life and in turn my creative life had turned arid, my soul parched.

Seeing it so clearly in my mind's eye, I recognized immediately what the boulder was and why it was there. I had given in to the notion that I had to be the rock for my entire family. I had come to believe that the health of our household depended on my ability to be steady, forbearing, patient, and strong. I was the one who had to keep it all together, not just our insane calendar but our sense of stability and harmony as well. If I faltered one little bit, the whole fragile ecosystem would come crumbling down.

Talk about pressure. I had sold myself an entirely false narrative, which was that as a mother, my job was to be the cornerstone holding up other people's lives, namely my children's and my husband's.

Christians know that the chief cornerstone is supposed to be Christ. The metaphor makes sense to us, but in ancient Judea, its significance would have hit home quite literally. The Gospels of Matthew, Mark, and Luke all recount Jesus asking the crowds if they recall the prophecy about the stone, the one that the builders rejected (Matthew 21:42, Mark 12:10, Luke 20:17). Those in attendance would have known the reference—it is to Isaiah 28:16, when God makes known that he is "laying in Zion a foundation stone, a tested stone, a precious cornerstone, a sure foundation"—and they would have understood its message. These were people who built their own houses and temples. They were present, if not actively involved, in construction projects. They knew without question that the singular most important element of any structure was the cornerstone. It was the first stone set and therefore the one that determined the structure's alignment and integrity. Claiming Jesus to be the chief cornerstone was not in any way equivocating. He was to be the savior of the world, and he would live this out from a position solidly *beneath*.

DEEP WELLING

Until that watershed moment on the porch swing with Molly, I really had no idea how exhausting it is to try to be a cornerstone when you're not one. With the best of intentions, I was mistaking my job for God's. What I craved deep in my core was not control but freedom, and somehow I knew that finding it was not going to come from climbing back up to those familiar high places. A mountaintop transfiguration was not in the cards. I needed to get down to the actual foundation and feel bodily what that really is. I needed to go down to where that boulder was sitting and learn to dislodge it. I needed to go into a dark cave and abide in stillness, no matter who might be calling my name from upstairs.

And so one day—one Saturday not long after my session with Molly when by some divine miracle we had no basketball games on the docket and no birthday parties to rush to—I resolved to transform the half-finished, mouse-riddled, junk-piled basement hideout in our home into a meditation room. I'd make it a room of my own—not for work but for communing with God.

Hauling out the half-full storage bins, broken skateboard, and random chair, I swept, vacuumed, mopped, and then mopped again. Collecting several promising items from around the house, including a set of string lights, a Moroccan floor cushion, a wrought iron lamp (half-broken), several Target pillows (all cream or white, most with stains), and a few dusty hurricane lamps, I set about creating a space where I could ground myself, literally and spiritually.

Fixing up this space, which I was now calling my meditation room, I had an exposed water pipe to contend with, but I wrapped it in an old piece of burlap and stuck an Ikea shelf on it, discovering that I had inadvertently made an altar. On the altar, I set a small vase with a feather, a turtle shell, a simple wooden cross, and a rock I had found in the river at our family's farm, which bears a strange marking not unlike an ancient rune. The final touch was a wooden basket with all the paraphernalia of my contemplative life: several books of poetry, whatever books of spiritual nonfiction I was reading at the time or intended to read soon, a Bible, a journal, a pencil, an assortment of crystals, a stick of palo santo, a candle, and a box of matches.

The next morning, I rose early and descended into the meditation room. I lit a candle and sat on the ground, feeling the very foundation of my home beneath the weight of my body. Closing my eyes, I began the process of what I have come to call *deep welling*.

Deep welling is a sacred time of meditation, prayer, reading, and journaling that takes place in a low bunker of our soul. It is an exercise in resuscitating feminine energies: of going inward and learning to breathe all the way up and all the way down our bodies. This corridor of oxygen proves to be a corridor of divine energy, as ancient tradition promised it would. Even that word *corridor* shows itself anew. The more yet-dark mornings we wake early to go sit in a cave of our own making, be it literal or metaphorical, the more we are able to traverse that *core-i-door*: portal to true self, threshold to the Source of all being.

That first morning, abiding in silence and solitude, I pulled from my basket of books a copy of Flannery O'Connor's *A Prayer Journal*, which had been a gift from my friend Eva several years prior. I had been saving it for the right time, and the right time had arrived. I was only four pages in when I encountered this line of astounding, even providential, relevance: "Please help me to get down under things and find where you are." Her words matched my exact actions. There, in my little room under the stairs, I, too, was praying to get under things. Under the surface. Under the chop of daily life. Under patterns of behavior and patterns of belief. Under the obvious. Under what I had been taught and told. Under my own skin.

What I sought was deep, deeper even than the cornerstone. I could sense, as Gerard Manley Hopkins penned in that same poem about brooding breast and bright wings, that "there lives the dearest freshness deep down things." I wanted to get down to *that.*

Over the next weeks and months, through profound silence and guided meditations offered by various apps, I felt myself descending. I visualized myself entering subterranean spaces often accessed by steep sets of stairs. Occasionally while in these deep meditative states, I would meet others: my maternal grandmother who passed when I was young, archetypal figures both male and female, and Christ in forms traditional and radical. This might sound strange, but it felt natural and profoundly true. I was slowly accessing the layers of my subconscious, getting closer to that deep-down freshness that I could not see or name.

In hindsight I can see that I was undertaking the rigorous and sacred work of integrating along the vertical axis. But the way, at times, felt more like a complicated labyrinth than a corridor. When I talked about my experience with another wise friend of mine, Blaire, an expert in integrative health and an uncanny seer into the soul, she asked if I felt myself to be in a process of *gathering* or a process of *shedding. Shedding* was my emphatic answer. I was shedding layer upon layer of creeds and rules, monikers, and mandates. All this I was shedding, trying to get at whatever was *under,* trying to get to the essence *beneath.* For just as God is in the topmost summit and awaits us from above, it was becoming clear to me that God is also in the undermost deep and awaits us in the beneath.

UNDERWORLD

Mythology is rich with stories of deities dwelling in the mountains but also in the underworld. In Greek mythology, the deepest bowels of the earth are presided over by Hades and his wife, Persephone, whom he abducted. Pulled into the netherworld, she becomes its queen, assuming reign over the souls of the dead. And yet despite this fate, Persephone maintains the legacy given to her by her mother, Demeter, one of the twelve original Olympians and goddess of the harvest. Alternating time between the underworld and the above-world, Persephone rules as goddess both of death and of fertility. The two are inextricably linked.

In Sumerian myths, the goddess Inanna also experiences a descent into the underworld that proves transformative. Her story, "The Descent of Inanna," was etched into clay tablets in the third millennium before Christ and has come to be considered the first epic poem ever written. Its opening lines make use of repetition to underscore the goddess's calculated decision to indwell the "Great Below." In translation, it reads: "From the great heaven she set her mind on the great below. From the great heaven the goddess set her mind on the great below. From the great heaven Inanna set her mind on the great below. My mistress abandoned heaven, abandoned earth, and descended to the underworld. Inanna abandoned heaven, abandoned earth, and descended to the underworld."

The narrative arc of Inanna's experience once she makes her obligatory descent—of betrayal by loved ones, of being stripped naked, of being hung on a hook to the point of death, of being resurrected three days later, of returning to the earth and again to the heavens—will be familiar to Christians. The story of Christ, with its roots in ancient mythology, underscores the imperative of death as a pathway to resurrection. It also confirms the dual nature of the Divine: both supernal (coming from on high) and chthonic (of the underworld).

What is it about the summits and the depths that inspire their association with the Divine? Both are places of imposing beauty and mystery characterized by an intrinsic unknowability and an element of danger. Neither is readily accessed. They are and will remain the last frontier: places only God can claim and only a select few can visit, and even then only briefly. In this way, God Above and God Beneath are conceptually kindred: both shrouded, elusive, and formidable.

When I looked again and closely, I found in Scripture a God "who shall bless thee with blessings of heaven above but also with blessings of the deep that lieth under, blessings of the breasts, and of the womb" (Genesis 49:25 KJV). What a revelation to discover language about God the Mother bestowing blessings of the breasts and of the womb!

What a revelation to discover a fearful yet generative God who operates not only from a position of power Above but from a position of power Beneath as well.

This shift in my conception of God proved seismic. I was able to experience the mystical union that I had been seeking, not as an idea to be grasped but as a depth to be mined. The Divine became the ever-hiding, ever-revealing, elusive but inevitable next layer down. As the mystic Julian of Norwich articulates: "[God] is [the] Ground in whom our Soul standeth, and He is [the] Mean that keepeth the Substance and the Sense-nature together so that they shall never dispart. For our soul sitteth in God in very rest, and our soul standeth in God in very strength, and our Soul is kindly rooted in God in endless love."

ROOT

Our soul *is* rooted in God, and yet many of us suffer from a "root problem." We have no roots, or at least no reliable ones. We are always on the go, lost in a chop of our own making, untethered from our true selves, from the earth beneath us, and from God. And we don't even know what we are missing.

Richard Powers opens his novel *The Overstory* with a woman leaning against a pine tree that speaks to her in "words before words." In chorus with more trees farther away, the pine says: "All the ways you imagine us—bewitched mangroves on stilts, a nutmeg's inverted spade, gnarled baja elephant trunks, the straight-up missile of a sal—are always amputations. Your kind never sees us whole. You miss half of it, and more. There's always as much belowground as above. That's the trouble with people, the trees go on to say: their root problem."

Though this "root problem" feels like an affliction distinct to modern-day life, it seems to have been true of first-century Judea as well. Jesus felt compelled to warn his followers of the root problem, using the parable of the sower and the seed to illustrate his point.

When he told this parable, such a large crowd had gathered to hear his teachings that Jesus had to climb into a boat to gain some space before addressing them. I can imagine Jesus standing on the prow, raising his arms for quiet. He is direct and unequivocal but not harsh or angry. He lays out the facts clearly: The seeds that fall on the surface quickly get eaten. The seeds that get sown in rocky soil grow fast but burn the minute things get hot. The seeds that get sown among the thorns get choked out. But the seeds that get sown in good soil grow steadily and bear ample grain. These are the seeds that grow roots and fruits. To the crowd, Jesus then says, "He who has ears to hear, let him hear."

I suspect there were some soulful thinkers in the crowd who understood Jesus's metaphor, but the disciples did not get it. Later they had to ask for clarification. Jesus tells the parable all over again, adding a few more details. The birds that devour the surface seeds are temptations. The sun that immediately burns up the seeds sown in rocky soil is a form of tribulation or persecution. The thorns that choke out some seeds are cares of the world and delight in riches. On the last point, Jesus explains that the seeds that are sown in good soil are the ones that "hear the word and understand it" (Matthew 13).

Jesus's teachings in this parable echo the wisdom of the ancient goddesses worshipped by agrarian societies the world over. They tell us that what's important is what's beneath, as symbolized by the seed and the root. Clarissa Pinkola Estes makes this point in her best-selling book, *Women Who Run with the Wolves*, when she writes, "If one has the root stock, the basis, the original part, if one has the seed corn, any havoc can be repaired, devastations can be resewn, fields can be rested, hard seed can be soaked to soften it, to help it break open and thrive. To have the seed means to have the key to life."

What happens when we settle down—when we stop racing along the blacktop, making our lives busy but fallow—is that we develop ears to hear. We hear not only the hidden meanings in Jesus's parables but something else also. We tune in to what Estes calls the "*canto hondo,* the deep song, the words of which come back to us when we do the work of soulful reclamation." To us is offered so much rich soil, so much sacred space in which to root.

The trees in Richard Powers's story pause, but they are not finished talking. They have one more thing to say: "If your mind were only a slightly greener thing, we'd drown you in meaning." The trees are like Jesus, impelling the crowds to incline an ear and to listen, to hear and to accept, to still and to deepen. Accessing God is about greening our mind. And faith is a matter of rooting, of seeping our way into that which truly nourishes us and gaining our stronghold there. It is as Christ explains in a different yet related parable: "I am the vine; you are the branches. Those who abide in me and I in them bear much fruit, because apart from me you can do nothing" (John 15:5).

All the nourishment we need—all the sustenance, all the stability—is buried beneath the surface of earthly things. Root into the fertile loam of the Divine, and we are promised to "bear fruit, thirtyfold, and sixtyfold, and hundredfold" (Mark 4:20 ASV). Such is the harvest of the soul.

GROUNDING

A dip into middle school science reminds us that the Earth has several layers: the crust, the mantle, the outer core, and the inner core. The inner core is approximately 4,000 miles beneath our feet. For reference, the distance between San Francisco and New York City is about 3,000 miles. Go all the way across the country, and you'd still have 1,000 miles to go before you hit the core of the core. For further reference, the deepest humans have ever drilled into the earth is a mere 7.6 miles. Even giving us a couple inches, that's about 0.002 percent of the way down. There is so much *beneath* that we cannot access, and yet we do know a great deal about its nature. The inner core of the Earth is extremely dense, formed primarily of nickel and iron. It burns at 9,800°F, a mere 200° cooler than the surface of the sun. Atop this burning hot center flows the outer core, which is also comprised of nickel and iron, but in liquid form that churns and flows. This churning and flowing creates convection currents that in turn generate electrical currents that form the Earth's magnetic field.

The magnetic field enables the Eurasian reed warbler to winter in sub-Saharan Africa and return to breed in Europe. The magnetic field enables the monarch butterfly to migrate from the Rocky Mountains to central Mexico and back over several generations. The magnetic field enables a sea turtle to swim from North Carolina to North Africa and home again to lay her eggs. The magnetic field, which is generated thousands of miles beneath us, serves as a navigational guide for a diversity of species that possess the proper sensitivity to it. Homing pigeons. Lobsters. Honeybees. Humpback whales. Even ants. All these creatures are capable of magnetoreception, a skill that allows them to detect the Earth's magnetic fields and use those fields to guide them. Humans, not so much, though we are ever learning.

One way to tap into the nourishment of this electric depth is through a therapeutic practice called *earthing* or *grounding*, which helps us tune into the Earth's charges for a variety of healing benefits, ranging from improved cardiovascular health to reduced inflammation. Grounding entails pretty much anything Mary Oliver articulates in any one of her poems, such as "At the River Clarion." Sitting for a time on the bank of the river, the poet begins to hear murmurs. The water, the stones, "even the moss beneath the water" have messages for her, not unlike the trees in Powers's novel. Their message, when received, is clear: "I am part of holiness."

It really is that simple. When we go out in nature and tune in to that which is beneath us—the trees and the roots beneath the soil, the springs and the mosses beneath the water, the garden and the seed beneath the shoots—there comes over us a sense of serenity and a sense of connection and ultimately a sense of the sacred. Novelist Lauren Goff articulates this moment of enlightenment in her novel *The Vaster Wilds* when she brings her protagonist to the lip of death and invites her to rewrite—to re*wild*—her understanding of God. "She had once believed that in the deepest reaches of everything was a nothing where men had planted god; but now she knew that deeper within that nothing was something else, something made of light and heat. It was this light and heat that endured, that was everlasting. At the center was not nothing, no. Out of the light and the heat all goodness poured." The God that the girl comes to fathom is not a deity of dominion but of upsurging depth. This God is not an abstraction of mankind but the generative and relentless power of Creation.

In *Freeing Jesus*, Diana Butler Bass articulates her own story of deepening to God Beneath. Having explored the various roles Jesus played in her life—Friend, Teacher, Savior, Lord, and Way—Bass closes her book with a final chapter titled Presence. She writes:

> Jesus is not far away in the sky, but here. He came here on purpose, surrendering the glories of heavenly realms for this humble earth. Emptying, tumbling down the mountainside, the rubble on the ground. That rubble, however, is not trash. . . . The fall, the surrender to gravity, releases energy; the moving thundering rocks, what seemed eternally stable, become something new. . . . This is the way that the earth births itself over and again, Indeed, this is the very meaning of "Mother Earth." Sometimes we imagine "Mother Earth" as a frolicking figure, a kind of white-robed goddess. However, Mother Earth births in the falling rock, the flooding waters, the winds of the haboob. Rock is not static, not permanent or stable. . . . Rock is generative. . . . Jesus is not Lord above the earth; instead, Jesus is earthy lord. Jesus is the birthing one. The rock. All the breaking, falling, and thunder; all the growing, nurturing, and gentleness: all of a piece.

Bass's description of Jesus places him in a lineage of the Divine that dates back many, many millennia. She connects Jesus to those distant ancestors of ours for whom the Divine was Mother Earth, and in doing so she underscores a powerful truth put forth by Paul Tillich, a German theologian of the early twentieth century. Tillich resisted the notion of God as *a* being (a who or a what) and insisted instead that God was beingness itself. He described God as the "ground of being": the core of the core that enlivens us but that also tethers and upholds us.

This language echoes that of fourteenth-century German theologian Meister Eckhart, who preached that God's ground is our ground, and our ground is God's ground. The term Eckhart used for ground was "grunt," which offers several layers of meaning. It refers to the physical earth beneath us. To the underside of something more generally. To the origin of something. And also to the inmost core of it: its true essence. We are reminded of Peter's description of Christ as the "living stone" (1 Peter 2:4–8) and Paul's description of Christ as a "spiritual rock" from which we can drink (1 Corinthians 10:4). These are not confused or mixed metaphors on the part of the saints. These are geological and spiritual accuracies.

The ground that undergirds us is indeed living; it is capable of quenching our deepest thirst and hunger, both physical and spiritual. And, at the deepest level, God's essence and ours are one, no matter what we have done or left undone, no matter how high or how low we may feel, no matter how grand or how inconsequential. Just as everything that rises must converge, everything that descends must converge too. The truth about the Great Chain of Being is thus realized. That which is Above and that which is Beneath coexist in a dynamic relationship that was established at the very outset of creation.

It is revelatory for me how aligned these two words prove to be, despite being opposites. Integrating God Beneath need not and in fact does not deny the truth and goodness of God Above; rather, it affirms them. Likewise, praising God Above need not and in fact does not deny the truth and goodness of God Beneath; rather, it affirms them. God is both apex and nadir. It is as the thirteenth-century Spanish rabbi Moses de Leon wrote: "The sublime, inner essences secretly constitute a chain linking everything from the highest to the lowest, extending from the upper pool to the edge of the universe. There is nothing—not even the tiniest thing—that is not fastened to the links of this chain. . . . The entire chain is one. Down to the last link, everything is linked with everything else; so divine essence is below as well as above, in heaven and on earth. There is nothing else."

KATABASIS

We are trained to want to be high on that chain, but at some point in time, in one way or another, we all find ourselves at the bottom. Our descent is rarely desired and our landing rarely supple. Regardless, the way to God is often down before it is up.

In his *New York Times* bestseller, *Iron John: A Book About Men*, Robert Bly delves into an ancient myth about a Wild Man who initiates a young boy into manhood and extracts truths that illuminate so much about how and why men today are suffering. In Chapter 3, Bly investigates what must happen to the hero when he has reached the pinnacle of youth, when he has become an "ascender" and is viewed as a *puelle aeterna* (holy or eternal boy) but has not yet learned of poverty and depravity. There's only one way for the kid to go, and it is down. Descent—*katabasis* as the Greeks called it—is not a pretty business. It is characterized by "ordinariness, heaviness, weightiness, and soberness." It is what happens when life, at any stage, discharges us, and we unwittingly find ourselves at rock bottom, perhaps from loss of a marriage or a job, or from addiction or illness or disillusionment.

Few of us would wish rock bottom on anyone, and yet it is often the place where we—with mud in our teeth, alone in the dark, cold, and terrified of what we have done or what will become of us—meet God. In this way, descent, the kind we most fear and resist, also becomes what Bly calls a "holy thing." It is what enables us to increase our "tolerance for ashes" and our "stomach for terrifying insights," he writes. It is what deepens our ability to understand the sorrow of the world so that we learn to shudder with compassion.

Bumping our heads and egos on the hard *humus* (Latin for earth), we learn humility. This crucial work happens at rock bottom, and, like you, I have been there. I have been on the floor, wracked by my own sobs that felt like retching. I have answered the phone when a friend found the rug—the entire rug of a shared life with its marriage, its children, its coffees, and its lovemaking—pulled out from under her, gone. I have been witness to stories of suicide, by gun, by rope, by overdose, shared by ones left behind, ones left breathing, barely. I have taught brilliant, beautiful adolescent girls who made A's on their papers and took razor blades to their wrists. I have sat vigil by a man who went walking with a loaded gun and used it. No one is immune to the echoes from the bottom, crying for mercy.

Katabasis is a critical part of the spiritual journey, and so we have to learn to sit achingly in anguish. There is no escape hatch or quick fix, no way to numb it out. We have to stay until we know with certainty that the ground is solid beneath us. This is the God Flannery O'Connor seeks when she writes that there is something "down there . . . which is holding me in."

Times of suffering are agonizing invitations into trust: trust that we will not be swallowed whole but will instead develop endurance and subsequently character and ultimately hope (Romans 5:3–5). The hope that derives from meeting the Divine through katabasis is not the naïve optimism of the ascender. It is the holy fortitude of one who has descended and found herself or himself yet alive. The ground proves both hard in the landing and also strong for the standing.

As David Brooks notes in his book *The Second Mountain*, "seasons of suffering have a way of exposing the deepest parts of ourselves and reminding us that we're not the people we thought we were." They help us discover that there is another layer we have been neglecting, "a substrate where the dark wound, and the most powerful yearnings live." Going down is how we find our humility. It is also how we find our humanity.

LOWERING

This humanity is the last thing Jesus teaches and models before he is hung up to die. On what was his final night on earth in human form, which he *knew* would be his last night, Jesus chose to lower himself, demonstrating beneathhood as an expression of love.

Getting up from the table, Jesus takes off his outer robe, wraps a towel around his waist, pours water into a basin, and gets down on his knees. Calling his friends one by one to sit, he tenderly places their feet in the water and begins to wash them—feet that had been walking in the dust all day in sandals, feet with toenails that I can only imagine were thick and curled and yellow. "You do not know now what I am doing, but later you will understand," he explains in a voice calm and wise (John 13:7).

Once Jesus has washed the feet of all the people in the room and carefully dried them, he stands, puts back on his robe, and resumes his seat. "You call me Teacher and Lord, and you are right, for that is what I am," he tells them before continuing: "So if I, your Lord and Teacher, have washed your feet, you also ought to wash one another's feet. For I have set you an example, that you also should do as I have done to you. Very truly, I tell you, slaves are not greater than their master, nor are messengers greater than the one who sent them. If you know these things, you are blessed if you do them" (John 13:14–17).

In this moment, Jesus is uncharacteristically direct. He has little time left to speak truth to power. He has little time left to prophesy. He doesn't want them to miss the message here, which is that when we are instructed to imitate God, we are being asked to lower ourselves into loving service, precisely as God did. When God "came down" and assumed a place in humanity, he lowered himself amply. God became a baby. Who was born in a barn. To a poor teenager who appeared to have cuckolded her fiancé. It's a real shocker when you frame it that way, but that's not even the sum of it. God, in Jesus, opted to be not a king but a carpenter, not a master but a servant. Jesus did not come to be served but to serve (Matthew 20:28). He, with all possible richness, chose to be poor (2 Corinthians 8:9). Episcopalian priest and author Cynthia Bourgeault emphasizes the humility, the *beneathing*, that Jesus consistently displayed. "In whatever life circumstance, Jesus always responded with the same motion of self-emptying," she writes: "To put it another way, of the same motion of descent: going lower, taking the lower place, not the higher."

How might the world change if we, one by one, bit by bit, dedicated ourselves to such lowering? If we cultivated beneathhood? How might the world change if we took to heart the advice Paul gives to the Romans when he says, "Be devoted to one another in love. Honor another above yourselves" (Romans 12:10 NIV)? The ego will vie for a place above, but the soul, if given the opportunity, will relish going beneath.

Putting ourselves beneath someone else is not a meek act. It is not an act at all, it turns out. It is, rather, a way of being: the precise way of being that God modeled for us. God is, after all, the Root of the root. The Rock of the rock. The Deep of the deep.

A PRAYER TO GOD BENEATH

God Beneath,
You are living stone and moss,
radiant core and regolith and loam.

You are the rich feed of our roots,
the birthing rock of our earth,
the ground of our being.

You are the freshest deep down thing.

May we go looking for you with our bare feet.

May we stand, as a tree, rooted in stillness
and want for nothing.

May we palm a stone
and see it as nothing less than a sacrament.

May we hit rock bottom
and find that what we fall onto is you.

May we get on our hands and knees
and wash the soles of your children.

Amen.

CHAPTER THREE

Near

Draw near to God, and God will draw near to you.

James 4:8

I have a capacity in my soul for taking in God entirely.
I am as sure as I live that nothing is so near to me as God.
God is nearer to me than I am to myself;
my existence depends on the nearness and presence of God.

Meister Eckhart

Nearness is, by nature, a tease. It is intimate and close yet untouchable, untamable, unreachable by hands or words or reason. There is a necessary space to be maintained with nearness, which evokes mystery and in turn allure. The space lets in a little sizzle, as multi-Grammy winner Norah Jones sings: "It's not the pale moon that excites me. . . . It's just the nearness of you."

The Divine is like that. She is that which lurks, that which lingers, that which we intuit but cannot confirm. Christians call her the Holy Spirit or, as was the case in my Episcopalian upbringing, the Holy Ghost.

As a child, I knew about ghosts. The door to the attic was in my room, as was a sliding glass door that looked out over a cave and a creek: the very spot where they say a woman named Sally Pack had been murdered centuries prior. Sally had lived on the farm alone, keeping two big dogs for protection, but legend has it robbers slit the dogs' throats to get to Sally. Legend also has it they put Sally face down in the spring near the cave just outside my window. In my father's office, an aged newspaper clipping with the legend of Sally Pack hung framed on the wall. It was yellowed and ominous. When the floors creaked in the house, it was Sally, my parents said. She was a nice ghost, they assured us.

The spirit world avails itself to us in legends as in myths and poetry. It avails itself to us in the cover of woods or the cover of night. It avails itself to us in solitude and in nature, a truth I learned early. Growing up on that farm in the Tennessee countryside, I encountered the Holy Spirit often, especially when exploring alone outdoors. I climbed hay bales and wooded hillsides and waded among bluebells blanketing the banks of the nearby river. I tracked creatures of all kinds—lizards on the deck and snakes in the high grass, bumblebees burrowing into wooden railings and bullfrogs burrowing into the mud, water spiders prancing atop the surface of the pond, and lightning bugs blinking out love notes on the night air—sensing all the while some mysterious presence, a Spirit that hovers and thrums. I saw things die. Lots of things. And I saw plenty more things live. All around me, every day, a riot of living and dying, connected by some common source, some common force, near enough to sense but never near enough to name or hold. The air was pregnant with it: a delectable invisible. A God Near: a Holy Ghost.

I never quite knew whether this Ghost was real or not, except I also did know. I had heard the words we spoke in church, and I was beginning to make sense of them. God as Father was logical and comforting, God as Son was confusing and comforting, but God as Holy Ghost—that was scintillating, and pure magic, and to-the-bone true. This was the God that felt most real to me, however elusive she might be. I loved her and I feared her. She proved the hardest to locate and the easiest to lose.

ATTUNEMENT

In my experience, the Holy Spirit doesn't get a whole lot of attention for being a third of the Trinity. The Nicene Creed that gets recited on Sunday mornings in Anglican churches calls it "the giver of life" and notes that it should be "worshiped and glorified." The Bible Dictionary calls the Holy Spirit "a mysterious power" and pretty much leaves it at that. Scripture suggests that the Holy Spirit is responsible for breathing life into Adam in Genesis and is responsible for breathing life into Mary during conception. The Spirit is what enables the prophets to prophesy and the healers to heal. It is what descends on Jesus during his baptism and what Jesus promises to leave us after he is gone. The Spirit is, it seems, some force—pervasive yet proximal—that enables us to experience life more acutely, to know moments of truth in the raw, and to feel connected.

So much of life we plod through unexceptionally. We read pages that number 1, 2, 3 … 119, 120, 121 … predictable, sequential. We sit at the traffic light waiting for the red to turn green. We exist through countless series of Monday-through-Sunday. We measure out our lives in mundane tasks. Life is indeed doled out in T. S. Eliot's coffee spoons.

Yet perhaps you have sensed, beyond the safe ordering of our world, a wildness. An infinitesimal fluttering. And also a swelling: a contraction and an expansion. Perhaps today or last week or five years ago you suddenly sensed a wave that you can't see but that elephants can feel in their ponderous feet. There is a molecule of oxygen that your great-great-grandmother exhaled that just slipped into your bloodstream. There is an energy shifting that you have sensed. There is a shadow along the edge: animal or angel.

In a moment like this, you have stopped walking. You have stopped thinking, blissfully. You have stilled, the antennae of your very soul raised. You have trained your whole being to the presence of the Holy Spirit, the Holy Ghost, and in doing so you have touched the ecstasy of what it means to be alive. This is what it means to be exquisitely attuned to God Near, who is always exquisitely attuned to you.

This phrase, "exquisitely attuned," is one I first encountered in a book by brilliant clinical psychologist and author Lisa Damour. Damour is a "girl whisperer," and because my husband and I have three fast-growing daughters of our own, I devour any and all books she writes, podcasts she airs, talks she gives. It was in her astute book *Untangled* where I encountered a claim that she makes about the way teenage girls are "exquisitely attuned" to the adults in their lives, namely their parents. They are so tuned in to our emotions, our patterns of behavior, and our pitfalls that they can discern all kinds of nuances spoken and unspoken. Hyperaware social creatures, they possess incredible gifts of insight. They also know just how to push our buttons to elicit certain responses and how to craft appeals to get what they desire. It is the maddening gift of the teenage girl, this power they have of being exquisitely attuned to our shadows and much less attuned to their own.

I suspect we adults are like that as well. We are exquisitely attuned to those things we want to manipulate and control but less attuned to our own psyches and souls. What's more, we tend to be exquisitely attuned to the demands of the day but pitifully attuned to the peripheral and sacred Spirit. Most of the time, we go about our lives with little sense of the nearness of God. There is no spark of the divine, no electric charge of the sublime. There is, instead, lots to do.

If we feel near an edge, it is less likely to be divine revelation and more likely to be the cliff of our own sanity. God may be near us, but we would never know it. How could we, with our frantic pace, our feeds that don't feed us? To experience the nearness of God is a gift. It is also a discipline. A practice.

I first heard the phrase "practice the presence of God" in a sermon years ago. It struck me immediately, and so I wrote it in large block letters across the top of my church bulletin:

PRACTICE THE PRESENCE OF GOD

The phrase was coined by Brother Lawrence, a seventeenth-century lay leader in the Parisian Carmelite Order. He greeted each moment as an opportunity to relish God and encouraged believers to pray not through memorized words but through robust and serene devotion to the task at hand. For Brother Lawrence, the nearness of God was an absolute given. It was up to us to absorb it.

I reflected on this teaching in earnest in the weeks and months after that sermon, and the more I pondered it, the more its truths seemed to spool out in succession: the foundational assertion that God is present (or near), the assertion that we have the capacity to experience that presence, and the assertion that the experience of God is to some extent within our power.

Holy encountering is not a matter of whim but a matter of practice. What this means is, we can cultivate mysticism. The instructions are simple: "Draw near to God, and he will draw near to you" (James 4:8). The word *draw* is derived from the Middle English word *drauen*, which meant to give motion to by the act of pulling. We and God are like magnets, giving motion to one another by a pull that unifies us. If we pull toward God, God will pull toward us.

But how? How do we initiate that pull? Some of us may want to draw near to God but don't have any idea how to begin. We yearn and yet stall. Some of us may want to draw near to God and are good at starting but lack the ability to sustain it. We attempt meditation or prayer but determine that we are not good at it. We pledge to attend church regularly or volunteer regularly, but we fail to follow through on our own promises—or we follow through on them but without the exquisite attentiveness that sanctifies such actions.

So much barricades us from the experience of God Near. Busyness. Hurrying. Fixations. Preoccupations. Anger. Self-involvement. On it goes. On *we* go. What is required is practice.

We humans aren't hardwired to like practice. It requires sustained commitment, discipline, and work, which is a bummer. When my kids were learning to play violin, they hated practicing. The result? They never made it much past "Twinkle, Twinkle Little Star." Neither do I want to practice tennis, and so when I agree to play in a round robin, I double-fault and find my backhand friendly with the net. Likewise, when I go for a period of time without making it to my meditation cushion, unpleasant consequences await: I get testy with the ones I love and with other drivers on the road. I get caught up in what is next instead of what is now. When I return to the forgotten cushion and close my eyes, my mind spasms and revolts. It is astonishing how fast we can get out of spiritual shape. There is a reason we use the phrase "spiritual discipline." Pursuing and sustaining spiritual maturity requires discipline. It requires practice.

We know how practice works: The more we do something, the more skilled we become. Things don't get "easier," per se; in some ways they get harder as we ask more of ourselves. But our bodies and minds and hearts become conditioned. They learn its benefits firsthand. And so, over time, they desire it.

Practicing the presence of God is a consistent challenge but also a sacred invitation, for with it we are given agency. God gives us our very lives, appointing us our own time and space in which to inhabit this earth. As Acts 17:27 reminds us, we can seek God and perhaps reach out for her and find her, learning that she is never far from any one of us.

And the good news is that God doesn't get fed up with us for falling out of attunement. We need only consider the story of the prodigal son to know that. No matter how far we wander or how much we squander, God is always at the ready, nearby and eager to give another try.

ADJUSTMENT

The prophet Isaiah understands both our thirst for God and our feelings of inadequacy. He understands our relentless preoccupations and the opportunity that awaits us. "Come all you who are thirsty," Isaiah implores. "Come to the waters":

> You who have no money,
>   come, buy and eat!
> Come, buy wine and milk
>   without money and without cost.

> Why spend money on what is not bread,
> and your labour on what does not satisfy?
> Listen, listen to me, and eat what is good,
> and you will delight in the richest of fare.
> Give ear and come to me;
> listen, that you may live. . . .
> Seek the Lord while he may be found;
> call on him while he is near. (Isaiah 55:1–6 NIVUK)

God is near, Isaiah insists. *Come. Listen. Eat. Eat what is good*, he implores. These are all actions of attunement and of intentionality. Rather than buy into the demands or the definitions of success society places on us, Isaiah implores seekers, quench your thirst and hunger on the "richest of fare." That fare is the nearness of God. And it is free.

When we come, when we listen, when we seek, we are already beginning to eat what is good. We are initiating a period of adjustment, which comes from the root words *ad* and *juxta*: "to near." We let our eyes adjust; we let our ears adjust; we let our bodies adjust; we let our souls adjust. This period of adjustment is slow, and so we must give it grace. But gradually, beautifully, our practice becomes habit. We find that we draw near to God not only when we pray or meditate but also when we wash our hands and walk the dog. More practice, and we find that we draw near to God as we go about the office. Even more practice, and we find that we draw near to God in obstacles and conflicts. Our habit becomes a way of being. This is not so much about a moment of conversion as it is about an ongoing conversation, what David Whyte calls "the conversational nature of reality." "Put down the weight of your aloneness and ease into the conversation," he prompts us in his poem "Everything Is Waiting for You."

Drawing near to the God who is already and always near us helps us stay rooted in our bodies and in our faith. Over time, we find that drawing near to God is the means by which we "pray without ceasing" (1 Thessalonians 5:16–18). It is, as Isaiah promises, the labor that satisfies.

Praying through attentiveness rather than through memorized words, or any words at all, is exactly what Brother Lawrence practiced and taught. Prayer can and should be amorphous. It changes form: it changes shape: it changes appearance. We may relate to Mary Oliver, who famously penned the line, "I don't know exactly what a prayer is." If prayer is lying on your back in the grass and watching a grasshopper, wonderful. If it's listening to the wren in the privet singing, how lovely. If it's reciting Scripture or fingering beads, then by all means. If it's moving your body in the light of the moon or the sun, I say, Right on. If it's going to church on Sunday and reciting creeds in unison, do it. If it's seeing everyone who crosses your path as a child of God, praise be. If it is breathing, absolutely yes.

I have prayed, and try to pray, in all these ways. When it's not working—when the world is too much with me, when I lay waste my powers getting and spending, when I am out of tune, as Wordsworth helped us articulate—I take to the fields or the woods or the water banks as a way of seeking the Holy Spirit I know in my bones. For just as people talk of loving-kindness as a way to God, this is the path—and thrill—of loving-nearness: Draw near to God, and God will draw near to you.

STAYING POWER

When Walker and I married on a summer evening at the farm, one of the groomsmen read Philippians 4:4–5. Ed was an old friend with a deep and commanding voice. "Rejoice," boomed Ed across the lawn. "I will say it again. Rejoice! . . . The Lord is near." I swear even the dog cocked his head.

It was Saint Paul who wrote that verse, in a letter to the church at Philippi while he was under house arrest in Rome sometime around the year 61 CE. The early Christians in Philippi had sent Paul a gift upon hearing of his imprisonment, and so he was writing to thank them and to offer some counsel while the opportunity availed itself. The letter he wrote is relatively short, with four chapters total. It is in the final chapter, as he begins to wrap up his correspondence, that Paul gives the missionaries an important takeaway. "Rejoice in the Lord always," Paul encourages them, and then abjectly repeats himself in case they missed it the first time. "I will say it again: Rejoice!"

Some of those tasked with translating the original Greek text, which had no punctuation, chose to insert an exclamation point after the word *Rejoice* to demonstrate the level of fervor that Paul was seeking to convey. Exclamation points can be overused, but it would be hard to argue that this one is gratuitous. Can you really even use the word *rejoice* without an exclamation point? The act of rejoicing is itself an exclamation, from the Latin root *exclamare*, meaning to shout out! Though Paul was himself in lockdown, he proved undeterred from his rallying cry to rejoice.

Why was Paul so certain that we should rejoice? He gives one very specific reason: *The Lord is near.* The nearness of God is grounds for unceasing joy. What's more, the nearness of God eradicates worry. As Paul writes, "Do not be anxious about anything, but in everything by prayer and supplication with thanksgiving let your requests be made known to God" (Philippians 4:6–7). Go ahead and present your requests to God; God is near and can hear them, Paul assures the early Christians, and us two thousand years later.

If only this were so easy to believe. If only the nearness of God were so obvious.

We have all been there. When we heard the news of the death of a young person—to a freak accident, to a bullet, to suicide—we may have felt only God's stark and slicing absence. When we listened for the heartbeat inside our womb and it was no longer there. When we sat numb from drink and not numb at all, the promise of God Near may have fallen on deaf ears. Alone in front of Netflix, feeling for all the world like our life is a waste and no one will love us, we might have sworn up and down that God was anywhere but near. Indeed, the prospect may have seemed like the worst kind of mockery. This world has a wretched way of making God Near feel like a cruel joke.

But those are the times when God is most near. Out of vast love and compassion for us, God draws near to us in our anguish, in our suffering, in our self-loathing and trauma. As Psalm 34:18 proclaims: "The Lord is near to the brokenhearted and saves the crushed in spirit." God loves us, so of course she draws near when we are devastated. That's what we do for the people we love. That's what God does for us: she stays. Because she stays, there is no place we can go where God is not. No matter the events of any given life, of any given day, of any given moment, God is near.

In moments of agony, we can hardly believe this is true. Even Jesus reaches the breaking point of his faith. Hanging by nails, crowned in thorns, mocked by crowds, betrayed by friends, Jesus is dogged by intolerable anguish. He had known full well his fate. The script of his life story was no surprise; it had been prophesied for generations and preached in the Temple. The day before his execution, he announces to his disciples that his "time is near" (Matthew 26:18). The nearer his time draws, though, the more anguished Jesus becomes. He admits that he is "deeply grieved, even to death" (Matthew 26:38). He falls flat on his face in the dust, beseeching God to remove this cup. He begs his friends to stay close and keep watch. He goes off into the darkness to draw near to the God he has given everything to.

Come morning, despite his anguish, Jesus is steady in the face of the high priests and Pilate and the crowds who jeer and mock him. He is steady in the face of the soldiers who strip off his clothes and whip him. He is steady in the face of the condemned criminals who hang beside him and revile him. And he is steady as darkness covers the land, as his breathing grows shallow.

But at the ninth hour, the faith that had steadied Jesus through so much agony—the faith that his beloved Abba had been drawing near to him as he had so desperately drawn near to God—broke. Jesus cries out, "*Eli Eli la'ma sabach-tha'ni*?" which we know means *My God, my God, why have you forsaken me?* (Matthew 27:46). What Jesus experiences in this moment of crisis is the most acute anguish of all: abandonment. Abba gone away. God *not* near.

What, though, of God his Abba? How did God experience this pivotal, painful moment in time? I imagine the anguish God must have felt, watching Jesus's agony, wanting to rescue him but knowing that he can't, not yet. The anguish God must have felt when Jesus, after such devotion and obedience, believes that he has abandoned him. We have to presume that God could have done anything in that moment. He could have rained down holy hell in rage, smiting all. He could have talked himself out of the whole ordained story: He could have swept up Jesus and removed the cup, which would have meant reneging on the whole big promise, but who cared at that point? Maybe it had been enough; maybe it wasn't worth it after all. Or he could have left. He could have retreated into a disappointment and sorrow so profound as to have swallowed all creation. But God didn't. God stayed, whether or not Jesus still had the capacity to believe it.

God draws near to the brokenhearted, even as God is himself brokenhearted. When the curtain rips from top to bottom, I have to believe it is God's very heart ripping in two. And when the earth shakes so violently that the rocks split, I have to believe it is the shuddering sobs of a loving God. We know from personal experience that it is so much easier to be angry: to rage and blame. It is so much easier to withdraw: to walk away and shut up shop on caring. It is so much harder to stay, to draw nearer to pain. It's the hardest thing we do, and it's the hardest thing Jesus did, and it makes sense that it's the hardest thing God does.

As much as he may have wanted to, God didn't remove the cup or change the story or renege on the promise. Because the cup, the story, the promise assure us of this very critical thing: God does not forsake us. God always, *always* draws near, even when—especially when—we are in crisis, whether we feel it or not.

If we really believed that God was near, what rest such knowledge would bring! Our hearts would be flooded not only with joy but also with peace. That is precisely what God Near promises us. A peace that guards our hearts and aligns our minds with the mind of Christ. Instead of thinking about whatever is wrong, whatever is scary, whatever is disturbing, whatever is bad, whatever is unacceptable, whatever is worrisome, we begin to think about "whatever is true, whatever is honorable, whatever is just, whatever is pure, whatever is pleasing, whatever is commendable" (Philippians 4:8).

This is, after all, the menu for true wellness. This is the feast prepared for the soul. The only invitation needed is the nearness of God, and that invitation is always open.

A NEW AND LIVING WAY

For the prophets of the Old Testament, accepting this invitation was not a matter of preference but a matter of urgency. They liked the word *near*, though they brandished it less as a call to rejoice than as a call to reform. Ezekiel, Obadiah, Joel, Zephaniah, and Malachi all used this preposition in relation to God. In each case the prophet used the word to refer not to the Lord directly, but to the *day* of the Lord. *The day of the Lord is near*, they proclaimed, over and over again.

These warnings were dire and went largely unheeded. It reminds me of a classroom in which the teacher has stepped out for a bit. In her absence, the class gets increasingly unruly. They throw paper across the room and write bad words on the board. Then they start bullying a kid with glasses and high socks. They steal his lunch money and taunt him. It only gets worse from there. One kid doesn't like what his classmates have been doing and knows full well what will happen if the teacher comes in and catches them. The consequence, when the teacher opens the door and sees what has become of her students, is going to be bad for everybody. He hears footsteps. *Get in your seats!* he scolds. *The teacher is coming! She's near the door!* By that point, his classmates cannot hear him. They do not listen, nor do they care.

I assume that God—like all good teachers—knows exactly what is happening in her classroom. She is hardly a fool. But her response is not what one would expect. God doesn't storm back in, issuing expulsions. Instead, she sends another teacher in there—a young one, a patient one, a courageous one who enters the scene humbly and whose first order of business is to minister to the boy with the glasses. Only then does that new teacher call for a new way. He does so by telling stories and by using familiar analogies. Many of the kids in the class listen to him. But the ones who are used to calling the shots don't.

We know what happens here. It's *The Lord of the Flies*, and the good one gets killed.

But once again, God refuses to rage. Just as she knew what was going on in the classroom the first time around, she knows what will happen the second time around. She is not worried about her beloved assistant: him, she has already picked up and brought into glory. As for those unruly kids? Well, she chooses to stay close to them. Not in the classroom, ruling them with an iron thumb, but just outside the door. Near enough that they know she is there. Near enough that they can come to her for help. Near enough that peace is possible, but only if they choose it for themselves. Only if they seek what the author of Hebrews describes as "the new and living way" (Hebrews 10:20).

This author of Hebrews, who was likely a friend and apprentice of Paul's, invites us—as the members of God's class—to this new and living way. It is a powerhouse phrase, one that I love: so fresh, so hopeful. It is the way modeled and made possible by the young rabbi, Jesus. All we need to do to embrace this new and living way is to "draw near with a sincere heart and with the full assurance that faith brings . . . hold unswervingly to the hope we profess, and consider how we may spur one another on toward love and good deeds" (Hebrews 10:20 24 NIV).

With this Scripture and this preposition, we are called into action—though the direction is more obtuse than it is with above and beneath. We can fathom what is required of us to rise above and likewise to lower beneath; but in drawing near, how do we know which way to go?

This verse tells us that a "sincere heart" will be our best guide in attuning to God. It also tells us that we must turn outward, drawing near not only to God but also to others. Doing so, we can spur them toward goodness and love. All this with the full assurance that faith brings.

The notion of a God Near, who is present but with a bit of distance, provides the perfect conditions in which our faith can grow. Knowing that God is close by but not right upon us provides us with a profound sense of peace but also space for personal choice, for searching, for doubt. The nearness of the Spirit leavens our faith that it may indeed be the richest of fare.

A PRAYER TO GOD NEAR

Holy Holy Spirit, keen and stealthy,
queen of sacred longing and attraction,
you draw near to us, delectably.

You cannot be anywhere other than here,
near your beloveds,
in our times of supreme joy
and our times of supreme sorrow.

Help us to practice your presence.
Help us to be exquisitely attuned to you,
as you are exquisitely attuned to us.

Help us to adopt a new and living way,
setting our minds on that which is
true, honorable, just, pure, pleasing, and commendable.

Help us to eat what is good,
what is free.
The richest of fares indeed satiates.

Help us to shed our worry
and Rejoice!

Amen.

CHAPTER FOUR

With

Though I walk through the valley of the shadow of death,
I will fear no evil, for you are with me;
your rod and your staff, they comfort me.

Psalm 23:4 NKJV

We call upon all that we hold most sacred,
the presence and power of the Great Spirit of love and truth
which flows through all the Universe, to be with us to
Teach us, and show us the Way.

Chinook blessing

Once I started noticing prepositions, they seemed to crop up everywhere—in morning devotionals, in podcast discussions, in verses of the Bible, and in sermons. One Sunday, early in the writing of this book, our priest took to the lectern and wasn't three sentences in when I felt my heart quicken. She had asked the congregation to reflect on what the most important word in the Bible might be, and I immediately knew what was coming. I mouthed excitedly to my husband across the tops of our daughters' heads: *She's talking about the word "with"!* He furrowed his brow, confused. He was still not as enthralled by prepositions as I was.

There is a scientific name for this phenomenon, when you start to notice something and it then appears everywhere. It is called, rather uninspiringly, the Baader-Meinhof phenomenon or the frequency illusion. It asserts that once we become attuned to something new, like a word, and suddenly start to notice it a lot, the reason is not because the appearance of that new thing has increased in frequency but rather because our awareness of it has increased. Our inclination to believe the contrary is cognitive bias—aka folly. Our inclination to believe that the universe or the Holy Spirit is sending us signs? More abject folly.

Maybe. No matter. I believe in a Divine that impels synchronicities and communicates in codes and connects all creatures. The collective unconscious is a blueprint of this Divine, and prepositions must have been blinking in there, like flashes of gold to miners, all along. "With" is one of those prepositions.

After all, Immanuel—the name for Christ Jesus—means "God with us." The very first chapter of the very first book of the New Testament makes this bold and substantive assertion: "'The virgin will conceive and give birth to a son, and they will call him Immanuel' (which means 'God with us')" (Matthew 1:23 NIV). The implication, which our Sunday sermon indeed reinforced, is that a key premise of Christianity is contained in the preposition *with*. It is arguably the most important word in the Bible.

The Messiah is *Immanuel:* God With. He is the one able to perform miracles, able to endure suffering, able to triumph over death, and able to illuminate the way. That's why we call him Lord and worship him. That's why Christianity is called *Christ*ianity. It is all about Christ: the living embodiment of God, the one who reveals the nature of God to be not merely above or beneath or even near but also, profoundly and potently, *with*. In Jesus, God's relationality proves not only suprapersonal—that which transcends us—but also interpersonal—that which connects with us on a personal level. Jesus reveals that God meets us where we are, *on our level.* This proclamation is astonishing, inconceivable, and universe-altering.

But we might have seen it coming. God was revealing himself to be with us long before Jesus came along. In fact, Scripture has a lot to say about God With, going back into the Old Testament, as far as Genesis, and also moving forward in the New Testament, as far as Revelation. We know that "In the beginning was the Word, and the Word was with God, and the Word was God" (John 1:1). This verse tells us that *with* is the primary relationship characterizing the triune God. God *is*, and God is *with*.

We tend to focus on God as an entity when the truer nature of God is as relationality. And the relationship that seems to characterize God on a foundational level is this one.

PEACE

The reality of this claim is so significant that it's hard to wrap our heads around it, even though we have no doubt learned it before and "know" it already. In the form of Jesus Christ, yes, and likewise before, in Eden, God *withdwells*.

The image that beautifully captures this idea is God walking in the garden in the cool of the day. God has made the morning and the coming night. He has made the garden, its lush abundance, its teeming life. God has made humans, male and female, two beings yet one flesh (kind of like *is* and is *with*). As God is strolling, assuredly content in the glory of his creation, he senses Adam and Eve nearby and calls out to them amiably. We have to expect that God already knows about the fruit and all that. It was surely no surprise. But God didn't come hunting them down to rage and blame. He simply took his evening stroll and called for them. This was their pastime, walking together in the cool of the evenings.

What a lovely conjecture of heaven this is. Might heaven be, first and foremost, a withdwelling: companionable, familiar, lovely? When we come to the end of our lives, the promise of returning to Eden, of being with God who is also with us, is really all we could ask for. The "way of with" may well be the way of eternity. It certainly seems foundational to "the peace of God, which surpasses all understanding"

(Philippians 4:7), a peace that is emphasized reverently in the Episcopalian liturgy of my upbringing.

For most of the worship service I attend, we are in the pew, either sitting or standing, either listening or reciting. Rarely are we at liberty to talk among ourselves. The one exception is in what we call "The Passing of the Peace." This is our invitation to turn to our neighbors, to offer our hand and our hope: *Peace be with you*, we say, or simply *Peace*.

The practice echoes the words Jesus used to greet and comfort the disciples the evening of his resurrection. There they were, huddled in a room with the doors locked, fearing persecution, perhaps even their own crucifixions. Any little sound would have sent shock waves through them. Any promise of hope would have seemed absurd. Everything they had believed in, everything they had given their lives for, was apparently worthless, laughable, untrue.

Into this bleak, fear-riddled nightfall came a voice, a familiar voice, which spoke not quietly in fear but loudly with rejoicing: *Peace be with you!* And there was Jesus standing with them, showing them the wounds of his hands and his feet yet smiling with the fullness of a promise made and a promise kept, however impossible seeming. The words Jesus uses are in turn the words that Paul uses in his letters to the early churches in Rome and in Corinth (Romans 15:33, 1 Corinthians 1:3), and they capture the fundamental hope we continue to have for one another and for ourselves. When we boil it all down, distilling our many petitions and intercessions and glorifications into a comprehensive one-liner, it tends to hinge on this one preposition *with*.

In the Episcopalian liturgy, the Great Thanksgiving (which includes Communion) follows The Passing of the Peace in the order of worship. The celebrant opens the Great Thanksgiving by saying, *The Lord be with you*, and the congregation responds, *And also with you*. In this way, we move from praying that peace be with us to praying that the Lord himself be with us. This is our one true need and therefore our one true prayer: that the Divine be with us, now and forever. The appearance of Jesus in that room validates this prayer. The appearance of Jesus in that room affirms that death has no power to diminish divine withdwelling. Christ resurrects, just as the green of nature resurrects each spring, just as the sun resurrects each morning, the cycle coming around whole. Even that which seems to be gone forever returns.

COMFORT

It's hard to believe this, though. Just as it is hard to believe that God is near, it is also hard to believe that God is with. Absence makes the heart yearn and the mind burn. How can we trust God With when all evidence is to the contrary? Jesus, *Immanuel*, ascended, and we are down here, bereft and alone, waiting. The notion of God With, like the notion of God Near, may well be the sickest of jokes. The worst unfulfilled promise. It seems so sometimes, doesn't it?

The week I was set to begin work on this chapter, at a school less than three miles from the desk where I was writing, and less than two miles from the desks where my children sat learning, a gunman broke in and opened fire, killing three children and three adults. The loss of those lives, the trauma to those present, gashed the community. We found ourselves ripped open and bleeding. When I heard the news, I could not breathe. A wailing came from so far inside me, my eyes water again to think of it. My own babies were not the ones locked in a closet, trying not to breathe for fear of making a sound. The bodies of my own babies were not the ones in a coffin, impossibly small, returning to dust. And yet those babies were babies, someone's, and in turn ours. Those families grieve excruciatingly. We all grieve excruciatingly. All the time, we grieve. For all the woe and horror of the world, we grieve. What solace do we have?

Our dean and rector at the time, Father Timothy, sent out a prayer in the days following this horrific wounding. It read:

> Lord of all mercies: abide with us when the darkness deepens and we suffer loss, pain, and grief. Help us to know and

> understand you are with us even when we cannot feel your presence. Let your saving help shine through the shadows as you hold your cross before our eyes, reminding us that you share our sufferings and have overcome death so that we might rise again with you. Let morning break upon our sorrowing hearts; abide with us in life and in death, Lord, so that we may live in your peace and rejoice in your love. Amen.

I don't know where Timothy found this prayer, but I do know that I found great solace in it. The words did not eliminate my grieving, but they did offer consolation. And as I reread them, fervently praying them, I understood why. Every single sentence in the prayer contains the word *with*. In three of the sentences, God is with us. In one of them, we are with God (rising with God, as it were).

This simple relationship proves the ultimate source of comfort, the only source of comfort in the bleakest, most devastating hour. Perhaps it is no surprise that the psalm that so often gets recited at funerals, the one many of us know by heart, echoes this truth. Rereading it again, we are invited to discover a potent little word that we may not have ever paid attention to before. "Yea, though I walk through the valley of the shadow of death, I will fear no evil: for thou art with me; thy rod and thy staff they comfort me" (Psalm 23:4 KJV). There it is: *with*.

When God Above is too far away, when God Beneath is too buried, when God Near is not close enough, we turn and return to God With.

God With is the next breath we are able to take, the next step we are able to take, when all else has gone to shadow. It is the knowledge we rest in when all else fails, and the prayer we offer when no others suffice. In the aftermath of that shooting, I prayed versions of a with-prayer, over and over:

> Please God, be with those families.
> Please God, be with those teachers.
> Please God, be with those first responders.
> Please God, be with us.

Please God, be with.
Please God, with.
With. With. With.

Jesus knew this would be our most fervent prayer and our deepest need. Before his death he made a promise. He said, "I will ask the Father, and he will give you another Advocate, to be with you forever. This is the Spirit of truth. . . . You know him because he abides with you" (John 14:16–17).

When he says this, Jesus knows that his time on earth has come to its inevitable end. He knows that he can no longer be with his friends or followers in the flesh. He knows too that his absence has the power to negate all the good work of God that he performed during his lifespan. With Jesus gone, God becomes a mere idea at best, and quite probably a farce. To combat this likelihood, Jesus recruits God to send another Divine With. In doing so, he shifts the role of Immanuel from himself to the Holy Spirit. The Spirit will be *with* us forever.

Jesus then goes ahead and answers a question he suspects we will ask. That question is: How will we know? If we can't see it, as we can see you, Jesus, how will we know it's there? You know this Spirit already, Jesus consoles. This is a knowledge that does not come by way of vision or reason. It is not a matter of the material, which can be seen, nor is it a concept of theology, which can be thought. It is, rather, a matter of familiarity. Like our cat or our spouse or our child or even our favorite chair or houseplant, the Spirit lives with us, occupying space in our homes, both literal and figurative. In the way that we can walk into our house and sense the presence of a loved one, so it is with God. There is a warm companionability, a felt sense, a knowing that we are not alone because of this Spirit.

Yes, Jesus *was* God with us. Yes, the Holy Spirit *is* God with us. The promise is scriptural, and the evidence is experiential. We know him because he lives with us. And because he lives with us we know him. It is a knowing unique to love.

Without it, we cannot even begin. With it, however, we can not only begin, but we can endure, hope, prevail, and flourish. The nature of God is to be with. There is no other way for God to be.

SHEKHINAH

"The Fall" or "The Expulsion," which has been dramatized in much of Christian art and history, might suggest otherwise. This story tells us that we are exiled—banished from that warm companionability of God—and that it is our fault. Hearing this narrative, we envision God kicking Adam and Eve out of the house and slamming the door after them.

But that is not how the story unfolds. Even though Adam and Eve disobeyed God and he asked them to leave, he did not kick them out naked, in any sense of the word. God readied them for their journey by making clothes for them (Genesis 3:21), using the skins of the wild animals of paradise. He designed, cut, and sewed the garments. God helped Adam and Eve put them on, teaching them how to dress, since it was the very first time they had ever worn clothes such as these. God adjusted the fit, making sure that all was just right, before he readied them to go, explaining what to expect.

Scripture presents God's words as a curse, but I read them as fair warnings. In the same way that we might warn our children of dangers and trials that might befall them when they venture out on their own, so too does God with his children. Because Adam and Eve know the full breadth of reality now—youthfulness and aging, joy and suffering, living and dying—things are going to be different. God wants them to know what reality holds. Childbirth will be painful, he tells the woman. Planting and harvesting food will be tough work, he tells the man. Your body will give out, he tells both of them. They listen. And then in response, Adam turns to his wife and tells her that he will call her Eve because she will be the mother of all the living (Genesis 3:20). He does not seem crushed in spirit to me. He seems almost excited, hopeful.

It is sometimes said that Adam and Eve "fall from God's grace," but there is no falling from grace. That's not possible when it comes to God. There is suffering to face and toil to endure for us, as there was for them, but never alone. Never without the companionship—the clothing, as it were—of God With.

Further reading of the Old Testament upholds this interpretation. No matter how angry and punitive God is portrayed to be, God nevertheless promises to be "with" his people, giving them the courage to face the inevitable hardship that awaits them. "Do not be afraid, for I am with you," God promises (Isaiah 41:10). "When you pass through the waters, I will be with you," he emphasizes (Isaiah 43:2). "Be strong and courageous. Do not be afraid or terrified," Moses encourages the Israelites when he breaks it to them that he won't be crossing the Jordan with them; "The Lord your God goes with you; he will never leave you nor forsake you" (Deuteronomy 31:8 NIV). This offering of steadfastness no matter how disloyal or disobedient we may be, this willingness to forgive no matter how egregious our trespasses, is what Christians have come to call grace. Grace is the withdwelling of God, and it is linked to the Jewish theology of *shekhinah.*

Shekhinah is a Hebrew term often translated as dwelling. It refers to God's abiding presence in the world as a protector and comforter. It is not a word that appears in the Hebrew Bible, but it appears in the Mishnah and in the Talmud often. Early Jewish mystics came to associate it with the Divine Feminine. I first heard it at a wisdom retreat led by spiritual teacher and author Rabbi Rami Shapiro, and then encountered it again soon thereafter in Diana Butler Bass's book *Freeing Jesus*. Bass defines the term *shekhinah* as "the presence of God dwelling with the world." It's a definition that reinforces our understanding of a God who withdwells.

Children often let us into their inner worlds, unexpectedly, at bedtime. When we are tucking in the blankets or getting ready to say prayers, they will come out with that one question or that one confession that knocks us back. I was putting my youngest child, eight years old at the time, to bed when she asked me a question in a soft, searching voice: "Mom, do you ever get lonely?"

She is a third child with older sisters, five years her senior, who are identical twins. They sleep in rooms beside one another on the ground floor. She has parents, two of them, who are married and sleep in the bed beside one another on the main level. But she is all alone, on that top floor of our house, with the best view but with no one to accompany her save a hermit crab named Natalie and myriad stuffed animals.

My daughter's face, lit by the twinkle lights that were draped over her curtain rod, betrayed a deep sorrow. "You and Dad have your thing, and Sissies have theirs, and I feel like I am alone in this family," she told me, bravely, crushingly.

Who among us has not known loneliness? Who among us has been spared the anguish of feeling that we have no one *with* us: whether we are lying solitary in the dark of night, or amid a lively throng of people, or in a classroom with others raising their hands, or in a relationship that is revealing its weaknesses, or in a cell for actions we can't undo and for which we have no opportunities to make amends? It is the agony of feeling forsaken. It is the agony of believing that God is not near or with. God is nowhere apparent, nowhere felt.

But the preposition *with* gives the assurance that no matter how lonely we are, we are not actually able to be alone. God is not capable of being away from us, from strolls in the garden of Eden all the way up through the end of time and everywhere in between. "See, the home of God is among mortals. He will dwell with them; they will be his peoples, and God himself will be with them and be their God" (Revelation 21:3). As theologian and mystic Howard Thurman writes in his seminal book *Meditations of the Heart*, "God is with me, in the sense that He is the Creator and the Sustainer of life. This is a part of my general thought and experience."

God is and will be precisely as God has always been: with us. There is no expulsion from God With.

WITNESS

When the resurrected Jesus repeated the words *Peace be with you* to that cramped room of disciples, he did something else. He breathed the Holy Spirit onto them, the very Spirit he had promised would help them and be with them, and he said something else: "As the Father has sent me, I am sending you" (John 20:21). The disciples don't get to hang out in perpetuity in a locked-away room with Jesus. Nor do they get to sit on the shore and blissfully gorge on all the fish they caught. They don't get *Peace* as they might define it. Quite the opposite: The comfort of God With becomes, in turn, a calling. *Feed my lambs*, Jesus tells Simon Peter. *Take care of my sheep*, he says. *Feed my sheep*, he repeats a third time. The message is clear. As God sent Jesus to be with us, so Christ sends us to be with others.

For nearly twenty years now, I have been blessed with the friendship of a woman named Tanya. She has watched my children grow up, as I have watched hers. She has comforted me during my breakdowns and delighted in my joys, as I have hers. Tanya was widowed when her children were practically babies, and she set about providing a life for them by cleaning houses. Resolving to provide a future for them with economic stability and opportunity, she signed a lease-to-own contract on a house and for nearly two decades dutifully paid her monthly bill with the dream of one day being able to bequeath the home, free and clear, to her beloved children.

But then Covid happened. As people sealed themselves away in their houses, sheltering in place, there was no work for her. Funds got tight. Tanya sometimes fell behind with the rent, but she always managed to make the payment. Fretting over these delays, Tanya was reassured by the landlord's wife that all was well: It was a hard time for everyone.

Then one day Tanya received a new housing contract in the mail. It billed itself as a simple renegotiation of terms, but the payments she owed monthly would be tripled and her rights to ownership diminished. The fact was, house values in Nashville had skyrocketed. The landlord knew he could get four times the amount for the house than was on the original lease. What proceeded were unpleasant exchanges, evasions and lies, and a court date. The life Tanya had so devotedly sought to build was one jerk away from crumbling. She was scared, and she was sad. But she spoke to me of an unbroken faith. *God is with us*, she told me, looking me level in the eye. Tanya is not defiant, nor is she stubborn. She is quiet and hard-working and faithful. *I feel that God is with us*, she repeated to me.

The judge, having hardly heard the case, gave Tanya thirty days to sign the new contract. Not doing so would mean losing 100 percent of the equity she had established plus losses on the repairs the family had made through the years out of their own pockets. Plenty of people felt like it was a no-brainer. *Don't throw it all away. Keep paying it down,* they counseled her. But Tanya did not want to be shackled to a person she could not trust. She did not want her children associated with someone who was, as she said, "not good," and so she walked away. Not cowardly, not stubbornly, but courageously, by faith.

I am reminded of the prophet Samuel who once he understood that the voice he kept hearing was not the old man in the next room but God, answered the call with openness and devotion, saying simply, "Here I am." God's response was to be "with Samuel as he grew up" (1 Samuel 3:19 NIV). And so it was with Tanya. She was welcomed into the home of a relative with five children of her own and a sixth on the way. Quarters were tight, but it proved a joyous time. Tanya helped watch and care for the children; in turn, she had a place to live and to belong. Soon thereafter, she became a grandmother. Soon after that, she found a home outside of town with a beautiful backyard where she can hear the birds sing. When all evidence was to the contrary, Tanya was right: God was indeed with her. No amount of money could take away God With. No amount of anything can take away God With.

Because of her faith, which calls her into trust and also into action, Tanya and her daughter Vanney have recently adopted a teenage refugee who was orphaned when his father was killed. This, despite the financial and emotional demands it makes on their family. Why? Because they too had lost a dad, and because their faith called them into withness.

The word *withness* is only one letter away from *witness*. The principle of "Christian witness" in its truest expression is not a tell-all of our own personal conversion nor even the elated news that Jesus came into the life of someone else. It is, rather, one of the deepest invitations of the faith tradition—one that has no need of words, no need of testimony, no need of being born again. It is a humble and abiding way of living that seeks, finds, and serves Christ in others, all of them.

To witness is to stay, and to see, and to express the essence of the Spirit of truth bequeathed to us by Jesus. Committing to be *with* others, those we love and those in need, enlarges us and deepens us. It makes us wiser and more gentle. We learn this way of being through our friendship with the Divine, whom we know because he lives with us. We practice this way of being through our friendships with one another. As David Whyte eloquently and astutely expresses in his book *Consolations*, friendship is an exemplary act of witness and withness: "The ultimate touchstone of friendship is not improvement, neither of the other nor of the self: the ultimate touchstone is witness, the privilege of having been seen by someone and the equal privilege of being granted the sight of the essence of another, to have walked with them and to have believed in them, and sometimes just to have accompanied them for however brief a span, on a journey impossible to accomplish alone."

This life is indeed a journey impossible to accomplish alone. We need friends, and we need God.

In the Septuagint translation of the New Testament, the Greek word chosen to express the Hebrew word *shalom* is *eiréné*. A feminine noun, *eiréné* suggests inner harmony and true welfare. It is derivate of the root word *eirō*, which means to join together into a whole.

When we say *Peace be with you*, we are praying not only for abiding harmony but also for wholeness, an unsunderable weddedness. Though we tend to use this verse solely in the context of marriage, it is as revelatory, if not more so, in the context of our connection with the Divine: "What therefore God hath joined together, let not man put asunder" (Matthew 19:6 KJV).

It is incumbent upon us not to dispel the truth of the Divine withdwelling. Not to interfere with the grace of the Divine withdwelling. Not to hoard the goodness of the Divine withdwelling. "As the Father has sent me, so I am sending you. . . . God himself will be with you" (John 20:21). We are not exiles of Eden; we are companions of Christ.

A PRAYER TO GOD WITH

Loving God,
you are with us.

You are with us in our highs
and in our lows
and in our ordinaries.

You are with us in our loneliness
and in our companionships,
and in our communities.

You are with us
as Jesus,
as Spirit,
as friend in Eden.

What you offer is
comfort and courage,
peace and wholeness.

Help us to open ours hearts,
our minds,
and our very lives
to your divine withdwelling.

Help us to heed the call
to be with others,
to pay witness,
to abide in our foundational connection.

Amen.

CHAPTER FIVE

Alongside

He has told you, O mortal, what is good; and
what does the Lord require of you
but to do justice, and to love kindness, and to
walk humbly with your God?

Micah 6:8

May the road rise up to meet you.
May the wind be always at your back.
May the sun shine warm upon your face;
the rains fall soft upon your fields and until we meet again,
may God hold you in the palm of His hand.

Irish Blessing

The dolphins, a whole pod of them, are astonishingly close to me. They are swimming, and I am in the water, swimming alongside them. The effect is euphoric.

My twin daughters and I are on spring break off the coast of Florida, on an expedition to swim with dolphins in the wild. I remain so proud of my girls to this day—mere kindergarteners at the time—brave enough to slide into the deep waters of the Gulf of Mexico. That the guides, and that *I*, as the mom, permitted two six-year-olds to enter the open waters of the ocean alongside a pack of undomesticated animals is questionable to me now, many years later. But at the time I didn't worry about it one bit. It was an opportunity I simply could not deny them. Their yearlong obsession with these mammals—all those books they read, all those drawings they made, all those random facts they collected and shared over bowls of cereal—merited an encounter with the magnificent creatures in their natural habitat.

More often than not, we hear the dolphins before we see them. Their squeaks and high-pitched beeps reverberate throughout the substance of the water, clear echoes in a dense chamber. Usually they are off to the side or far below us, shadows gliding with grace and speed. When the captain positions the boat and gives the signal, in we go, the three of us clumsily together. It's not easy trying to situate our bodies to see them, with our goggles fogging up and saltwater gushing down our breathing tubes, but we do it—over and over again—and it's incredible.

After countless plunges, my girls have had their fill and are content to rest on the deck of the boat in the sunshine. And so, on this particular dive, which the captain enthuses will be a good one, I go in alone. With the help of my solitude and my flippers, I am able to keep pace. For the first time, I am not just above the dolphins or near the dolphins or with the dolphins. I am not merely beside them. I am *alongside* the dolphins and they are alongside me. In our fluid connectedness, it is as if we are one. I have no thoughts. I have no fears. I have no body even. I have only joy and surrender. The result is nothing short of magic.

SYNCHRONIZATION

We call this type of experience "being in the zone." It occurs when we tap into a rhythm so easeful that we feel as if we could go on forever effortlessly and buoyantly. Such is the high of the long-distance runner. Such is the rhapsody of the pianist on a keyboard, the abandon of an enthralled artist. I imagine surfers riding waves, neurosurgeons rewiring pathways, and basketball players lifting off and lithely dunking the ball. All are compelled by their own competence but also by an unseen, unerring, generous, and exalting force. We know what this feels like—these snatches of glory—when what is often extremely difficult feels, all of a sudden, easy and free. It's like we get scooped up by God and carried along on a tide of his making. We are passengers on a sacred, synchronized ride.

This synchronized ride is happening on a molecular level, it turns out. Photons—the very entities of light—can become engaged in something called "quantum entanglement." Quantum entanglement is a state of interconnectedness in which bits of light bounce in direct correlation with one another, forever interlocked and intertuned.

My mind had already been blown by the essential fact that light is at once both wave and particle, its paradoxical nature affirming, for me, the multiplicity at the heart of trinitarian theology. And then this! Not only is light itself nonbinary; light is also capable of—and proven to exhibit—infinite interconnectedness with other light. Relationship—*sustained* relationship—is evidenced in the very light of the world. It consociates even while it moves and shifts and has its own being. The preposition for this roving togetherness, for this holy harmony, is *alongside*.

Alongside is kin to the prepositions *with* and *beside*. They are all in the family of words expressing closeness and connection. But *alongside* is unique in the way it refers to a sustained and evolving congruence. Whereas *with* tends to be immediate, even fixed, *alongside* suggests motion. I may be with you now but not later. I may go with you but then leave. *Alongside*, on the other hand, promises an enduring alliance. It assumes growth and change.

And whereas *beside* can incorporate motion, it lacks the critical feeling of connectedness. I may run beside you, I may swim beside you, but the implication is that you are there and I am here. You're in your lane; I'm in mine. The preposition *alongside* takes away the lanes. When I run alongside you or swim alongside you, we share a physical and emotional rhythm. This word orients us one to another in an ongoing way. It means togetherness, cooperation, coexistence in perpetuity.

Alongside those dolphins that day, I was on that ride. I was in that zone. I was interconnected such that we two—we many—were one: exquisitely uninhibited yet harmonized. It was a spiritual experience; I would even say a mystical experience. And reflecting on it a decade later, I can recognize that the sublime nature of it had everything to do with that preposition *alongside*.

RIGHT HAND

This particular kind of alongsiding is elating. It is also rare. More often than not, alongsiding is a steady, tender, caring slog. It may well be the least glorious of all relationalities. And because of its steadfast nature, it tends to get stale. Over time, we fail to notice it and in turn to appreciate it. But those who have experienced a sustained relationship, be it marriage or friendship or a partnership of any kind—and even those who have *witnessed* such a partnership—know that alongsiding is the most beautiful, humble, and essential of creaturely connections. It is what matters most at the end of the day or the end of a life: to have someone there, at our right hand, holding it and seeing us through.

References to the "right hand" abound in the Bible. One count suggests this phrase appears 166 times in the Christian Scripture. A lot happens by God's right hand. It is capable of extending victory and blessing, of igniting fires and planting seeds. It is capable of quelling enemies and pointing the way and holding stars. The right hand of God is the source of strength, wisdom, comfort, and protection.

The right hand of God is also, generously and tenderly, something we can hold. When God spoke to Isaiah, he made this explicitly known: "For I, the Lord your God, hold your right hand; it is I who say to you, 'Do not fear, I will help you'" (Isaiah 41:13). This language is echoed in Psalm 73:22–24, when its author confesses, "I was senseless and ignorant; I was a brute beast before you. Nevertheless, I am continually with you; you hold me by my right hand." And ever so beautifully and reassuringly, the psalmist says in Psalm 63:8: "My soul clings to you; your right hand upholds me." What does it mean for God to hold us by the hand? It means that God is alongside us as both a trusted protector and a beloved partner.

I hold hands with my husband sometimes. If, by supreme good fortune, we do not have a late soccer game or a choral concert or a gymnastics practice to contend with, we walk after dinner in the low light of evening and we hold hands. Hand-holding can be somewhat clumsy. It can be inconvenient. It only works if two people keep the same pace and are committed to connection. My husband and I hold hands because we love each other and because we are making our way together.

I hold hands with my child sometimes. If we are crossing a busy street, I will hold out my hand to her and she will take it, and we will venture forth together, keeping one another close and safe. She sometimes resents this hand-holding. She wants to be capable of crossing thresholds on her own. But she holds my hand because she trusts me to protect her. She holds my hand because we love each other and because we are making our way together.

So it is—or can be—with God. God Alongside keeps pace with us, committed to connection, and keeps us safe as we cross tricky thresholds. God is indeed "our refuge and strength, a very present help in times of trouble" (Psalm 46:1). It is beautiful to think of holding hands with God. The image reveals the fundamental truth that we love each other and are making our way together. When Jesus speaks of being at the right hand of God, this tender connection is surely part of what he meant. Jesus's feelings echo those of his ancestor David, who praises God, saying: "In your presence there is fullness of joy, and in your right hand are pleasures for evermore" (Psalm 16:11).

Jesus's comments, however, were—and often still are—taken to mean that he exclusively claims a place of authority alongside God. The right hand of God is the presumptive seat of power. It is the second in command. To be alongside God in heaven is to be, as Paul describes it to the Ephesians, "far above all rule and authority and power and dominion, and above every name that is named, not only in this age but also in the age to come" (Ephesians 1:20–21). That Jesus elevated himself to such a position was cause for acute alarm, accusation, and ultimately execution.

But the people who made the accusations and sentenced him to be executed lacked the ears to hear what Jesus was saying. It wasn't about being *above*, it was about being *alongside*.

When Jesus declares that he will be seated at the right hand of God, he has already been betrayed and accused. The priests were well aware that Jesus's teachings had threatened their authority, and they were eager to pin him with a punishable offense. They had already arranged for Judas to betray him. To seal the deal, they eagerly sought false testimony. When someone stepped forward and offered the very evidence they sought—that Jesus had proclaimed he could destroy the temple of God and rebuild it in three days—the high priests seized upon these words as evidence of Jesus's blasphemy. They assumed that Jesus would jump to defend himself, as most of us would. But Jesus did not. Instead he stood quiet. "Have you no answer? What is it that they testify against you?" they demanded (Matthew 26:62). And yet still Jesus stood quietly. It is only in response to the priest's next statement that Jesus broke his silence. "Then the high priest said to him, 'I put you under oath before the living God, tell us if you are the Messiah, the Son of God.' Jesus said to him, 'You have said so. But I tell you, From now on you will see the Son of Man seated at the right hand of Power and coming on the clouds of heaven'" (Matthew 26:64). At this the high priest rips his robes and cries blasphemy. At this the crowds affirm: Jesus deserves death.

The final straw was Jesus's declaration that he would be seen seated at the right hand of God. How dare he presume such authority, such equality with God? Anyone with this audacity deserves to be hung from a tree. But that is exactly what Jesus was willing to die for. He was willing to die for the truth of the claim that he—and by extension we, each of us—*belong* at the right hand of God. This is, I believe, how he "washed away our sins." He deemed us worthy of such proximity and intimacy with God, no matter how unworthy we might otherwise seem. We get to sit right by God's side. We get to hold God's hand.

The way that Jesus seemed to know this truth was by the way he lived it. Jesus prayed constantly. He spoke to his Abba intimately. He trusted God, turning things over to him, asking for guidance, for courage, for help. In effect, he asked God to hold his hand, which is how he knew that God would accept him at his right hand in turn. It was also how he knew God would be there through his labors, both the labors of his living and the labors of his dying.

I am reminded of a metaphor that Sue Monk Kidd uses for God: "How did we ever get the idea that God would supply us on demand with quick fixes, that God is merely a rescuer and not a midwife?" she asks. What does a midwife do? A midwife comes alongside a mother during her labors, helping her breathe through the pain, helping her steady her flashing mind, helping her bring new life into the world safely. The process takes an agonizing series of seconds, minutes, hours, sometimes even days, all awash with anguish and elation, suffering and euphoria. The midwife is alongside her the whole time, participating in labors that are not hers, seeing her through.

God is the midwife to our labors and our life-making. God was physically and emotionally at the "right hand" of Mary when she was laboring. He was physically and emotionally at the "right hand" of Jesus when he was laboring. And he is physically and emotionally at the "right hand" of us when we are laboring. We know what this alongsiding is. It is Love: the one thing that "bears all things, believes all things, hopes all things, and endures all things" (1 Corinthians 13:7).

JOURNEYING

Because Jesus lived alongside God and God lived alongside Jesus, there was work to do. The two did not disappear into the garden and stroll together forever. Bliss was not the aim. Relationship was, and is. To live alongside God is to live alongside all that God loves and all that God is in the world. It is a commitment to the "other." It is a commitment to accompany him or her, it or them, not by preaching hellfire but by holding their hand, as Jesus did.

The whole point of Jesus's teachings and ministry—indeed the whole point of his life—is to come alongside people: not just upstanding citizens and priests but small children, tax collectors, prostitutes, foreigners, and those with disabilities. This Savior, this incarnate God, pulled the deity down from an elevated throne into the messy struggle of life and proved that divine rule is not only prescribed from a place of authority but also enacted from a place of intimacy. And he showed that a true Savior is not one who grants immunity or issues pardons from on high but one who engages in active caretaking, appearing at street corners and deathbeds and prison cells, holding the hands of those most in need of healing touch. Jesus eschewed strict rules about uncleanliness and modeled this purer way of being, this one of alongsiding. Because the Messiah is at the right hand of God with a name above all other names, the Messiah is also and always alongside us as we navigate this painful, beautiful, brief, hard, blessed life.

This is why *alongside* is the very preposition Father Richard Rohr chooses to embody the "God the Son" member of the Trinity. He writes, "I understand Jesus as God alongside us. Jesus is the accompanying God who walks with us, especially through the mystery of death and resurrection."

When Rohr shared this reflection in the Center for Action and Contemplation daily email, it was December 2022. I was deep into making my own discoveries about the power of prepositions and attempting to write about them, piecing together day after day, discovery after discovery, this portrait of a multidimensional God. Seeing the same idea sitting in my inbox one hectic Advent morning was exhilarating and even, dare I admit, threatening. My ego leapt into proprietary mode, wanting to copyright the ideas for myself. But the wiser part of me understood how affirming, how hopeful, and even how self-evident this overlap was. Of course we were gleaning shared truths and finding similar verbal tools. They were and are right there for the taking.

Rohr's articulation of Jesus as God Alongside reflects the "divine pattern" of "loss and renewal, death and resurrection" that Jesus embodies. In other words, God the Alongside (Son) proves our steadfast companion, the one accompanying us on the full duration of the soul's journey, with its highs and its lows, its losses and its renewals, its deaths and its resurrections.

The Bible is full of such journeys. Noah journeys over the waters in an ark of his own construction. At age seventy-five, Abraham packs up everything he possesses and sets out from Haran to the Land of Canaan. Moses leads the people out of Egypt. Naomi and Ruth journey from Moab back home to Bethlehem, arriving in time for the barley harvest. David journeys from Bethlehem to Hebron. Rehoboam journeys from Jerusalem to Shechem. And in one of the more famous journeys, Mary and Joseph journey to Bethlehem, only to find it overcrowded. Jesus himself journeys across Galilee, also traveling north to Syro-Phoenicia, east to the Decapolis, and south to Judea, among other places. And then begin the journeys of the followers of Christ: first the magi and the shepherds, later Barnabas, Paul, and Peter. On and on this goes, throughout time, right up to today.

Nearly all the forenamed journeys were direct responses to divine commands. God tells Noah, Abraham, Joshua, Ruth, Daniel, Paul, and the three wise men, among others, where to go and what to do, and they do it. In this way, the journey itself is a form of surrender and an act of faith.

We tend to think that we "do" life, but over and over again we find that life actually does us. We respond to the call of love and marry, only to discover how much we must release to stay the course. Likewise with parenting. Or launching a company. Or creating authentic art. We feel a calling—or perhaps it is more of a pulling—toward these endeavors, and they become our life journeys: more arduous than we ever anticipated, with demands to self-sacrifice and a courage we doubted we possessed. We each have a sleepless night on the mountain, praying fervently for protection, for guidance, for help. We each wrestle with truths we don't want to face and fears we don't want to name. We each climb until we find ourselves dumbfounded by the views, which show us not only what is beautiful and possible but also how far we have come.

The summons from God, when distilled, is relatively basic: travel great distances spiritually and keep God as our constant companion. This is something we purposefully do, but it is also something that happens despite us. When we *recognize* God Alongside us, when we *enable* God Alongside us, when we *embrace* God Alongside us, the journey—with its long days and nights, its hungers and nourishment, its challenges and celebrations—becomes a crucible. What emerges from our ongoing and intimate partnership with the Divine—a relationship built on trust and characterized by endurance—is our truest self, our most authentic self.

In this way our lives are journeys of devotion. They are walks in love. They are adventures of alongsiding.

YOKEFELLOW

Early twentieth-century writer and Christian speaker S. D. Gordon penned a series of essays titled *Quiet Talks On*, in which he addresses a wide range of topics from "Quiet Talks on Power" to "Quiet Talks on Calvary." In a short essay on the topic of service, Gordon draws on the image of a yoke to illuminate our relationship to the Divine. He describes the way a yoke has two loops, which are used to harness two service animals, be they cows or mules or horses. The yoke locks the two animals alongside one another so that they can work side by side in the field. Their shared rhythm and effort as "yokefellows" proves far more focused and efficient than if one were working alone.

Gordon suggests that Jesus is our "yokefellow." "Our yokefellow is always there alongside," he writes. "Every temptation that comes to us He has felt the sharp edge of, and can overcome. Every problem, every difficulty, every opportunity He knows, and is right there, swinging in rhythmic step alongside." What Matthew tells us about yoking to Christ is that it will ease our burden: "Come to me, all you who are weary and are carrying heavy burdens, and I will give you rest. Take my yoke upon you, and learn from me, for I am gentle and humble in heart, and you will find rest for your souls. For my yoke is easy, and my burden is light" (Matthew 11:28–30).

Gordon makes another point too. Linking up with the Son of Man lightens the heavy load that is this life, and it conditions us to help others with their load as well. "It's yoked living and yoked service," Gordon asserts. The idea that being alongside Christ not only supports us along our journeys but also positions us for a life of service is echoed in Paul's second letter to the church in Corinth. As Eugene Peterson paraphrases it in *The Message*, Paul insists that "[God] comes alongside us when we go through hard times, and before you know it, he brings us alongside someone else who is going through hard times so that we can be there for that person just as God was there for us" (2 Corinthians 1:3–5). Alongsiding begets alongsiding, it seems. Goodness begets goodness.

This idea—that goodness begets goodness—is encapsulated in the very nature of a triune God. The revelation is that alongsidedness is not just what God *does* but also what God *is*. We made a similar discovery with the preposition *with*, and we can see how it extends now too into the preposition *alongside*. The Divine is manifested in several ways, each of which functions alongside the other. God the Father and God the Son and God the Holy Spirit—or God For and God Among and God Throughout, or any other myriad expressions and combinations—are themselves yokefellows. They are swinging in rhythmic step alongside one another. One is not a threat to another. One is not better than another. Unlike the deities of Greek mythology, who play out dramas that involve power struggles and revenge, the triune God upholds the virtue of unity in diversity. As one in three and three in one, God embodies the efficacy and the beauty and the inevitability of quantum entanglement.

The takeaway, which gets modeled for us and passed down to us, is this: "We who are many are one body" (Romans 12:5). When we come alongside one another in faith, hope, and love, we who are many are one body. We belong to one another.

Believing this—living into this—yields the power to transform the world. This is how we create a world in which there are no sides. There's no your side, my side, the winning side, the losing side; there is only alongside.

A PRAYER TO GOD ALONGSIDE

Holy and Gracious God,
you are ever and always alongside us.

You journey alongside us
through trials and storms,
through labors and unspeakable loss.
You do not leave our side.

You journey alongside us
through incomparable wonder,
through blessed discovery and delight.
You are our steady companion.

We are holding hands
because we love each other
and because we are making our way together.

We are light entangled.
We are creatures yoked.

Help us to heal this broken world.
Help us to nurture a sacred alongsiding.

Amen.

CHAPTER SIX

Before

Before time—I am. Before beginnings—I am.
There were as yet no oceans when I was born,
No springs deep and overflowing.
I am older than mountains.
Elder to the hills, the valleys, and the fields.
Before even the first lumps of clay emerged—I am.

Proverbs 8:23–26

Something undifferentiated was born before heaven and earth;
still and silent, standing alone and unchanging,
going through cycles unending,
able to be the mother of the world.

Lao Tzu, *Tao Te Ching*

Most Christians would say they know what happens "in the beginning," when "God created the heavens and the earth." Even those without a mental Rolodex of Bible verses know this one. It's the first sentence of the Old Testament, and the first glimpse into the behavior of God. What does God do before anything else? God creates.

But what do we know about the God that did the creating? What do we know about the God of *being* prior to this God of *doing*? We know that it existed. It is the subject of the sentence preceding any verbs. *In the beginning, God.*

The Greek word for this abstraction is *alpha*. The preposition for it is *before*. As eleventh-century Islamic theologian Al-Ghazali posits: "God is the beginninglessly pre-eternal with nothing before God." God is as *before* as before can get.

Something that is eternally *before* is impossible to get our hands on or our words around. By its very nature, it exists out of the frame. The closest I can get to fathoming it is in my memory of caring for my third daughter, freshly delivered into this world, into my arms.

By the time she was born, the iPhone was ubiquitous but social media was yet nascent. The monolith Facebook was being demoted by the newer, shinier Instagram, neither of them aware that they would one day be bedmates. I was wary of social media from the beginning, mostly because my body pricked with unease whenever I scrolled through images of other families all bright and perky on their summer excursions and holiday ski trips. I recognized quickly that this form of friend-tracking was not good for me. I did not want to begrudge anyone else her life. And also, I wanted to be precisely and abundantly present where I was, which was holed up in a yellow nursery with my baby. A sublime baby girl whose physicality—whose warm, pulpy body—made my mouth water.

I learned the word *synesthesia* in high school. A literary device often employed by poets, it means a mixing of the senses. It is what happens when our brain routes sensory information through multiple unrelated pathways, which causes us to experience more than one sense simultaneously. Fourteenth-century Japanese poet Ryushu Shutaku relied on this device to articulate the otherwise inarticulable experience of Zen, or what he calls the "mind set free in the Dharma-realm." For such sublimity, only mangled logic will do. Seven hundred years before I stayed up nights, nursing my baby and gazing into the darkness outside, Shutaku was sitting up late and early too. He wrote, "I sit at the moon-filled window / Watching the mountains with my ears, / Hearing the stream with open eyes."

Beholding my baby girl was a synesthetic experience of this kind. The flush across her cheek while she slept tasted like a summer cantaloupe. I could smell the round curve of her belly and nearly hear her eyelashes, impossibly long, going about their work of protecting the precious eyes behind them. Divine love disturbs our standard sensory processes, it seems. We hear with open eyes.

Suffice to say, I was besotted, and I needed to do something with all that adoration beyond staring and suckling and shushing and swaddling, and so I created an Instagram account, its handle her initials, then tapped to make it private and posted pictures without hashtags or followers. It was a wholly private endeavor, a love letter spelled out in small square images. It was how I absorbed her new perfect separate self, and also how I *reabsorbed* her into my being. The thing is: My body longed for her body. It had known her inside it; it had made space for her and made sustenance for her. My cells held the memory of *before*, when her flesh was multiplying and morphing inside my own flesh, which also was multiplying and morphing.

My body had been a vessel of beforing. My body had sourced that which was and was also yet to come.

TEHOM

A God that exists as a beginning, as a *before*, presumes something to come. Its being—its very *beforeness*—is its doing. It is all that will be. In this way, God reveals herself to be not only inherently ancient but also inherently generative, not only infinite retrograde but also infinite potential. As the ultimate vessel of beforing, God not only *has* the capacity to create; God *is* the capacity to create.

And because God's creative capacity is entirely self-contained, the distinctive kind of creating that God does is *begetting*. God is ever and always in the process of generating new life and new self out of its very Life and Self, even while existing out of the frame, pre-eternally. That is the transcosmic nature of the One Source: God Before.

This sounds like heady stuff but it's not really. God is the womb of the womb. Mentally, this theology might confound us, but cellularly, we remember it. If we sink into silence and stillness, distancing ourselves from preoccupations and itches and inclinations to complete the sentence, and if we enable ourselves to settle absorbingly into our own lush emptiness, we might get a sense of the sheer being, the primordiality, of God Before.

This "beginninglessly pre-eternal with nothing before" of Al-Ghazali's is the *deep* of Genesis 1:2. It is a deep upon whose face was darkness, when the earth was yet formless and void. I can imagine this deep. It is supple and warm. Elastic. Thick. Rich. The Hebrew word for it is *tehom*. The sound of that word, *tehom*, on the tongue is lovely. It is strong yet hollow, trailing into bass vibrations that return us phonetically and prophetically *home*. In meditation, I sometimes chant this word—*tehom*—as a way to slide into the ancient timelessness and spaciousness of "God" well before it acquired such a name, when it was merely, purely, and forcibly *before*: a fecund deep, formless yet omniformative.

Texts from across the world's great religions echo this language of God, Goddess, Source, Ultimate Reality, Brahman, Tehom—whatever we desire to call it—as a formless deep or fertile womb. One that I cherish is from *Tao Te Ching*, which reads: "So deep! It seems to be the source of all things. . . . So indistinct! It seems to exist / I do not know whose offspring it is / Its image is the predecessor of God." Another is an excerpt from the Bhagavad Gita 7:4–7, in which Krishna explains himself by saying: "Know that my Superior Nature is the very Life which sustains the universe. It is the womb of all being; for I am That by whom the worlds were created." Yet another is Psalm 139.

When I collected into a little square booklet the myriad photographs I had taken of my daughter as an infant, Psalm 139 was the text I chose for the opening dedication. This psalm manages to personalize God Before without reducing it. The psalmist writes:

> You created my inmost being;
> you knit me together in my mother's womb.

I praise you because I am fearfully and wonderfully made;
your works are wonderful,
I know that full well.
My frame was not hidden from you
when I was made in the secret place,
when I was woven together in the depths of the earth.
Your eyes saw my unformed body;
all the days ordained for me were written in your book
before one of them came to be. (Psalm 139:13–16 NIV)

This beautiful and comforting psalm assures us of God's beforeness and also of our own. Before we were born into these bodies, God was wonderfully and fearfully making us in our mothers' wombs. Even before that, God was weaving us together "in the secret place." God was making us "in the depths of the earth," in the depths of its—we might say, *her*—very self.

Even though it may at first seem preposterous or even blasphemous to claim our eternality alongside God's, this olden song of Scripture inclines us to understand that just as God existed in the abstract *Before*, somehow we did also. Our conception is ancient. Our souls existed on some level before they were manifest in this particular time and space, just as our souls will continue to exist on some level afterward. We exist beyond birth, just as we exist beyond death.

SANCTIFICATION

In the most beautiful, simple way, Psalm 139 also reinforces our understanding that not only does God form us and ordain us; God *knows* us through and through. This is because God was weaving not just our bodies but our moments of being, not just our matter but our consciousness, not just life but its inherent meaning. The psalmist writes:

You have searched me, Lord,
and you know me.

You know when I sit and when I rise;
you perceive my thoughts from afar.
You discern my going out and my lying down;
you are familiar with all my ways.
Before a word is on my tongue
you, Lord, know it completely.
You hem me in behind and before,
and you lay your hand upon me. (Psalm 139:1–5 NIV)

God *searches* us: How lovely is that? She is curious about us even as she can anticipate what we are thinking and what we might say. This curiosity is an act of love. It is the way of mothers and fathers. They delight in their children's developments, even as they know to expect them.

Laying a hand upon us, as the closing line discloses, is also an act of love. It too is the way of mothers and fathers. The child who is sleepy, who is sick, who is cuddling, who is busy eating her banana or jetting off to school receives a touch, be it a caress on the cheek or a quick squeeze of the shoulder. The laying on of the hand is a spiritual reflex. It does itself.

There is a photograph of my youngest daughter, taken by a nurse, that captures the precise moment of her birth. She is being lifted up out of my womb. Though her body is covered in vernix, she is nevertheless bathed in a white light. It is not the hue of fluorescents but somehow otherworldly, as if aglow from within. Her eyes, capable of seeing contrasting forms if anything, are translucent. She has about her the aura of the Divine.

What I mean is that she was birthed of God far more than of me. She was *begotten*. As such, this birth—her birth, my birth, your birth—is in essence an ordination. Psalm 139 tells us this. The God of Before was not only writing our days; she was *ordaining* them. This is not a matter of predestination but rather a matter of *presanctification*. Each and every day, hour, minute, second that we live, including this one, has been conferred by holy order.

We often say that time is sacred because it is fleeting. But in truth, time is sacred because it is divinely spawned, divinely soaked, and divinely directed. This moment, each and all, has been consecrated.

What does this mean, aside from the astonishing glory of it? It means that the living that we have been given to do is not accidental, nor is it random. It eliminates on a spiritual level the possibility of any kind of void. In his book, *Man's Search for Meaning*, Holocaust survivor and psychotherapist Victor Frankl notes that "having been is the surest kind of being." Here Frankl is referring specifically to what he calls the "full granaries of the past" in an individual's life: the storehouse of that person's decisions. But he is drawing on a truth of larger proportion as well. The granaries of the past, Frankl suggests, are deep-reaching and sacred. Taking the long view—not only of our own past or even of our ancestral past but of our spiritual past—enables us to re-member ourselves to the sacred body to which we belong.

Our lives, yours and mine, have meaning because they were conceived and consecrated by the Divine. As we wrestle with what it all is and what it all means—God and our lives and our purpose and our death and our love and our worth—we can find assurance in the truth that all creation has been conferred with holy orders. Sanctification characterized our utmost origin, and it characterizes our lives now, and it will characterize what is to come, no matter what befalls us.

Jesus makes this very point just prior to his betrayal and crucifixion. Standing before his disciples, Jesus talks aloud to Abba, saying: "Father, the hour has come . . . glorify me in your presence with the glory I had with you before the world began. I have revealed you to those whom you gave me out of the world. . . . Now they know that everything you have given me comes from you. . . . Sanctify them by the truth; your word is truth. As you sent me into the world, I have sent them into the world. For them I sanctify myself, that they too may be truly sanctified" (John 17:1, 5–7, 17–19 NIV).

In this, his final teaching, Jesus explains with clarity what his purpose was. His purpose, as the Word, was to reveal the truth of God.

And that truth is that *we are all sanctified.* We know this because we all originate from the same Abba, Mother, Source, One. The same God Before. *Begetting* us, bringing us into being, is the original act of love. It is what starts it all.

When we then talk about "God's plan" for us or having our days "written in a book before they came to be," we are claiming that our lives are God-*led*, such that it is impossible for us to enter a terrain, whether temporal or spatial, that is untrespassed by God. When you think about it this way, God gets to our future before we do. Crafting the path of our life and our death before us, God anticipates it but also clears the way. This is how we grasp that God can be "the Alpha and the Omega, the First and the Last, the Beginning and the End" (Revelation 22:13). This is how we understand God's answer to Moses, when Moses asks what to say if the Israelites demand to know God's name. God says, "I AM WHO I AM" which can also be translated I WILL BE WHAT I WILL BE (Exodus 3:14). The translations, taken together, underscore the paradox and fullness of God Before for whom time and space are nonbinding.

The word *before* proves especially revelatory here, because not only does it take us backward; it also takes us forward. *Before* means "formerly" or "previously" with respect to time, but it also means "in front of" with respect to space. The Divine who comes before us (in time) is also the Divine who goes before us (in space).

PROTECTION

I have been to Africa one time in my life, a long time ago. Memories abound from that trip, but I recall one instance vividly. We were visiting the Masai Mara National Reserve, staying in a chain of huts that unfurled like a tail from the central body of a dining hall. The path along the huts was lit by torches but otherwise open to the plains and therefore to the animals that roamed its wild expanses. Guides from the Masai tribe escorted any visitor who was ready to retire for the evening or who was hungry for breakfast come morning. One was never to walk the path alone.

After dinner on our first evening, I was introduced to the guide who would escort us to our hut. Bright beads hung from his neck, and in his hand was a long spear with a point on its end that I would not have tested against the pad of my finger, however gingerly, for any prize. As we set out along the torchlit path, I could see that beyond the glows of light cast intermittently by the lamps there was a darkness as impenetrable as a wall. One could see nothing, or at least *I* could see nothing. I do not know what our guide could or could not see, what he could or could not hear. He walked slightly ahead of us on the side of the open plains. He was not visibly tense, but he was hardly strolling. In the flickering shadows, I could see his profile. Without considering whether I really wanted to know the answer, I asked him if he had ever used the spear he carried. *Yes* was his deep reply, his eyes never ceasing to roam the vast night.

After that I was quiet. If I had not understood it before, I understood it then: My life was in his hands. My safety depended on the keenness of his awareness, the quickness of his instincts, the mastery of whatever skills were needed to take down a wild cat in the dense dark with only a spear. Not to mention the courage and the commitment to self-sacrifice required to do the job. Most nights, standing sentinel outside the huts of sleeping travelers proved uneventful, but there was always the possibility that any moment would be the one prepared for, any second might bring its intractable flash of danger. And so the job of our guide was to walk out into the soft and potentially deadly night before a set of strangers and save them if need be.

This is what it means to go *before* another. The one who goes first is the one with the most demonstrated courage and composure. The one with the most trusted decision-making. The one willing to be ambushed and even killed on behalf of others.

Not unlike Jesus.

There is ample Scripture about Jesus going before us. Jesus goes *before* us to make the rough places smooth (Isaiah 45:2). Jesus goes *before* us to prepare a place (John 14:3). Jesus goes *before* us to light the way (John 8:12). This must be why Jesus is always calling people to follow him. Thirteen times in the Gospels, Jesus invites and implores onlookers to become followers. *Follow me*, he says. *Let me light the way for you. Let me forge the darkness for you. Let me risk—and ultimately—give my life for you.* He knew it was part of the job description. He knew it was the way of love.

Jesus had studied the Torah. He had absorbed the teachings of Moses and learned from Moses's example. As the leader of the Hebrew people during the Exodus, Moses wisely and steadfastly guides his people across a wilderness abhorrent to them. He stands before them to speak God's commandments, and he walks before them to part the waters of the sea. The people assume that Moses will go before them for the duration, ushering them all the way into freedom. But when he nears completion of this arduous journey, having made it within sight of the promised land, Moses finds that his place is no longer as the front man. There comes a time, even for him, to relinquish charge.

I can imagine Moses—his richly browned skin with moats of wrinkles around the eyes, his white beard, his feet caked in dust and calluses—standing before his flock. He clears his throat, raises his palms, and addresses the weary pilgrims. "I am now a hundred and twenty years old," he says to them. "I am no longer able to get about." I imagine the collective gut punch at that news, the panic poised to rise. But Moses holds his hands and his voice steady. He explains that he has received word from God that he, Moses, will not, after all, cross the Jordan but that "The Lord your God himself will cross over before you" (Deuteronomy 31:2–3). This is the primary message Moses gives his people. He keeps circling back to this essential point, repeating it again and insisting that they hear. "It is the Lord who goes before you. He will be with you; he will not fail you or forsake you," he assures them. "Do not fear or be dismayed" (Deuteronomy 31:8).

When one by one the people lose their resolve and want to turn back, Moses is the one who keeps on. But at the climactic moment in the story, when the guide is poised to lead his people through the final peril to freedom, Moses adheres to the call to step aside. He does this not out of cowardice or faithlessness but out of the deepest truth: that he, Moses, isn't in charge after all. God is and always has been. It is God who was "going before them in a pillar of cloud by day to lead them on the way, and by night in a pillar of fire to give them light" (Exodus 13:21 RSV). It is God who "has gone out before them . . . making the sound of marching in the tops of the balsam trees" (2 Samuel 5:24).

Reading these pieces of Scripture with an eye toward prepositions, we note the word *before* when before, rather ironically, we might have missed it. We discover that God not only goes alongside us; God also goes before us. God is not only companion; God is also leader. Our invitation therefore is to hold the hand of God and also to follow God's footsteps.

Way back around 975 BCE, King David wrote a song about that very combination. David was the youngest brother in the household of Jesse and least likely to be the chosen monarch. He was out in the fields with the sheep when his father presented his brothers, one after the other, to the prophet Samuel to be the next chosen king. Of the seven presented, none would do regardless of his stature, looks, or military prowess. Those were irrelevant when it came to the kind of leadership God was seeking. Sacred leadership, it turns out, was honed in the fields with the sheep. David's role as a shepherd foreshadows Jesus's role as the good shepherd: what unites them, in addition to bloodline, is their shared understanding of how to lead so that others will follow, how to guide so as to protect. God chooses leaders capable of this particular brand of leadership because this is the kind of leadership God exhibits and values. This is the leadership of a God who goes *before* the others, showing them the way. To follow God is, according to David, a matter of listening to one's heart. As he writes in Psalm 16:7–8: "I bless the Lord who gives me counsel; in the night also my heart instructs me. I keep the Lord always before me; because he is at my right hand, I shall not be moved."

I imagine David, the unlikely king, staying up late into the night after the servants of the house have retired for the evening. He sits in contemplative prayer, attentive to the counsel of God. Inspiration strikes him, and he sets about composing a song. David discerns the truth not by what his advisors and strategists tell him, nor by what his purse strings tell him, but by what his heart tells him. The fact is: In meditation, in prayer, in moments of fullness, we know. We know whose we are. We know whose hand we are holding and whose path to follow. We trust that God will lead us "not into temptation," as we say in the Lord's Prayer, but into the promised land of the present moment.

Maybe we feel as if we are watching the mountains with our ears. Maybe we hear the stream with open eyes. Maybe our own confusion is a sign of clarity.

You and I are strangers, and we are also siblings.

God is above us and also beneath us. God is somewhere near us and also right here with us. God goes alongside us and also before us. We are experiencing more than one sense simultaneously, and more than one preposition simultaneously, and it strikes us as truer than logic. This is what happens when our minds are set free and our bodies do the remembering: the re-membering of our individual selves back to the One Body, the God that begot us all.

A PRAYER TO GOD BEFORE

Ancient Divine who came before us:
You knit us in our mother's womb.
You wrote our days in your book.
You ordained them.
Help us to remember our shared and holy origin.

Light Divine who goes before us:
You clear the way and absorb all darkness,
delivering us from evil.
You lead us not into temptation,
never forsaking us.
Help us to follow your lead.

Amen.

CHAPTER SEVEN

For

And we know that in all things God works for the good of those who love him. . . . If God is for us, who can be against us?

Romans 8:28

Everything is laid out for you.
Your path is straight ahead of you.
Sometimes it's invisible but it's there.
You may not know where it's going,
But you have to follow that path.
It's the path to the Creator.
It's the only path there is.

Chief Leon Shenandoah

The job description of a parent is long and distinguished. Boss, nurse, scapegoat, stylist, garbage collector, chauffeur, Sherpa, housekeeper, teacher, storyteller, line cook, disciplinarian, tutor, cheerleader, hairdresser, hugger, arbiter, and advocate, to name a mere few. Sometimes the job at hand is obvious. Cuts call for a nurse, tangles for a hairdresser. Other times it's less obvious what role we are to take. In any given situation, we may see fit to intervene, or we may choose to sit back and let things play out. We may permit a monumental mess to be made, or we may mandate an immediate cleanup. We may walk out on a fit of tears or sit and cuddle. We may stand up for our kid or encourage our kid to stand up for herself. In the moment, it can be hard to know how best to proceed.

One spring afternoon a number of years ago, I received a call from an administrator at my daughter's school. She was very cordial, assuring me that everything was fine but that my daughter had been involved in "an incident." She laid out the details of the story for me in a way that was tidy and succinct. Later I realized that it begged a number of questions, but in that moment, with the school leader on the other end of the line, I didn't register any holes, and I certainly couldn't begin to formulate any questions. I was feeling mostly dismay, closely followed by a mighty swell of condemnation. I was primed to lay into my kid.

I didn't get a chance to see her until several hours later. Where I had expected to find remorse, though, was desperation. Seeing her pleading, red-rimmed eyes, I understood with calm clarity the role I was to take in this moment. Not judge but advocate. What she needed was not to be reprimanded but to be heard.

I took a deep breath and showed up as openly and lovingly as I possibly could for her. I asked her to walk me through what happened, and I listened. Listening is in itself a form of advocacy. When I made space for my daughter to share her experience, I reinstated the voice that had otherwise been denied her.

The following day, I reached out to the school administrator, and we had a productive discussion that brought to light some missteps in the way the incident had been handled. When I picked up my daughter from school, I was able to relay the nature of that conversation to her and the apologies the administrator had extended. The look on her face is hard to describe. It expressed relief and gratitude, something like pride, and something else in there too, something deep. It was the look of someone who felt not vindicated but protected, cared for, *unalone*. This is exactly what we, as children of God, are: Protected. Cared for. Unalone.

ABBA

The characterization of God as Father is meant to convey this very kind of protective and caring love. But it can register as both gendered and static. Reducing God to one role, that of Father, feels like a gross underestimation of all that God is. What of the dark womb, the viewshed, the fertile deep? What of the stealthy shadow, the indispensable witness, the steadfast fellow sojourner?

But then, did I myself not just name all the multifaceted roles that a parent takes, from scapegoat to nurse to advocate? To be a mother or to be a father: isn't it to be an exemplar of unity in diversity, to "contain multitudes," as Whitman states it, on any given day and in any given moment?

It is for this very reason—for the great many demands of the job, for the great many faces that need to be worn, and for the great many discernments needed to fathom what response is appropriate in what situation—that God is the paragon of parenthood. Of course, God is Father. And also Mother. God is the person in authority who listens to us, who comforts us, and who stands on our behalf with conviction and courage and strength and, above all else, love.

The term *Abba*, which Jesus uses for God, means Father but in a tone that more aptly matches *Dad*, or *Pa*, or even *Dadda*. It is so intimate as to be like the babbles of a baby when it first speaks of its parent: *Babbabbababba*. The baby's sounds—her gurgles and coos—are the first response of love to this most intimate and trusted person: a very different image than a strict disciplinarian or enthroned monarch. This is a Dadda who has eyes only for his baby, who will do anything in the world—anything at all—for her. And there it is: a powerhouse little preposition. *For.*

The term *Abba* seeks to convey that quality of *for-ness*. It is not formal. It is not even reverential. It is deeply personal, benevolent, intimate, and trusting. When he reframes the Trinity in terms of prepositions, "God for us" is the synonym Richard Rohr uses for "God the Father." He writes, "God, like a good father, is *for* us and is protective of us. You can just as easily call God Mother, or Inherent

Goodness, or Primal Love." Ultimately, God For, out of a love that is unconditional, exercises power to help and protect. He is "the Father of mercies and the God of all consolation" (2 Corinthians 1:3), our shared Abba.

When I think about God's promise to be *for* us in light of that one small experience of advocacy on behalf of my daughter, I understand that being for someone is a supreme act of devotion. Old Testament characterizations of God's power incorporate thunderbolts and raging storms, but the essence of God's power resides not in his capacity for destruction but in his unassailable fidelity—not ours to him but his to us! As Paul articulates in his letter to the Romans: "If God is for us, who is against us? . . . Who will separate us from the love of Christ? Will affliction or distress or persecution or famine or nakedness or peril or sword? No, in all these things we are more than victorious through him who loved us. For I am convinced that neither death, nor life, nor angels, nor rulers, nor things present, nor things to come, nor powers, nor height, nor depth, nor anything else in all creation will be able to separate us from the love of God in Christ Jesus our Lord" (Romans 8:31, 35, 38–39).

I have read and heard that verse plenty of times. What used to catch my attention was the poetic litany that Paul takes pains to write, naming not only all manner of suffering but also those angels and rulers and dimensions. He really wants to make his point here. And the point he makes is all contained in that one very small word, that easily overlooked preposition in the opening question: *for.* That word is mighty enough to stand against any and every potency. If God is for us, who (or what) is against us? No one. Not one thing.

SOLIDARITY

When we internalize the truth that God is for us and that nothing at all can be against us, we are freed to do all sorts of big, bold, beautiful, vital work in the world. Jesus, the humble carpenter who took down all the establishments of the day—political, social, and religious—models this. So much of Jesus's ministry involves advocating for those on the margins.

Fresh from his forty-day trial in the wilderness and ready to embrace his divine calling, Jesus walks into a synagogue and is met with a man possessed by an unclean spirit, who begins shouting at him (Mark 1:23). Most of us would walk away or at least avert our eyes. Not Jesus. He immediately turns toward the man to help, recognizing a soul deserving of healing. Straight from there, Jesus is escorted to the house of Simon's mother-in-law, who had fallen ill. Most people want nothing to do with someone who is feverish. They steer clear until the fever has abated, fearing contagion. Not Jesus. Jesus not only comes near the woman; he holds her frail hand and heals her. Word spreads fast, and so that very same night, there comes a throng of every single sick or deranged person in the entire village, pounding at his door. One by one, Jesus lets them in, and one by one, he cares for them. These are people—someone's grandfather, another person's child, yet another's sister—who have been long ostracized for their ailments, who themselves may have lost any hope for a healthy life or a happy one. Along comes Jesus, the one person who would care for them. From his position of compassion, of mercy, of justice, and of love, Jesus is able to perform miracles.

On this goes, throughout the story of Jesus's life and ministry. He stands up for and cares for myriad people society has deemed unworthy: a leper, a paralytic, a cripple, a girl taken ill, an epileptic boy, a tween presumed dead, a woman hemorrhaging, a blind man, a deaf man, a demoniac, a woman accused of adultery. So much of what made people want to call Jesus Savior and Redeemer was his willingness to be *for* others, all others, no matter their lot. And yet few people in Jesus's day had eyes to see the glory of the work he was doing. They found him threatening to the status quo. They found him to be a heretic and a blasphemer. They feared his message and his miracles and therefore sentenced him to death.

The lives of so many of humanity's greatest heroes share a similar storyline. These are people, ranging from John the Baptist to Joan of Arc, from Mahatma Gandhi to Martin Luther King Jr., who advocated for the lesser-thans and were killed for it. And yet, as is evidenced by the rise and endurance of Christianity itself, death was never much of a plug in the tide of love. Jesus died and martyrs have died, but their actions have inspired countless others to carry forth the mission of the gospel. And what the gospel calls for is what Jesus modeled: compassion for others and persistent advocacy on their behalf, especially those who cannot advocate for themselves.

This kind of servant-heartedness is surprisingly communicable. Seeing one person care for someone else inspires another to do the same. And another. And another. In this way, God For initiates and sustains revolutions of loving goodness throughout time and place. No possible force can stop this tide.

This happened in Jesus's own day, before his death and subsequent resurrection, which then paved the way for the acts of the apostles and the formation of churches across Greece and Asia Minor. The disciples, having witnessed days and months of Jesus's unending acts of mercy and healing, become empowered to perform miracles of service themselves. It wasn't that hard once they knew how to do it. One day they, like their Lord, "cast out many demons and anointed with oil many who were sick and cured them" (Mark 6:13). Then other "ordinary people" followed suit, including a man the disciples insisted was not a proper follower. Unsure of his ancestry and his motives, the disciples tried to prevent him from advocating in the name of Christ, but Jesus would have none of it. "Do not stop him," Jesus told his disciples; "Whoever is not against us is for us" (Mark 9:39–40).

This is a loose definition of faith that Jesus gives, and a generous one. We don't have to be big believers. We just need not be haters. Jesus gives the benefit of the doubt, quite literally. Doubt he does not condemn, only aggression of the hand and of the heart. And to that he responds with acts of nonviolence, with invitations to repentance, with understanding and promises of forgiveness. Jesus is against certain attitudes and certain actions, but he is not against anybody. Which means that Jesus is *for* everybody. A core tenet of Christianity, understood in the personhood of Jesus and illuminated in Scripture, is God's absolute *for*-ing love.

CHEERLEADER

It is true that in advocacy, there is an opportunity for beautiful reciprocity: God is for Jesus, and Jesus is for God. Jesus is for the leper, and the leper is for Jesus. This is less "You scratch my back and I'll scratch yours" and more "I got you and I know you got me." That's the way love works: without demand. For just as God For has no restrictions, neither does God For have stipulations. We get to have the Divine on our side regardless of how "in or out" we may be at any given moment. What changes is not God's steadfastness but our awareness of God's steadfastness. It's not whether God is for us but how for God *we* are.

This is so often the case, isn't it? We don't know what we don't know. I smile when I think about the way Jesus responded to his disciples when he was trying to teach them things. With deep sighs, he would marvel at how much they—the ones closest to him, the ones most devoted to the cause—missed. The people more able to absorb the fullness of Jesus's message were the ones he advocated for directly; everyone else was enthralled but largely confused.

This is in part because Jesus was not exactly direct. When teaching, he speaks in parables whose meanings are hard to discern and easy to misconstrue. Why? I think this is another, more subtle form of Jesus's advocacy. Refusing to spoon-feed answers, he impels his followers to think for themselves so that they might act according to an understanding and a set of principles that they have developed rather than one dictated by a person in authority. Jesus is the reigning champion of critical thinking.

And critical thinking is hard. We'd rather just to be told the answer, but teachers, the best of them, know better. They are *for* their students in a way that might seem at first like being against them. Diann Shoaf was one of those.

The viciously challenging teacher of AP literature at my high school, Ms. Shoaf was an imposing person: slight and pale, with cropped dark hair and black clothes. All year, every single day, she wore only black clothes. And her voice, it warbled with a sort of elitist intelligence as to be almost stylized, and yet she was putting on no airs. She assigned us *Absalom, Absalom!* by William Faulkner—which would have been wretched any time of year—over spring break. *The Scarlet Letter*, a book I detested to such an extreme that I videotaped myself throwing it out of a window, had been summer reading. (This was before cellphones, and so I had used a hefty camcorder to capture the dramatic act.) *Hamlet* we read together, but *Moby Dick* was "reading on the side," with an occasional pop quiz that featured obscure questions like "What was the content of the painting that hung on the wall in the inn?" That question nearly killed me. There I was slugging through thousands of pages of whale blubber, and Ms. Shoaf wanted to know what was in the painting.

It was maddening, and yet I understand now. She was training us to notice even the smallest, seemingly most inconsequential thing. She was sharpening one of the most valuable tools in our life-box: our *awareness*, the very skill we must use to detect all these prepositions. And we just thought she was being nasty.

She was not. Ms. Shoaf was resolutely, boldly, faithfully *for* us. She was so for us, in fact, that she refused to shortchange us the opportunity to be for ourselves: to prove to ourselves what we were capable of. On the last day of class, Ms. Shoaf threw us a party and baked us a cake and actually smiled. She was visibly delighted. We had swum the whale-infested waters and survived. Not so much with us or even alongside us, still, she had been *for* us since day one, and that stance was what had taught us the most.

Being for someone is not always easy. Sometimes it requires us to take courageous action and stand on behalf of the weak. Sometimes it requires us to hold back and hold space for failure, no matter how desperately we want to step in and soften the suffering. My classmates and I had no idea that Ms. Shoaf loved us or believed in us. We would have sworn the opposite was true. But her love was what they call tough, maybe not just for us but for her also. She willingly accepted our assumption that she was mean, scary, distant, and uncaring if it meant that we would come out stronger, wiser, more capable, and more enriched in the end. She was more for us than she was for herself, it turns out.

Ms. Shoaf would scoff at an analogy that compares her to God, and she would likely give me a B minus on this particular work of nonfiction. But she helps me understand something critical about the way God approaches teaching. God loves us and believes in us, which is precisely why he doesn't jump in to save us from suffering. Gives us the tools needed to survive, yes. Trains us to see with wiser eyes, yes. Cheers from the bank, yes, even when we're underwater and can't hear him.

We might easily assume there is no God. Or that there is a God, but he is patronizing or masochistic or punitive—or all three. But I believe we are being guided on paths of fulfillment that we may lack the perspective to see. Indeed, Jesus promised his disciples, and promises us in turn, that an Advocate has been sent to help teach and guide us (John 14:26). This Advocate, also translated as Helper, Counselor, Comforter, and Paraclete, is not only God With and God Alongside but also God For. This God is at work in the world, soothing, protecting, guiding, and teaching each of us on a daily basis.

ALTRUISM

What is our response? Are we against Jesus, or are we for him? Or are we somewhere in an amorphous middle? And what are the consequences of our stance?

These questions sound like they have to do with "being a Christian," but they don't necessarily. Jesus isn't asking us to believe in him or to join a religion around him so much as he is asking us to form a way of *being* around his deeds and teachings. "Believe the works," Jesus tells the crowds who wish to stone him at the Festival of Dedication in Jerusalem (John 10:38). This isn't about me, he implies.

The more appropriate questions may well be: Are we against the *teachings* of Jesus, or are we for them, or are we somewhere in an amorphous middle? And what are the consequences of our stance?

One consequence, as Jesus explains it, is that to condemn the teachings is to be condemned (John 3:18). Condemnation does not mean going to an afterlife of hell. Condemnation means residing in a hell of our own making, one that is oriented toward surface self (ego) rather than true self (soul) and the welfare of others. This hell renders life empty, lacking, unfulfilling, disconnected, angry, and painful.

To be for Jesus's teachings, on the other hand, is infinitely generative. As Jesus explains rather hyperbolically: "Truly I tell you, there is no one who has left house or brothers or sisters or mother or father or children or fields for my sake and for the sake of the good news who will not receive a hundredfold now in this age—houses, brothers and sisters, mothers and children, and fields, with persecutions—and in the age to come eternal life" (Mark 10:29–30). This is happy news, but it is not a teaching we much like—or understand. How are we supposed to leave our mothers when a commandment is to honor them? Why abandon our children when we are instructed to bring them up in the way of God? How is this remotely even possible, and why would it be God's will for us?

I would venture to guess that Jesus is using extremes to make a point. What Jesus wants is for us, first and foremost, to be for God and for the gospel. That's why he says the first commandment is to "love the Lord your God with all your heart and with all your mind and with all your strength" and why he says the second is like it: to "love your neighbor as yourself" (Mark 12:30–31). Implied in that second commandment is the wisdom that in order to love others, we have to first love ourselves—our truest selves as opposed to our false selves. Perhaps what Jesus was doing those forty days in the wilderness was uncovering his own truest self. That period of solitude, during which he wrestled with temptation and discerned his own power, was a deep dive into soulwork, into learning to love himself. From there, he could turn that love toward others, whether through prayer, healing, teaching, feeding, or forgiving.

Everything Jesus did was for the love of others, as he loved himself, and for the love of God, his Abba. By naming these two commandments as the most critical, Jesus insists that we be *for* ourselves and *for* others and *for* God too. Indeed, the whole of the gospel may well be summarized as a campaign of *for*-ness.

When you think about the verbs that typically pair with the preposition *for*, you can see that they are a powerful bunch: Care for. Pray for. Apologize for. Long for. Wait for. Work for. Stand up for. Be there for. Thank for. Love for. Anytime we do any of these things, we are likely in gospel territory.

And let's not forget the phrase with the preposition "for" that gets touted most of all in Christian teaching: *Die for*. The "proof" of Jesus's abiding love tends to be the crucifixion. From an early age, children raised in Christian churches hear that Jesus died for us. It's the big news. The grand act. The defining moment.

Another astonishing and disruptive and heartening truth dwells at the core of Christianity too, though. It is this: God not only dies for us, God *lives* for us also. God's will to live, God's desire to live, God's capacity to live is *for* us—for the purpose of us and the hope of us and the love of us. As is declared in 1 John 4:16, "So we have known and believe the love that God has for us. God is love, and those who abide in love abide in God, and God abides in them."

We believe not only in a God willing to die but also in a God willing to live. This God grants life—ours, yours, and mine, right now and also ours, yours, and mine, eternally. Christianity is a faith system that testifies to the fact that death is not final but is rather a critical component of life—of unbound, abundant, persisting life. And living is God's ultimate gift for us.

BIG LOVES

My mother has always been a stickler about writing thank-you notes, and so I come by it naturally. Beginning in childhood and continuing now well into adulthood, I have written thousands of thank-you notes, many to the same people year after year (Sally, Barry, Betty . . .). After all this time, the words "thank you" feel stale. They fail to convey authentic gratitude, becoming almost embarrassing in their inadequacy. But I keep writing, addressing, stamping, and sending: a process that is wholeheartedly for the recipient but is also for me. It is a reminder for me to cherish what I am given, to take time to express thanks, and to reflect love back to the giver.

So it is with spiritual praise and thanksgiving. We know we are supposed to praise God for all God is and all God does for us. And yet we may feel like our words fall flat. We may find our prayers—all those invisible notes we send out into the ether—woefully inadequate. They aren't. They are a sign that we are receiving what is given. They are a sign that we are accepting the bold, life-giving love that God has for us and saying thank you for it in return.

My mother has also always been a robust tag writer. Birthday gifts and Christmas presents come adorned with tags that take anywhere from thirty seconds to three minutes to read. That may not sound like a long time, but when you're a kid ready to rip into some wrapping paper, it definitely is. These tag-notes are repositories of lavish praise, which inevitably begin *For Varina*. Even if the tag has a preprinted *To* on it, my mom will cross it out to write *For* instead. The distinction matters to her. She doesn't just give a gift *to* someone; she chooses a gift *for* him or her. The giving is not just a transactional handover but rather an intimate expression of love and genuine knowing.

Just as these tags never open with *To*, they also never close with *From*. She crosses out that word also. In its place, my mother will occasionally write *Love* but in most cases will write *Big Loves*, a shortened version of a longer statement spoken often in our household. My parents did say "I love you" plenty, but it was also common to hear them say "I have big loves for you." That is a mouthful. The phrasing makes a point by being spacious, even cumbersome. It demands hearing. It also shifts "love" from a verb to a noun—which makes room for that potent little preposition, *for*.

Love is not an action, hopping from an "I" to a "you." Rather the "I" has the love, keeps it, lives with it, experiences it, all while also giving it—specifically, grandly, and altruistically—to the "you." "I have big loves for you" is life-enriching for both parties, but the emphasis is on *for you*. This happens to be the exact same nuanced phrasing that Jesus uses when he says, "By this everyone will know that you are my disciples, if you have love for one another" (John 13:35).

The abiding truth here is this: God has love—big loves, as it were—for you. This may sound cutesy, but it is not. Divine love is an unconditional, sacrificial, merciful, joyful, elemental, eternal devotion. It is always oriented outward: It is always *for.*

A PRAYER TO GOD FOR

God, you are for us
when we cannot be for ourselves.
Humbly we praise you.

God, you call us to be for one another,
especially the poor and the destitute,
the lowly and the infirm.
Humbly we beseech you
to give us the conviction and courage to do your will.

God, you invite us to be for you,
to listen for you,
to stand for you.
Humbly we ask that you strengthen our faith.

For us, you live and die and live again.

For you, we live and die and live again.

We give thanks for you, God.

As you have big loves for us,
so we have big loves for you.

Amen.

CHAPTER EIGHT

Through

It is not you who speak, but the Spirit of your
Father speaking through you.

Matthew 10:20

Christ has no body now on earth but yours,
no hands but yours,
no feet but yours.
Yours are the eyes through which is to look out
Christ's compassion to the world.
Yours are the feet with which he is to go about doing good.
Yours are the hands with which he is to bless men now.

Attributed to Teresa of Avila

I used to sit on the vestry at our church in downtown Nashville. Sitting on the vestry is like being on a board of trustees. The focus is business, and the meetings are conducted using parliamentary procedure, which means they don't begin until they are called to order and discussions don't occur until there has been a motion to initiate them and a second to actually launch them. In general, things don't happen unless someone declares them so moved.

This was all very hard for me to get used to, as I was not well versed in parliamentary procedure. In my work as a teacher, writer, and content strategist, I ask probing questions, draw out truths, and embrace the potential in pauses. To stop a discussion in order to formally initiate it with the requisite "so moved" was anathema to me. To have to *second* motions in order to validate them? It bordered on offensive. Though I understood why we utilized this procedure, it nevertheless had an alienating effect on me. Rather than feeling so moved, I often felt removed.

At the time I also happened to be reading Richard Rohr's book *The Naked Now: Learning to See as the Mystics See,* and I came across a sentence that arrested my attention. We, as humans, "are always and forever merely seconding the motion" of God, Rohr writes. I underlined that one. And starred it. And came to ponder it often. *We are always and forever merely seconding the motion of God.*

The implications became clear over time. God is the one who set things in motion (past tense), which makes sense. God is the author of creation. God is also the one who sets things in motion (present tense), which also makes sense. God is moving and inspiring and guiding and using us all the time. In this way God is not only Before and For, but she is somehow also Through. In trinitarian theology, this would fall into the camp of *God the Holy Spirit.*

Even as I have struggled to understand the person of Jesus, I have never struggled with the concept of the Holy Spirit. Throughout my life, I have consistently felt and believed in the Holy Spirit, with all her beguiling nearness, because I have known the feeling of being so moved. As a child, I was so moved by the shades of violet, indigo, and purple around the angel's wings in the stained-glass window in the sanctuary of our church. As a teenager, I was so moved by Wordsworth's evocative poetry: "Let the moon / Shine on thee in the solitary walk; / And let the misty mountain winds be free / To blow against thee." And as an adult, I was so moved by the first sound I heard from my newborn daughters. Before I could see them, I could hear them, like geese honking, announcing their arrival. *So moved*: there is that phrase and yet in a context so vastly different than our weekly meetings.

In countless ways daily, I continue to be so moved. By music, by trees, by kind notes, by expressions of suffering. I cry easily. I get goosebumps a lot. Not just my heart but my body registers divine motion. I used to think that joy was elusive. As I take baby steps toward wisdom, I understand that joy is not elusive. Joy is the natural consequence of allowing oneself to be so moved.

We experience this joy across a spectrum of emotions. It is the delight that springs from being tuned in to the natural world. It is the serenity that floods our bodies when we stand in awe. It is the gladness that accompanies an act of service or of generosity. It is the passion, erotic or platonic, that we feel toward another human being. And it is the conviction we possess to persevere toward a calling, no matter how unconventional or daunting it may seem. Always this joy is a response of the soul rather than the ego. It is the soul allowing itself to be an instrument. "The essential religious experience," Rohr surmises, "is that [we] are being 'known through' more than knowing anything in particular [ourselves]." Likewise, we are being "done through" rather than doing anything on our accord, and "prayed through" rather than praying ourselves. "No wonder all of the great liturgical prayers of the churches end with the same phrase: through Christ our Lord, Amen," Father Rohr notes. "We do not pray to Christ, we pray through Christ. Or even more precisely, Christ prays through us. If God does indeed live for us, so too does God live through us. We are always and forever the conduits, the tuning forks, the receiver stations of the Divine."

This understanding of the Divine as a kind of through-force is true of Christianity and yet not exclusive to Christianity. The Bhagavad Gita, the sacred text of Hinduism, for instance, echoes this claim closely:

> Those who are free from selfish attachments,
> Who have mastered the senses and passions,
> Act not, but are acted through by the Lord.

> Listen to me now, O son of Kunti,
> How one who has become an instrument
> In the hands of the Lord attains Brahman,
> The Supreme consummation of wisdom.

The language is convincingly parallel. The Lord is acting *through* us, and we are her sacred instruments: trumpets of a holy music, prophets of a holy word, disciples of a holy calling, agents of a holy love. When we free ourselves of selfish attachments, we free ourselves to be acted through by none other than God herself. Sometimes this comes by our own fierce devotion: We have practiced the presence of God deeply enough to channel it, as was the case with Mary Magdalene. Other times this comes like a jolt of lightning, unexpected and unbidden: We have rejected the presence of God fervently enough to conduct it, as was the case with Saul, who became the apostle Paul.

Many of us know the story of Saul's conversion. Pounding on doors from house to house in the city of Jerusalem, Saul spent his days hunting any and all disciples of Jesus—male or female, it did not matter. He vowed to lock them up or in some cases put them to death by stoning for the faith they professed. Saul was dogged and successful in his efforts. Having outed believers in Jerusalem, he obtained special permission from the high priests to track down and arrest offenders in foreign cities as well, including Damascus.

It was on the road there that he was famously flattened by a flash of light. Issuing forth from this light was a voice clear enough to be heard by all traveling the road that day. This voice did not profess murderous threats to match the murderous threats of Saul, however. It was not eager to smite or proclaim destruction, though one could argue such a response was merited. This was the voice of the Christ, and it asked a question: a simple, patient, pained question: "Saul, Saul, why do you persecute me?" (Acts 9:4). I hear in the repetition of Saul's name a gentle, deeply intimate tone. It does not sound angry. It sounds composed and genuine. It sounds wise and loving, despite the infractions of the man involved. It sounds injured but also curious and tender.

Jesus proves less gentle with Ananias, the other figure in the story. Ananias is quick to answer the voice of Jesus, enthusiastically responding *Yes, Lord* when Jesus summons him. But Ananias's willingness is short-lived. When Jesus tells him his mission—go to Straight Street and intercept a native of Tarsus named Saul—Ananias backs down from his ready eagerness. *I have heard about that guy,* Ananias tells Jesus, in essence. *He is really dangerous, and he has the authority to arrest us, and that does not at all sound like something I want to do.* Jesus does not repeat Ananias's name. He does not ask him a question. He gives him one directive—"Go!"—along with one explanation: "This man is my chosen instrument" (Acts 9:15 NIV).

And what an instrument he proves to be. Blind for three days, Saul thereupon resurrects as Paul, the apostle responsible for spreading the gospel throughout Anatolia and Greece. He is the author of many of the biblical passages that elucidate the nature of a universal Christ, a saint who surrendered to a gruesome death to uphold the faith. God worked through Paul boldly and fruitfully. God worked through Ananias too, for Ananias did go to the house on Straight Street as he was called to do. He laid trembling hands on a man hell-bent on murdering him and he called him Brother. It was by Ananias's touch that Paul rose, newly able to see through the eyes of Christ, newly ready not to act according to his opinion and will but instead to let God's wisdom and will work *through* him. Indeed, Paul was so moved by what happened on the road to Damascus that he devoted his life and his death to seconding the motions of the God that struck him.

In those vestry meetings every Monday night in a corner room at our church, we used that phrase "so moved" in order to facilitate a good and fair discussion. What had felt to me like rigidity was in fact equity in disguise. I came to understand that truth, and the longer I stayed, the more open I was to learn. I also came to realize that—though we were down to business—a sacred force was working through us for things likewise good and fair.

We never have to make the first move, nor do we even get to. The first move is always God's, and it is through that motion that transformation, healing, and love occur. All we have to do is be so moved that with faith and courage we second that motion, letting God work through us. This is what transforms an ordinary person into a disciple or a prophet or a mystic or an angel. Once we experience it, we understand its sublime power.

I am reminded of that piece of Scripture my friend Sarah gave me in middle school and now have eyes to see it anew: "I can do all things through him that strengthens me" (Philippians 4:13). There it is, this revelatory preposition, showing us how we can do all things through Christ just as Christ can do all things through us. This is how we become holy instruments and why Saint Francis of Assisi prays his familiar, sacred request: *Lord, make me an instrument of thy peace.* Each of us has our melody to play.

VIRGIN

The Bible is overflowing with examples of people who become holy instruments of God's peace. These people are often the least expected or deserving of the task. When called by God, they protest, make excuses, politely decline, and adamantly resist. Ananias went from very willing to very disinclined in a matter of seconds. Sarai literally laughed in God's face, viewing herself as way too old for childbearing. Jeremiah, on the other hand, viewed himself as way too young and told God as much. Moses argued that he was a bad public speaker. Jonah tried running away, as if God could not track him to foreign shores.

The most esteemed example of a person willing to be an agent of God's will is Mary. Mary, the Mother of God. The Virgin Mary.

With limited contextual knowledge, Christians have often understood the term *virgin* to mean sexually chaste, but doing so has meant that we collectively have missed a critical aspect of what the Mother of God has to teach us. Mary's story exists within a larger framework of the Feminine Divine, one that often associates a sacred female figure with virginity. Many of the goddesses of antiquity were considered virgins, from the Chinese Holy Virgin Shing-Moo to the Babylonian Ishtar. These goddesses also had many lovers and bore many children. They were not virgins sexually by any stretch of the imagination. As Jungian analyst M. Esther Harding explains, the word *virgin* "cannot be used as denoting a factual situation, for the quality of virginity persists in some unexplained fashion despite sexual experience, child-bearing, and increasing age." Virginity, "of either the Virgin Mary or of the virgin goddesses of other religions" has little to do with sexual chastity, as it were. When we are able to "recognize religious concepts as symbolic and interpret these contradictions psychologically," writes Harding, "we realize that the term 'virginity' must refer to a quality, to a subjective state, a psychological attitude, not to a physiological or external fact."

The term *virgin*, as it was used in reference to women living at the time of Mary, had little to do with chastity either. To be a virgin was to be unwed, and to be unwed was to be independent. When a woman married, she became the property of her husband, thus abdicating her right to personhood. But as a "virgin," she was her own authority, able to accept or refuse sexual advances as she so desired but, even more significantly, able to act in all things according to her own discernment and decisions. Harding explains that a virgin "belonged to herself alone, she was 'one-in-herself.'" To be a virgin is to be self-reliant, free, and autonomous.

Such was the quality, the psychological attitude, the state of being of the Virgin Mary. Mary was possessed of both openness and agency. She could make the will of God her own if she so chose. When the angel spoke to her, explaining what was to come, Mary listened, asked a question, and then replied, "I am the servant of the Lord. Let this happen to me as you say" (Luke 1:38). Whatever incredulousness she had gave way to absolute trust and surrender. She was her own woman, free to make her own choices, and we know the rest of the story. The inspiration of the Holy Spirit was so potent, and Mary's willingness to receive it so absolute, that she became a conduit of the Divine. As a true virgin, one able to *authorize* herself, she agreed to let God use her and effectively incarnate through her. She agreed, in effect, to love God and to be God's lover, and the result was the conception of a new life, a holy way.

To equate Mary's virginity merely with sexual purity strips us of a very rich takeaway, one that might have altered the course of Christianity for centuries and one that still has the capacity to do so. We tend to put Mary on a pedestal, touting her virginity as proof of the miracle of Jesus's birth. But in the same way we miss that the mind of Christ is in us and not just in Jesus, we also tend to miss that the virginity of the Divine is also in us and not just in Mary, should we cultivate it. We, like Mary, are capable of being sacred conduits for the Holy Spirit, which seeks to inspire and impregnate us, as it did her. Like Mary's, our souls are capable of magnifying the Lord. This happens when we choose, boldly and courageously, to second the motion of God.

LABOR

Seconding the motion of God is a holy but sometimes grueling assignment. Agreeing to let God incarnate through her, the Virgin Mary was thereby agreeing to labor. Actual labor. The various writers of the Bible, none of whom experienced labor themselves, liked to reference labor pains to encapsulate the holy terror invoked on creation by God. Jeremiah, Isaiah, Micah, Paul, and various psalmists all use the metaphor. I can imagine these men, when a woman's time drew near, retreating to another room. Yet they were likely unable to escape the sound of the wailing and the sharp screams of their womenfolk as new life came forth from their bodies. I can imagine them averting their eyes but still glimpsing her brow drenched in sweat, her bedcovers soaked in blood. This, after nine months of ripening, of drawing smaller and smaller breaths, of aching backs and swollen ankles.

In the book of Genesis, God is said to have caused labor pains as a consequence of sin, but God knows what those writers did not. Throughness is not easy. No deeply good thing is. Labor is not a consequence of sin but rather a crucible of salvation.

Near the end of my first pregnancy with our twin daughters, my feet were so swollen that I could wear no shoes, only slippers. I was a high school teacher then, and so I plodded through the halls in my slippers. I suggested to the teens in my class that if they were not ready for all this, my hand floating up and down the engorged frame of my body, they ought to take care to avoid activities that produce such transformation. They listened with wide eyes, eyes that betrayed a mix of disgust and wonder. There was a miracle being witnessed, but also a repulsion at the making of it.

As for me, having two bodies growing in my body—becoming, literally, room and board for other living people—was worth whatever I might go through. That included, when I reached thirty-five weeks of pregnancy, something more than any of us anticipated: the resolute, systematic, and highly dangerous shutdown of all my internal organs, one by one.

The acronym for this syndrome is HELLP, of all things. I did not know this was happening to me. Neither did the nurse who answered the phone when I called, the nurse who said if my contractions weren't less than five minutes apart, I should stay home. Neither did my husband, who promised to stay up with me in my agony but was snoring in less than thirty minutes. I don't blame him one bit. If I could have been snoring, I would have been. Instead, I was lying on the floor on my side, my bloated body sweating and aching, pain ripping through every cell of me, tears pooling in the rough nodules of carpet beneath my cheek. It was nightlong agony, and I had to go through it. And when we eventually went to the hospital and the surgeon made a neat incision across my lower abdomen, pulled open my flesh, and tugged out first one healthy baby girl and then another, I finally understood the fruits of all that nine-month-long labor. I finally understood that *what you go through is what you become.*

Once those children were alive and thriving in the world, I often read them the board book *We're Going on a Bear Hunt* by Michael Rosen and Helen Oxbury. The book features an intrepid family of five—six if you include the dog—that sets out on an afternoon adventure and discovers all manner of obstacles: mud, blizzards, raging rivers, and scary forests. They were not unlike the band of weary travelers trying desperately to make it to the promised land. At each obstacle, the family repeats the mantra of the familiar chant: *Can't go over it. Can't go under it. Gotta go through it.* And onward they plunge, squelching through mud or angling against torrents of rain. The family perseveres in their journey because they are impelled by an attitude of throughness.

Like it or not, God gives us ample opportunity to develop our throughness muscle. It is one of the things we like least about God and one of the things we *understand* least about God too. If God is benevolent and merciful, good and almighty, why does God allow such things as blizzards and mud fields to bar our way? Why do we not get the part or the job or the girl? Why do relationships have to end? Why can we not get pregnant? Why do lovely people get cancer? Why war and acrimony, abuse and crisis of all kinds? Why, why, why the suffering?

The pain of the world seems antithetical to a God who is Love. It might be easy for us to determine once again that there is no God. Or that if there is a God, she is punitive and not much worth worshipping. Reason would tell us this, but wisdom says something different. Reason would tell us suffering is something to be avoided, but wisdom would tell us that suffering is an opportunity for transformation. Reason would tell us suffering is a sign of an angry god or an absent god, but wisdom would tell us suffering is a path into the very heart of God.

With suffering, we can't go over it. We can't go under it. We gotta go through it. The experience of that hard throughness infuses our understanding, forms our identity, and informs our way of being in the world. Addiction and recovery. Illness and treatment. Loss and grief. Trauma and therapy. Labor and birth. Going through any of these, we cannot but come into new being. We cannot but *become*. This is what throughness is: the very hard but also very sacred work of becoming.

I have a close friend who lost her first child just weeks before he was due. He died inside her, and she had to bring him into the world to take no breath at all—unbearable suffering for a woman whose faith is resolute and whose wisdom has been a balm to many. In that gutted space of the aftermath, in the weeks and months of the afterward, she grew a philanthropy to give clothing and blankets to babies born in our area who come into the world in poverty. The philanthropy, Strick's Gift, is named for her son who came into the world without breath but who nevertheless *became*.

Ever so bravely, my friend enabled her suffering to be creative. Unlike "neurotic suffering," which is untransformative, creative suffering is, according to Sue Monk Kidd, "the pain we encounter in confronting our lives honestly, expanding our vision, choosing a new way, owning our shadow, and healing wounds." This kind of suffering is the through-work of God.

Jesus models it for us, bravely and faithfully, when he gets betrayed, arrested, tortured, and executed, only to rise again in three days' time. Only through the agony of crucifixion is there an experience of resurrection. Suffering guts us, and in that emptiness, the living waters rush through.

FLOW

In the Hindu tradition, the mother goddess is Shakti. She is responsible for creation and destruction and creation again. Her very essence—that which enlivens, strengthens, eradicates, and resurrects all things—is flow, and her pattern, like Christ's, is cyclical. The writer of Ecclesiastes writes this about the Divine:

> The sun rises, and the sun goes down
>   and hurries to the place where it rises.
> The wind blows to the south
>   and goes around to the north;
> round and round goes the wind,
>   and on its circuits the wind returns.
> All streams run to the sea,
>   but the sea is not full;
> to the place where the streams flow,
>   there they continue to flow. (Ecclesiastes 1:5–7)

This is God, who set the earth spinning, sunrise following sunset persistently. This is God, who created for six days and then took a rest, establishing our patterns of work. This is God, who inscribed the process of birth, death, and rebirth in the genetic code of every living thing. This is God, the living water, the divine motion, flowing ceaselessly without ever filling. What she *does* and what she *is* is flow. Her way of being is therefore ever and always *through*.

God will move us through labor and through labyrinth. She will move us through life and through death. She will make rivers flow on barren heights and springs within the valleys. She will turn the desert into pools of water and the parched ground into springs (Isaiah 41:18). She will sate all thirst, cleanse all filth, soak all seed. A fountain will flow out of her house, watering the valley of acacias. From her hills will flow milk. From her mountains will flow wine. All the ravines will run with water (Joel 3:18).

Aligning with this flow is the aim of yoga, qigong, and tai chi. It is the aim of chanting, of chakra clearing, of breath work. It is the aim of meditation, mantra, and contemplative prayer. It is the aim of any spiritual work when it realizes it need not have any aim at all. The Flow flows. She courses through us, physically and spiritually, whether we are aware or not. We breathe in. We breathe out. The same air as Eve. The same molecules as Adam. "All is a procession," Walt Whitman opines. "The universe is a procession with measured and perfect motion."

We, like Whitman, can sing the body electric. We, like Mary, can second the measured and perfect motion of the universe. We are all possible channels for the Spirit, who works through us every day in ways bidden and unbidden, in ways large and small. We may experience the inspiration of the Holy Spirit when we find we have the right words to pray over someone. Or when we feel ourselves guided to a certain place, realizing later that our presence was needed there. Or when we are filled with the grace to forgive, to surrender, or simply to abide. We are opened to the workings of the Spirit when we abort our own agendas and the egos that fuel them. As the anonymous monk who authored *The Cloud of Unknowing* instructs: "Let it do with you and lead you as it will. Let it be the one that works; you simply must consent to it. Simply look at it, and just let it be. Do not interfere with it, as though you wish to help it on, less you spill it at all. Try to be the wood and let it be the carpenter."

Maybe that was the furtive message in Jesus's vocation. He: carpenter. Us: wood, ready and willing to be shaped into something beautiful, something functional.

Have you found that you somehow had the right words to console a friend when you didn't think you knew what to say? Have you found that you opened the door for an elderly woman who was, at that very moment, needing to be seen, helped, and respected? Have you found that you asked the right question at the right moment?

I was in Houston for work one weekend in early autumn, and I called a rideshare to take me to the airport. A middle-aged man picked me up, and I slid into the back seat and chose not to get out my phone. I learned that he had family still living in Nigeria, his country of origin, and also a sister living in London. I asked him if he had any children. His answer surprised me, and possibly him as well.

"I don't know," he said. And then he clarified: "I had a son who died at birth. I don't know if that counts."

The air in the car shifted. I could feel it shift, and I suspect it had something to do with the motion of the Holy Spirit.

"That counts, my friend," I said softly. "That counts."

He told me then of holding in his hands the corpse of his infant son. He became a father at eighteen years old, and yet he never got to be one. This, as the line of traffic blurred and stalled outside the windows of the car.

"I am sorry," he said. "I don't mean to be such a downer."

I gently refused his apology. Then we sat, he at the wheel and me in the back seat, in a space that felt to me suddenly cleared out, spacious and sacred. I felt profound sadness for his loss and also profound gratitude for his vulnerability, for having been invited to receive his story. None of what happened was me.

God flows through: That is her nature and her desire and her destiny. Our work is to open the valve of our strong and beating hearts. Our invitation is to second the motion. Our pleasure is to be so moved, so profoundly moved.

A PRAYER TO GOD THROUGH

Through my lips, God, speak.
Through my eyes, see.
Through my body, move.
Through my heart, love.
Through my suffering, transform.
Through my life, live.

Help me to be opened and ready.
Help me to second the motion of Love.
Help me to let you flow,
through and through.

Amen.

CHAPTER NINE

Into

Then the Lord God formed a man from the dust of the ground
and breathed into his nostrils the breath of life,
and the man became a living being.

Genesis 2:7

Out of himself he brought forth the cosmos
and entered into everything in it.
There is nothing that does not come from him.
Of everything, he is the inmost Self.

Chandogya Upanishad

"If you were a word, what word would you be?" Elizabeth Gilbert poses in her best-selling memoir *Eat, Pray, Love.* It is a question I pondered in earnest when reading that book and a question I encountered again later when consulting with high school seniors on their essays for college. The University of Chicago has a delightful list of unexpected prompts on their application, and one year this very question popped up. It's not hard for an admissions officer to spot a brilliant applicant with a question like this. It's the difference in picking the word *antevasin*, which is Sanskrit for "one who lives at the border" (and is Elizabeth Gilbert's word), and something like *confident* or *friendly.*

Antevasin is a word to envy: clever, original, memorable, if a tad unpronounceable. The example I always gave my students was far more mundane. "If I were a word," I would tell them with mounting suspense. "I would be . . . *into*." A measly four-lettered preposition that doesn't seem to mean all that much, *into* is the punchline that falls flat. It's the answer to the "what word would you be" game around the dinner table that gets the least number of ahhs. It's a weird choice, but secretly or not so secretly, I think it's awesome.

Into expresses a movement that is penetrating. It does not come *to* something and stop there; nor does it even go *in* something and then quit. The combination of *in* and *to* suggests engagement at the deepest, most sustained level.

So much of modern life skims the surface. We scroll through feeds. We rush through workouts. We see people in passing, rarely able to go past a quick *How are you?* and a promise to get together soon. Our pace is so fast that we rarely have the time or energy for a deep dive. I wonder sometimes if we collectively have even retained the *capacity* for a deep dive.

That's why I like the word *into*. It asserts the values of curiosity, intentionality, and connection as well as dedication, perseverance, and courage. Its mission is to live profoundly. A commitment to *into*-ing challenges us to sink into something substantive and more meaningful, asking that we let ourselves be surrounded, or even enclosed, by something else. It trusts and even seeks immersion.

The into-moving self is not lost in this process but instead enhanced, because this brand of movement begets newness and fullness. The experience is so completely absorbing as to be transformative. It is worth noting that the word that almost always follows *transforms* is *into*. The caterpillar transforms into a butterfly. Clark Kent transforms into Superman. Transformation is always an into-ing.

We engage in this kind of transformative into-ing when we immerse ourselves in an inquiry or study of some kind. We engage in this kind of transformative into-ing when we delve courageously into our fears, our trauma, our suffering. We engage in it when we lead with empathy, putting ourselves into someone else's shoes. We engage in it when we practice meditation, yoga, dance, or any other kind of somatic endeavor that unites body, mind, and spirit. And we engage in it when we commit ourselves to relationship.

What unites all these endeavors is that they are born of, and sustained by, hope. In this way, these labors are the work of the soul—derivative of and reflective of the creative Divine. It may well be that the entirety of the Christian faith is based on the essential claim that transformative into-ing is the nature and the behavior of God.

All of the prepositions we have explored so far have been moving us ever closer to this defining moment. We considered the ways God is both above and beneath, in proximities both distant and immediate. We learned about the God that draws near with a closeness that is at once reassuring and yet unreachable. Then God is with us and alongside us, a source of comfort and companionship. God is also before us in both time and space. With the preposition *for*, we contemplate not so much where God is but *why* God does. It's all for us. In order to enliven us and give us spiritual agency, God works through us. As such, we are invited to be virgins and angels, conduits of the divine.

But here—in the word *into*—is a new thing, a pivotal thing. In the hourglass of this book, we've reached the narrow space through which all things must pass. We're at the neck of it now, the passageway of all prepositional truth. Here is where God enters *into* matter, life, creation. This preposition reveals the astonishing practice of a God that offers everything, including God's very selfhood. Such is the doctrine of incarnation we hold so dear.

INCARNATION

I am no scientist and certainly no physicist, but I am enamored of the ways that scientific truths dovetail with spiritual truths and reinforce them. This makes absolute sense and really couldn't be any other way, since both science and spirituality fall into what we could call the full *Godscape*, which comprises all things seen and unseen. In the way that magnetic fields illuminate some of the mysterious power of a God Beneath, the Big Bang theory of the universe illuminates some of the mysterious power of God Into.

This theory postulates that 13.7 billion years ago, a "gravitational singularity"—an entity in which space and time were not distinguishable and for which physical laws did not yet exist—instantaneously and expansively dilated. Scientists have extrapolated that in the span of a hundredth of a billionth of a trillionth of a trillionth of a second, the universe doubled in size ninety fold. From there, it just kept going, and as it expanded, it cooled, thereby transforming into matter. A uni-point, existing outside any fathomable law, transformed itself instantly and eternally into a uni-verse: the vast and multifaceted sum of all matter, energy, and light. The word *universe* is itself derived from the Latin word *uni*, meaning one, and the Latin verb *versus*, meaning to turn. The universe originated with The One turning into all else.

In Christian mythology, the human species was generated by God breathing *into* inanimate matter. Forming the human body from the dust of the ground, God "breathed into his nostrils the breath of life, and the man became a living being" (Genesis 2:7). The story tells us that the living God sparks a living being through a process of into-ing. This is the process by which God's energy enlivens matter, the process by which God's existence animates all existence. In this way, *into* is the preposition that proclaims God as the animating force of all life. Rather than some distant and arbitrary judge, God is Ultimate Creativity: an original and generative force that penetrates, forms, and enlivens all that is, across the continuums of time and space.

Whether it began with a breath or a bang, the result is the same. Creation was and is God's original incarnation. As Richard Rohr explains it, we humans tend to believe that:

> *Everything that exists in material form is the offspring of some Primal Source, which originally existed only as Spirit.* This Infinite Primal Source somehow poured itself *into* finite,

> visible forms, creating everything from rocks to water, plants, organisms, animals, and human beings. . . . This self-disclosure of whomever you call God *into* physical creation was the *first Incarnation* (the general term for any enfleshment of spirit), long before the personal, second Incarnation that Christians believe happened with Jesus. . . . The incarnation, then, is not only "God becoming Jesus." It is a much broader event (emphasis mine on *into*).

Broad events, however, are hard to sink your teeth into. We may hear about children who are starving, but it is only when we are introduced to one or shown a picture of her and learn her name and just how little she has on her plate come evening that we are mobilized to care and to act. Factual reality, what author Tim O'Brien calls "happening truth," frequently falls on deaf ears. "Story truth," on the other hand, penetrates. It is what layers an emotional reality onto what are otherwise cold facts.

We cannot resist a good story: telling one or listening to one or reading one or believing one. Indeed our proclivity for story, and our facility with it, may well be what distinguishes humans from other creatures and from artificial forms of intelligence. Stories are the bedrock of our religions and our mythologies, our memories and our histories, our imaginations and our souls. Without them, it is all too broad—God included. Without story, God is intractably abstract. This is why God "sent" his only Son to be the redeemer of the world. Jesus is the character who reveals the nature of the artist: God himself, the Poet of the Uni-Verse, the Author of all creation and salvation. Jesus is many things, but for me and for my faith, he is the story truth that enables me to fathom a divine happening truth—one that would otherwise be infinitely too vast to access.

What God transforms into when God transforms tends to be an easy answer for Christians: Jesus. Jesus is the Son of God. Jesus is the one who came to save us from our sins. Jesus is the one who died, was buried, and on the third day rose again. Jesus is the anointed one, the messiah, the Prince of Peace. It is he whom we follow. It is he whom we worship. It is his story that we quote and his example that we try to emulate. But how does that make any sense? One guy who survived for a few flecks of decades amid the vast expanse of time? A carpenter in Capernaum two thousand years ago?

I said in the introduction to this book that I wasn't sure I was even a Christian anymore when I started writing it. I didn't have a clear sense of what "being a Christian" meant, nor did I have a full conviction about the figure of Jesus. But, for me, this preposition, *into*, unlocks the truth and significance of Jesus as the Christ. He is the way and the truth and the life, because his story reveals all that we need to know about who and what God is and does. Maybe that's why Jesus loved speaking in parables: He *is* a parable. His life is the short story that illustrates a profound truth. His life was a tangible manifestation of an otherwise abstract God, and it serves to illustrate the bountiful, willing, transmogrifying capacity of the Holy One.

The movement of God Into originates with creation, climaxes with Jesus, and extends pervasively and universally as Christ. In this very singular present moment, God's self-transformative nature and behavior are unceasing. The stories of the Bible, writes Sue Monk Kidd, often paint "a portrait of a patient God who enters into the experience of those who wait." There it is, that subtle but powerful little preposition telling us that God enters into our lives. We experience this radical infusion when we are connected to God, opened to God, remembering God, waiting for God, feeding on God, and loving God. In this way, the first Incarnation (Creation) and the second (Jesus) are all jumbled up with another (Christ), which is ongoing. When I sit in church and recite the words, *Christ has died . . . Christ has risen . . . Christ will come again*, I often mutter under my breath *and again and again and again*. This transmutes Christ's coming from some future Day of Judgment event into an everyday common occurrence.

Conceptualizing a God that "somehow poured itself into . . . could be Christianity's unique contribution among the world religions," Rohr asserts. That is how important God Into is. That is how this innocuous preposition became the linchpin of my Christian faith.

TRANSFORMATION

I have wondered, and you may have too: *Why?* Why would God transform into pitiful and temporary flesh? Why go from being eternal to mortal? From sovereign to fallible? This is *not* a lateral move.

The answer to this question is one we also know already but sometimes have trouble believing. It is love that motivates God's penetration into fleshhood. It is love that motivates God's transformation into new life. In truth, as Rohr says, "God loves things by becoming them." By becoming heat. By becoming proton. By becoming ice crystal and stardust and tides and, much later, by becoming turtles and tulips, wildebeests and willow trees. And later still by becoming *Homo sapiens*: woman and man. And some thirty-five thousand years after that, by becoming Jesus. And then by becoming you. By becoming me. By becoming the whole of it. All creation. The full body of Christ. We are the vast animation of God Into who penetrates and procreates abundantly.

If that sounds oddly sexual, I would argue that it is *purposefully* sexual. Christianity has villainized sexuality—anything "carnal" or physical—from the outset. In the story of the Fall, the direct consequence of sin was shame: Adam and Eve recognized their nakedness and sought to hide it. Expelled from Eden, they were expelled from their own bodies. As a result, the natural, essential, and beautiful intercourse of bodies became contaminated. How, though, can *incarnation* be good, but *carnal* be sinful, with their shared root words? Why did an action and expression of generative love instead become associated with shame?

Making love is exactly what God does. Franciscan author and scientist Ilia Delio articulates this beautifully when she writes: "God does what God is—love." Delio argues against seeing God "as a separate being over the world" and instead asserts that God is the very "stuff of existence for where there is energy of attraction, union, generativity, and life, there is God."

This brings to mind Bernini's life-sized sculpture of the ecstasy of Saint Teresa in the Cornaro Chapel at Santa Maria della Vittoria in Rome. The marble sculpture depicts Saint Teresa fallen back in a state of unmistakable ecstasy, her heart having just been penetrated by the arrow of a male cherub. A Spanish mystic, spiritual leader, and esteemed author of the 1500s, Teresa had experiences of the Divine that were unabashedly erotic. She writes of the penetrating love of God that sets her on fire and causes her to moan in sweet pain. Her brand of "bridal mysticism" dates back to the Gnostics and explores the idea of a masculine spirit penetrating a feminine soul and thereby producing a joy in Christ that is orgasmic in its rapture and surrender. This intercourse with the Divine is what consummates life, birthing us out of mundane ordinariness and into blissful union with God. Such is the ecstasy of experiencing, absorbing, and really fathoming God Into. God into you: your body, your soul, your life, your everything.

If God remained only above or beneath, everything would be vastly different in the landscape of our faith because its foundation would be separation. Worshippers of pagan gods made sacrifices because they believed that the gods needed to be appeased. Gods that need to be appeased are gods that are solely above; they are sovereign gods, but more critically they are *separate* gods. A separate god may well be subject to whims and inclined to smite people. A separate god may hurl thunder or repay gifts with favor. A separate god leaves us bereft and unsafe, pleading and fearful, and—in the end—alone.

But ours is a God Into, and this one truth serves to undergird all the others. God did not just make creation; God enters into it. Why? Love. How? Always by a process of self-disclosing. Always with the result of transformation.

God's ability to transform—and *our* ability to transform—are at the heart of Christian teaching, and so it makes sense that Jesus's first miracle is one of transformation. He is at a wedding feast where the hosts run out of wine. His mother prods him to solve the problem. Jesus is disinclined to do so. But good son that he is, he obliges his mother's request. He prompts the servants to fill the thirty-gallon stone pots typically used for ceremonial washing with water. Rather than use the water for cleansing, Jesus instructs them instead to draw a cup and serve it to the person in charge. The man takes a sip and marvels. It's a delicious *oinos*, even better than the variety served at the start of the party. The celebration carries on, and Jesus's glory is first revealed (John 2:1–11).

The fact that the first sign of Jesus's glory is his ability to transform one thing into another is surely not accidental. It references God the Father's transformation into God the Son, thereby reinforcing the procreative love of the Divine. It also foreshadows critical transformations to come, notably passing through death into new life. And it alludes to the possibility for human transformation as well, as encapsulated by the call for fishermen to become instead fishers of men. (All they needed was that little preposition "of" to transform their whole self-understanding!)

Ultimately, the transformation of water into wine announces that what seems impossible is in fact possible with God (Matthew 17:20). This is why we put our faith and hope and trust in God. Because with God transformation is possible. What's more, with God transformation is *inevitable*. If we falter in believing this to be so, we need only look outside, at God's first incarnation—at the changing light, at the changing seasons, at life cycles and moon cycles. Nature is the most splendid, bountiful reminder and example of God's transformative into-ing. It is ever-changing and ever-becoming, just like its Creator.

SACRAMENTS

It should come as no surprise that nearly all of the sacraments of the church echo the divine process of into-ing. The sacrament of marriage brings two people into union. The sacrament of confirmation ushers a person into the faith community. Holy orders and ordination elevate leaders into positions of authority. And the Eucharist, or Holy Communion, re-members us into the body of Christ.

At our church, we receive communion weekly, and so I am familiar with the words associated with that particular rite (mostly Rite II in *The Book of Common Prayer*). I am so familiar with them, in fact, that at one point I came to a place where I could hardly hear them anymore. The ritual was losing its power to inspire and transform.

But then one Sunday, something about the sequence of the liturgy struck me anew. I realized that the call for God Into begins well before we consume the actual bread and wine. It begins when the celebrant blesses God and asks that he "cleanse the thoughts of our hearts by the inspiration of your Holy Spirit." This prayer echoes the psalmist who long ago offered the supplication: "Create in me a clean heart, O God, and put a new and right spirit within me" (Psalm 51:10–12).

This cleansing of our hearts requires an in-breaking of the Divine. The Holy Spirit in-spires, or "blows into" us, thereby cleansing us emotionally so that we may be prepared to receive the Holy Communion physically. To partake in this cleansing, we are invited to kneel and "open our hearts," confessing the ways we have transgressed against God and our neighbors. To partake in the feast, we are then invited to kneel again, this time opening our palms to receive the gifts of God for us and our neighbors.

Rituals are outward manifestations of inward intentions. They overlay literal action with symbolic meaning. When we receive communion, we are literally ingesting the bread and the wine: bringing them into our bodies, where they will be metabolized and transferred into energy. Likewise, when we receive communion, we are symbolically ingesting the Divine: bringing the incarnate God into our hearts, where it will strengthen our union with Christ. Our bodies take over from there, doing what they know to do. Food, which has been broken down into its simplest forms—amino acids, glucose, fatty acids—gets absorbed into our bloodstream and then absorbed into our cells. It gets into everything. We not only ingest the Bread of Heaven; we digest it. The Bread of Heaven and the salvation it brings seep into every atom of our being: physical and spiritual. Christ gets into us, all the way.

While Holy Communion brings the Divine into us, its partner sacrament, Holy Baptism, brings us into the Divine. The word *baptism* derives from the Latin word *baptizare*, and the Greek word *baptizein*, which both mean to be dipped into.

The degree of dippage varies wildly among church traditions. So too does the age of the one being baptized. Newborns, toddlers, teenagers, twentysomethings, on it goes. One is never too old or too young. Baptisms at my church are reverent and relatively reserved affairs. They typically feature a baby in a white gown and a priest who scoops up water in the palm of his or her hand and splashes it over the baby's forehead. We do have a metal tub for families who prefer a full immersion, though I have witnessed that only once in all my years of worshipping there.

The church just down the street, also Episcopalian, does it entirely differently, however. Their baptisms are river affairs, Southern through and through. In late spring or early summer, the doors of that church are closed on Baptismal Sunday as parishioners gather instead at a nearby farm on a river. In their khakis and dresses, they greet one another, adding their fruit salad or potato salad or pasta salad to a long buffet table. They set up lawn chairs or lay out blankets, corralling their kids for the worship service, which happens over the barking of dogs and the rustle of the wind in the microphones. When it comes time for the "thanksgiving over the water" portion of the liturgy, however, they all get up and file down to the banks of the river, watching as the priest wades in waist deep, her vestments floating up about her, listening as she dips her hands into the muddy currents passing her and prays: "We thank you, Almighty God, for the gift of water. *Over* it the Holy Spirit moved in the beginning. . . . *Through* it you led the children of Israel. . . . *In* it your Son Jesus received the baptism. . . . *By* it we share in the resurrection."

It's a whole lead-up of prepositions that is building to the big one, the wet one, the dramatic and critical one. In this case, *into* is embodied rather than spoken as the baptized is dunked—church clothes, head, and all—into the flowing waters.

My godson was baptized this way, and as his godmother, I was right there in the river with him when it happened. Forming a circle around him with our arms, when the priest said, "I baptize you in the Name of the Father, and of the Son, and of the Holy Spirit" and went under with him, so did we: his parents, his godfather, and I. It was startling, as going under in cold water always is, but even more startling for the circumstances. There was no avoiding what the moment entailed, what the moment meant. There was no fussing over a lace bonnet or thinking about lunch to come. There was only that one invigorating, holy moment: the astonishing into.

When this happens, we are dipped into water and also brought into the body of Christ. Right after the priest raises the soaking, wailing baby to the crowd of onlookers and says, "Let us welcome the newly baptized," the very next thing she says is, "We receive you into the household of God." From that moment on, we are sealed therein forever. Having been received into the household of God, into the body of Christ, we are a permanent member of the family.

This is what baptism offers us: a transformative into-ing that can never be undone. It is a ritualistic embodiment of what already happened in the moment of our birth, when we came into the world. We are all, every last one of us, received into the household of God by the sheer act and miracle of our birth.

Baptism is also a ritualistic embodiment of cleansing away the worldly cares that shame us and reemerging as the beloved virgin souls that we truly are; for whenever there is a baptism to be performed, it's not just about the one getting wet. Each member of the congregation renews his or her baptismal covenant. We renounce whatever taints our faith, whatever taints our hope, whatever taints our love, and we relocate ourselves in the household of God where we belong. It is a cleanse of the purest kind.

This kind of cleansing happens in an official church sacrament, but it also happens in myriad other pursuits as well. The Spirit calls us into rituals of renewal in creative and compelling ways. We may submerge ourselves in cold lakes or scale mountains at sunrise. We may choose to fast or call loved ones to share in a feast. We may sit in solitude, or we may make pilgrimages alongside throngs of fellow believers.

No matter how, we find the way into God, as God has already found the way into us.

A PRAYER TO GOD INTO

Almighty God,
your love is so profound
that you not only create all things,
you also *become* all things.
We praise you and we thank you.

Almighty God,
you invite us to the table,
offering us spiritual food to take and eat
in remembrance of you.
We praise you and we thank you.

Almighty God,
you desire to pour into our hearts,
and you enter into all things,
cleansing and renewing our spirits.
We praise you and we thank you.

Almighty God,
you invite us to sink our bodies into water,
as we sink our souls into the mystery of faith
and are baptized into the family of all Creation.
We praise you and we thank you.

Almighty God,
beckon us into the deep.

Almighty God,
seal us in your household forever.

Amen.

CHAPTER TEN

Within

This is the Spirit of truth, whom the world cannot receive
because it neither sees him nor knows him.
You know him because he abides with you, and he will be in you.

John 14:17

I know the Immovable comes down;
I know the Invisible appears to me . . .
I, a frail, small mortal in the world,
Behold the Creator of the world, all of him, within myself;
And I know I shall not die, for I am within Life,
I have the whole of Life springing up as a fountain within me.
He is in my heart, he is in heaven:
Both there and here he shows himself to me with equal glory.

Symeon the New Theologian

The prepositions we have explored so far have moved us in steady progression toward a comingling of divine and creation, of God and self. When God comes into, another preposition immediately presents itself. Inevitably, God Into becomes God *Within*.

I will be honest: I did not want to write this chapter. It was too daunting to write, yet too critical not to. That God dwells within us is an obvious yet startling revelation. It cannot be proven and yet remains resolute. It is the most simple and the most impossible truth.

After his abrupt conversion on the road when Paul develops new eyes to see, the notion of an indwelling God is a point he preaches, even belabors. It is what drives him to evangelize on behalf of Christ until his own execution. With special attention to prepositions, he declares that there is "one God and Father of all, who is above all and through all and in all" (Ephesians 4:6). To the believers in Corinth, he beseeches, "Do you not know that you are God's temple and that God's Spirit dwells in you?" (1 Corinthians 3:16). To the Ephesians, Paul emphasizes that "Christ may dwell in your hearts through faith" (Ephesians 3:17). To the church in Rome, he explains "that which is known about God is evident within them; for God made it evident to them" (Romans 1:19 LSB).

Though Paul's letters consistently reinforce the notion of God Within, our default way of thinking is that God is separate. That separation is considered a natural consequence of our sin. Some of us learn that this separation is itself sin. We begin to believe that we were born this way, sinful, and if we were born sinful, then we do not, *cannot* possibly, possess God Within.

The notion of sin as somehow original was learned not from God, nor from Jesus, nor from the prophets, nor from the apostles, but from Augustine of Hippo (354–430). For Augustine, sin was original in the sense that it was committed by Adam (*originating* original sin) and thereafter inherited by us (*originated* original sin). In regular terms: Adam was the firstborn bad, and we have all been born bad too.

But in a little-known text from the Gnostic canon, Jesus refutes this outright. He acknowledges that sin exists, but he disputes the fact that sin is itself original. Our "proper origin," Jesus insists instead, in this telling, is not one of sin at all but one of divinity.

PROPER ORIGIN

This teaching of Jesus—that at our core we are sacred rather than sinful—has the power to radically transform how we understand the Christian faith. His words on this subject are made explicit in the Gospel of Mary Magdalene, a text first discovered in a bazaar in Cairo, Egypt, in 1896 and subsequently published in English in 1975. I came to it by way of Magdalene scholar Cynthia Bourgeault's work with the text in both *The Luminous Gospels,* published in 2008, and *The Meaning of Mary Magdalene,* published two years later.

This text and others like it, such as the Gospel of Thomas, were deemed heretical by the authorities of the day because they upheld an esoteric understanding of Christianity that was threatening. At the pivotal moment the Bible was being codified and the religious movement of Christianity was being spread, the focal point of the council of authority was on *preaching* God rather than *practicing* God. One might argue that Religion took precedence over Spirituality. It is also no surprise that the councils of Rome chose not to canonize a text by a woman, to whom they also denied the title of "apostle" despite believing that it was she who first beheld the risen Christ.

So much of this ancient text is revelatory and worth our consideration now. Written in the form of a dialogue between the resurrected Christ and his disciples—by someone we know was in the upper room—the Gospel of Mary Magdalene yields significant insights into the risen Christ's theology. The opening six pages of Mary's Gospel account are lost, and so the narrative picks up in the middle of the conversation between the resurrected Jesus and his disciples—among whom, Acts tells us, were "Peter, and John, and James, and Andrew, Philip and Thomas, Bartholomew and Matthew, James son of Alphaeus, and Simon the Zealot, and Judas son of James. All these were constantly devoting themselves to prayer, together with *certain women*, including Mary the mother of Jesus, as well as his brothers" (Acts 1:12–14, emphasis mine).

There they all are, Mary Magdalene included, trying to understand what to make of Jesus's resurrection and what it reveals about the nature of God. As the Gospel of Mary reveals, someone present asks about "matter" and whether it will survive or not. This question might seem odd, but it makes sense given that they are talking with someone who was once dead and now seems to have returned to life. Jesus, who was known for teaching in parable and metaphor, gives a different kind of answer in this text: abstract and metaphysical. Given that Jesus has just been through the experience of death, descent, and resurrection, it makes sense that his manner of speaking would be altered, his wisdom crystallized. He says: "All of nature with its forms and creatures exist together and are interwoven with each other. They will be resolved back, however, to their own proper origin, for the compositions of matter return to the original roots of their nature" (Gospel of Mary Dialogue One).

Again, this is not how Jesus normally talks. His comments are sophisticated, even themselves esoteric. But what Jesus tells us in this unprecedented moment is cardinal. Jesus knows what happens next. He has been there. What he declares happens is that "all will be resolved back." That word *resolve* derives from the Latin verb *solvere*, which means to loosen, to liberate. The prefix *re-* serves as an intensifier, and it also means back. We, all of us, will be fully unbound as we reunite with our origins, our Creator, our God Before.

What a tremendous promise this is! So tremendous, in fact, that it begs some questions. Peter, for one, is confused. If everything is interwoven, and everything will be resolved back to God, the original root of all nature, what about sin? What about suffering? What about all that? "Tell us one more thing," Peter says. "What is the sin of the world?" he asks.

Jesus responds to Peter's question without equivocating: "Sin as such does not exist," he says and then elaborates: "You only bring it into manifestation when you act in ways that are adulterous in nature" (Gospel of Mary Dialogue One). In other words, you sin only when you fail to stay aligned with your divine nature, the God within you. Sin is simply an aberration of your sacred soul.

Jesus does not wait for someone to ask about judgment or punishment or hell. He has an important point to add on that front as well. Yes, we sin when we fail to stay aligned with God, but that is not the end of the story. That is simply an impetus for God, or Christ, or the Holy Spirit to pursue us. Jesus says, "It is for this very reason that the Good has come among you pursuing its own essence within nature in order to reunite everything to its origin" (Gospel of Mary Dialogue One).

Reading this line of this text well into my exploration of prepositions felt like someone turning the light on.

Of course. Yes.

What all these prepositions are doing is illuminating the robust and complex nature of God's pursuit of us. That's why they are so spot-on. That's why there are so many of them. They evoke all the ways God is trying to reach us, as God "the Good" pursues its own essence within nature. The God out there is desperately seeking the God in here. It knows where it's hiding, and it wants to bring it into the light.

The message is a triumphant one, and yet, if we take it to heart, it demands a great deal of us. If the Divine dwells within us and yet we feel wracked by a sense of separation and sinfulness, we must work to integrate our actions with our origins. We must work to integrate our false self (our ego) with our true self (our soul). We must work to integrate our busy outer life with our sacred inner one. There is, as Bourgeault notes, "important integrative work to be done here." It's not so much that we need to be saved from our sins as that we need to realign with our sacred center.

When we aren't in alignment, the consequence, as Jesus explains to the people in the upper room, is "that confusion and disturbance resonates throughout one's whole being." The disciples must have known exactly what Jesus was talking about, as do we. Who among us has not experienced disturbance resonating throughout our entire being? Who among us has not felt agitated, confused, and anxious when we are out of alignment with our truest self and therefore out of alignment with God? "It is for this reason," Jesus continues, "that I told you to find contentment at the level of the heart, and if you are discouraged, take heart in the presence of the Image of your true nature" (Gospel of Mary Dialogue One).

In other words, shore up the Indwelling Divine. It is available right here, already inside you. This is what it means to be made in the image of God.

This teaching is not heretical at all. It echoes the well-known verse from Genesis 1:27 that declares that "God created humans in his image" and then immediately restates it, emphasizing the divinity of both male and female, in case anyone tries to limit or distort this vital truth. "In the image of God he created them; male and female he created them." Our proper origin, our true nature, is divine. That DNA is within us—all of us.

LIGHT WITHIN

Jesus is not quite done. In case the disciples still miss the point, he reiterates his message by blessing them and saying, "Peace be with you. May my peace reside within you. Guard carefully that no one misleads you saying, 'Look, he is here,' or 'He's over there,' for the Son of Humanity already exists within you" (Gospel of Mary Dialogue One).

Saint Luke records Jesus making this very same claim: "Nor will they say, 'See here!' or 'See there!' For indeed, the kingdom of God is within you" (Luke 17:21 NKJV). John testifies similarly. He records Jesus making an all-important promise to his disciples prior to his crucifixion: "I will not leave you orphaned; I am coming to you," Jesus vows. "In a little while the world will no longer see me, but you will see me; because I live, you also will live. On that day you will know that I am in my Father, and you in me, and I in you" (John 14:18–20). The revelation to be had, which Jesus makes perfectly clear, is that the Divine exists within and always has. It is as Paul affirms to the church in Philippi, "I am certain that God, who began the good work within you, will continue his work until it is finally finished on the day when Christ Jesus returns" (Philippians 1:6 NLT).

Saint Paul's teaching underscores the same message proclaimed by Mary Magdalene. We can fathom God because God is within us as our *proper origin* and the *root* of our nature. This is what it means to be made in the likeness of God. Mature spiritual thinkers throughout the ages have since echoed this wisdom. Eastern Christian mystic Symeon of the eleventh century declares, "I, a frail, small mortal in the world behold the Creator of the world, all of him, *within* myself. . . . I have the whole of Life springing up as a fountain within me." Two centuries later, Meister Eckhart asserts that "there is something in the soul that is so akin to God that it is one with Him." Twentieth-century Quaker mystic Thomas Kelly proclaims that "deep within us all there is an amazing inner sanctuary of the soul, a holy place, a Divine Center, a speaking Voice, to which we may continually return . . . It has a dynamic center, a creative Life that presses to birth within us. It is a Light Within that illumines the face of God." Poet Laureate Joy Harjo writes that "There is a spirit in every human. . . . That spirit is God's signature within us." And Rohr claims that "The Divine Indwelling is central to authentic Christian spirituality." For him, God Within is the final aspect of the Holy Trinity. God Within is the "code word for the Holy Spirit . . . that inner aliveness that heals people and awakens them from their wounds." The excerpts could be endless, their truth the same. God is the light within.

If it's all right there, spelled out so clearly in the Gospels and in the writings of spiritual trailblazers, why don't we know it? Why haven't we prioritized this teaching? In part, because it is threatening. As Princeton professor of theology B. B. Warfield fairly notes, "He who begins by seeking God within himself, may end by confusing himself with God." It's true that when we emphasize *only* the God Within—or only within *me* but not within *you*—we can end up with a privatized, even dangerous spirituality. Claiming *only* the God Within, to the exclusion of all other locations for God, can land us in a place of perilous hubris.

Yet for churches seeking to establish and expand the faith, and in some cases their power, the tendency was to sidestep the God Within. Risking the acknowledgment of an indwelling divine—which gives spiritual authority to all people rather than concentrating it in the hands of the ordained few—was unpalatable. People, like the sheep of the Bible, needed to be shepherded. They needed someone to guide them, effectively keeping them safe and also contained.

Politics was involved too. Declarations of a divine within are threatening because they have the potential to disrupt economies based on subjugation. One cannot readily own another human being and believe he or she possesses God within. One cannot have a wife one considers property while believing God is alive and well within her. And what would all those bishops and priests who had a direct line to God do if all the layfolk understood God to be within their very souls and bodies? This is, in part, why the church has been subject to so much corruption over the centuries. Perhaps even against its own will, it sought to keep God *out of* our very souls. Was it better to emphasize original sin than core divinity because that helped keep people on the hook?

Martin Luther contested this notion and advocated instead for universal priesthood, citing 1 Peter 2:9, which refers to the people of God as "royal priests, a holy nation, God's very own possession." In this view, which underpins Protestantism, professional clergy are no more or less spiritual than layfolk because all have access to the Divine, as all are God's own possession. The Quakers take this a step further by having no ordained clergy. They abide in the knowledge that "there is that of God in everyone" and name God as the Light Within or the Inward Teacher. The guiding principle of these Friends, as they are called, is a belief in the indwelling divine. It is for this reason that their worship services often consist of periods of deep silence and patient waiting.

This form of worship, which combines corporate contemplative prayer with witness, strikes me as a vivid example of the kind of mystical state encouraged by Howard Thurman, who advocates for a "central stillness of spirit," and also by nurse and activist Florence

Nightingale, who declares that we must put ourselves "in a state for Him to come and dwell in [us]." "This," she writes, "is the whole aim of the Mystical Life." In order to experience the divine, we must create space for it within.

VESSEL

For a supreme example of this kind of gestative state, we can turn once again to Mary, the Mother of God, who inarguably possesses God Within. That job might appear uniquely hers, as she literally carried Jesus in her womb. But, in the same way we set her apart as an icon of virginity, we also tend to set Mary apart as an icon of motherhood and therefore miss so much of what she has to teach us. We miss that Mary is a model for how we *ourselves* might incarnate the living God.

As it is told in Luke 2, the Nativity story unfolds sequentially, strung together with a lot of *ands*. *And* everyone went to register. *And* they placed him in a manger. *And* the shepherds were watching their flocks by night. The word *but* appears only twice. The first time is likely the better known. It's when the angel interrupts the shepherds' acute stress response: "But the angel said to them, 'Do not be afraid.'" The second time, it concerns Mary, but she's not interrupting things so much as responding to them in her own special way. "But Mary treasured up all these things and pondered them in her heart" (Luke 2:19 NIV). Everyone else—the shepherds, the wise men, those who heard the story secondhand—were "amazed" by what happened. Rather than sit with that amazement, they promptly went out and started telling about it.

But not Mary. Mary knew the story too well to be stupefied, having been its humble protagonist all along. She had been the virgin. She had accepted the call to carry the faith, literally, in her body. And she had *delivered* it, literally, to the people. What for her now? She sits and ponders, not with her mind but with her heart. She invites the Christ child, who no longer inhabited the manger of her womb, instead into the manger of her heart. She does this by quieting herself, by storing up all the spiritual treasures that have come to her, contemplating them, and "keeping them," as certain translations relay.

In this way, Mary the Mother of God models for us how *we* might mother God. She practices precisely what her son will come to preach. She says yes to aligning her soul with its proper origin, and it is in turn magnified. Thich Nhat Hanh makes a shockingly similar claim in his revelatory work *Living Buddha, Living Christ*: "The Buddha described the seed of mindfulness that is in each of us as the 'womb of the Buddha' (*tathagatagarbha*)," Hanh writes. "We are all mothers of the Buddha because we are all pregnant with the potential for awakening."

When I think about Mary, I am reminded of *matryoshka* dolls, or what I grew up calling nesting dolls. These are the wooden dolls that decrease in size, one housed inside the other in shrinking progression. The term *matryoshka* derives from the Russian word for mother. A mother is the one who carries another inside her and another inside that and yet still another. At just twenty weeks of gestation, a female fetus typically carries 6 to 7 million eggs inside her. In her nascent form, she houses the life source for more life. Some material part of me lived inside my mother inside her mother inside her mother—and onward too in the other direction. Some part of me lives in my daughter and in her unborn daughter.

This is true on a biological level and also true on a spiritual level. It is how we live at all. God the Mother begets God the Daughter in unbreaking sequence.

It's just that most of us identify as only the first few sets of dolls. It begins with the outermost persona: what we see when we look in the mirror and what people see when they look at us. Then, just one layer of self in, perhaps it's the name we have, what it speaks of our origins and our destiny. Then maybe the roles we carry—daughter, brother, friend, wife—and the jobs we have—teacher, doctor, electrician, analyst. Next down may be our faith face: Buddhist, agnostic, Presbyterian, healer, seeker. We may go so far as to unearth archetypes, a set of dolls that guide us along the soul journey. We may work with a therapist and open doll upon doll, edging our way toward the inner child, who deems herself unworthy or unlovable.

Go deeper still, and the way gets murky. Numinous. The forms no longer hold. There is no more doll. There is only the dark center, the formlessness around which all the other selves were defined and formed, what Thurman calls "the fluid area of consent . . . your crucial link with the Eternal." This center, this sacred space within, is worth investigating.

Pondering the indwelling Divine—to discover it, to realize it, to accept it, to tap into it, to nourish it, to effect it—is the spiritual calling of a lifetime. We are, each and all of us, a vessel of God—as Mary was, as Jesus was. We are each a series of selves opening unto what is and can only be a Sacred Center. What we find there is summarized potently by poet Ntozake Shange, when she writes, "I found god in myself / and I loved her / I loved her fiercely."

This is the invitation awaiting each of us. This is the joy to be had, the love to be extended. When we realize that we carry the kingdom of God within us, our awareness is altered forever. We see with new eyes, as Jesus predicted. We hear with new ears. We praise with new praise. We respond with new response. "We delight to do God's will, because God's law is within our hearts" (Psalm 40:8).

This is the good news of Christ. We are not merely followers; we are vessels. We are nesting dolls of the Divine. All we desire we have, deep within.

A PRAYER TO GOD WITHIN

Holy and Almighty One,
how is it that you might dwell in me?
I am not worthy, I think,
but you insist otherwise.

Holy and Sacred Center:
Help me to sink in and find you.
Help me to align my soul to you.
Help me to be resolved back to you.
Help me to let the Light Within shine.
Help me to keep you in the manger of my heart.
Help me to be a vessel of you,
the Eternal Indwelling.

Amen.

CHAPTER ELEVEN

Throughout

I am a God who is everywhere and not in one place only.
No one can hide where I cannot see them.
Do you not know that I am everywhere in heaven and on earth?

Jeremiah 23:23–24 (GNT)

O Almighty God!
I see in You the powers of Nature,
The various Creatures of the world . . .
I see You, infinite in form,
With, as it were, faces, eyes, and limbs everywhere;
No beginning, no middle, no end;
O Lord of the Universe, whose Form is universal!

Bhagavad Gita 11:15–16

When I was first hired to teach high school English, I was in my mid-twenties. I had no idea what I was doing and also big ideas about what I was doing. The head of the school called me into his office the week before classes were to begin. He invited me to take a seat across the desk from where he sat, leaning back in the comfort of his grommeted leather chair, his fingertips forming a pyramid in front of his chest. He smiled and made small talk, asking about my summer and my family. He then paused, and from the wall of shelves behind him drew out a hardback book. He handed it over to me and said it was mine. The book was Parker Palmer's *The Courage to Teach*, a treasury of wisdom for anyone inclined to teach, whether formally or informally.

I took the book home and devoured it amid diligent lesson planning. I underlined a lot and put plenty of stars in the margin, but one single line struck me. It would become my north star, first as an educator and then on into my parenting and now as a kind of mission statement for my entire vocational life. It's the sentence in the book in which Palmer defines teaching as guiding students toward "more truthful ways of seeing and being in the world."

More truthful ways of seeing the world, more truthful ways of being in the world: That was it. That was what I wanted to illuminate for the teens who came shuffling through my classroom door. That was the worthy pursuit, the genuine objective of all learning.

Palmer was speaking to a truth I understood only dimly at the time, and one I still fathom only partially, but his words resonated nonetheless. They sparked across my soul like a match along its strip: that modest little runway of powdered glass and red phosphorus that launches into fire. For me, it was never just going to be about teaching students how to diagram sentences or craft a thesis statement or even close-read Martin Luther King's *Letter from Birmingham Jail*. That would have been easier—to leave it along the surface of a well-constructed syllabus—but that wasn't the ambition. I wanted to help my students become better readers and writers, yes, but also better thinkers and ultimately better people. By better people, I meant people capable of more truthful ways of seeing the world and of being in it.

SOPHIA

I didn't realize then, teaching in my early twenties, that I was a mere student myself. And I still am and will always be. Developing truthful ways of seeing and being is a lifelong endeavor. Blissfully, there is no end to it. To some, we may be the guide. To others, we may yet be the pupil. One instant, we may have a flash of enlightenment. Another, all may be dim. But something impels us onward. Something begs us to seek. Something sparks that runway of the soul.

I recall vividly when I was a high school student myself and was assigned to read Wordsworth's *Lines Composed a Few Miles above Tintern Abbey.* There it was, on the willowy pages of my anthology: an expression of the experience of the Divine:

> I have felt a presence that disturbs me with the joy
> Of elevated thoughts; a sense sublime
> Of something far more deeply interfused,
> Whose dwelling is the light of setting suns,
> And the round ocean and the living air,
> And the blue sky.

Yes. Yes. Yes! I remember thinking. On I read, as Wordsworth further attempts to get at the ineffable:

> And in the mind of man,
> A motion and a spirit, that impels
> All thinking things, all objects of all thought,
> And rolls through all things.

Goosebumps—those physiological manifestations of recognition, those tiny swells of epiphany—texturized my skin. As a teenager, I had felt a presence that disturbed me with the joy of elevated thoughts, what I would later learn are termed *transcendent* thoughts. I had sensed something sublime that was deeply interfused. Not just *in*fused but *inter*fused: woven throughout and between, so as to secure connection. The dwelling place of this sublime presence was indeed in the setting sun. The air itself did seem to be living.

The spirit that impels, that rolls through all things, impels even now. Her way of being is not rushed nor brash nor offensive. Her way of being is wise. For just as God is love, so too is God wisdom.

In the century before Jesus's birth, King Solomon wrote a series of religious reflections that were initially excluded from the canon of the Holy Bible but were later published in the Apocrypha. His writings articulate the multidimensional nature of this wise Divine. Indeed, when I came upon the seventh chapter of his book, the Book of Wisdom, I felt like I had arrived home. I was elated, comforted, validated, and also angry. How had this not been shown to me before? How had this not been included in the lectionary at church? Why had this been hidden?

The way Solomon describes the Holy One, or what Jewish scholars know to be *Sophia* or Lady Wisdom, resonates with everything that I have experienced of the Divine in my most authentic and direct encounters. He writes:

> I learned both what is secret and what is manifest,
> For wisdom, the fashioner of all things, taught me.
> For in her there is a spirit that is
> intelligent, holy, unique, manifold,
> subtle, mobile, clear, unpolluted,
> distinct, invulnerable . . .
> because of her pureness she pervades and penetrates all things (Wisdom of Solomon 7:22).

Solomon's description of the Divine as unique, manifold, subtle, and mobile helped pave the way for this exploration of the Divine through prepositions. And his description of the way she "pervades and penetrates all things" underscores the veracity and potency of the idea in this chapter: that God exists *throughout*.

God Throughout is a common epiphany for people of deep searching and deep faith, no matter their faith tradition. As the cornerstone of perennial wisdom, it is an idea that unifies the world's major religions. The omnipresence of God is our common ground. The idea that God infuses and interfuses all matter is precisely what infuses and interfuses nearly all spiritual belief.

Texts from across faith traditions illuminate this core truth. There is the ancient Sanskrit text, *Svetasvara Upanishad*, which comprises 113 mantras, or sacred verses, one of which offers this sublime declaration of the prevalence of the pervasive Divine:

> God is one, hidden in all beings, all-pervading,
> the Self within all selves, watching over all doing,
> dwelling in all being,
> the witness, the perceiver,
> the single one, free from all qualities.

There is this excerpt from the *Enneads* by the ancient philosopher and father of Neoplatonism, Plotinus, who describes the "Soul" our individual souls encounter when we sit in contemplation:

> Let it observe how the Soul flows in from all sides into the resting world, pours itself into it, penetrates it and illumines it. . . . The Soul gives itself to every point in this vast body, and vouchsafes its being to every part, great and small, though these parts are divided in space and manner of disposition . . . the Soul is not divided, nor does it split up in order to give life to each individual. All things live by the Soul in its entirety; it is all present everywhere.

We have this verse from the second surah (or chapter) of the Qur'an, which testifies that:

> To Allah belong the East and the West;
> And wherever you turn,
> there is the Face of Allah.
> For Allah is omnipresent, all-knowing.

And this verse from the Bhagavad Gita (9:4–6), which proclaims:

> The whole world is pervaded by Me,
> Yet my form is not seen.

> All living things have their being in Me,
> Yet I am not limited by them. . . .
> As the mighty wind, though moving everywhere,
> Has no resting place but space,
> So have all these beings no home but Me.

Add to it Cynthia Bourgeault's synopsis of the parting wisdom of Christian theologian Father Keating, who affirms that:

> God co-inheres and interpenetrates everything, the ocean-in-drop and drop-in-ocean. . . . There is not a single place in all creation where God is not, because God is creation itself, endlessly outpouring, endlessly receiving itself back. From top to bottom, we live and move and have our being in a participative reality, every fractal joined to every other fractal in a symphony of divine becoming pouring forth from that infinite wellspring.

How glorious! God is a symphony of divine becoming, co-inhering and interpenetrating all that is, infinitely. Or, we might say, more simply: God *throughouts*. That is what God is, and that is what God does. The commonalities across faith traditions on this point are affirming and invigorating. When we conceive of a Divine Throughout, we place our faith in a lineage of spiritual thought that transcends age and nation.

I find solace in this knowledge. I find rest in it, and delight, even while I find it unsurprising. The pervasiveness of this line of thinking matches the pervasiveness of the thought itself. This truth is so simple that most children think it naturally.

I certainly did. My childhood, spent roaming open fields and studying pieces of lichen I peeled from the barks of trees, chewing the yet-sour cherries I plucked from laden branches and catching a glimpse of a dashing star, affirmed my experience of a God-infused world. Nature, in all its minute detail and vast grandeur, was the dwelling place of the Divine.

So too were books, where the magic of words, of poetry, of story felt soaked by an ineffable spirit. The embossed letterings of gold, the current of vowel sounds in a verse, the fantastic oddity of a word I had never before heard, the photographs of faraway worlds: All of it was soaked through with God, as was life itself. No thing, whether matter or spirit, was exempt. Wisdom, the fashioner of all things, was teaching me.

I was learning naturally both what was secret and what was manifest. I was a sponge and a scout for the omnipresent God. The All-Pervasive.

Christ or Allah or Reality or Source or Sophia: Whatever name we choose to use, it animates each and every one of us from the inside out—no matter the era in which we live, or the place or body into which we are born. No matter our political or sexual orientation, our job or level of education, our life circumstances. She is our shared origin; therefore, she cannot but be in our collective genetic code.

What's more, humans don't possess exclusive rights to this inner divinity. There was a time when humans believed they laid sole claim to a certain set of spiritual virtues. Humans alone could cooperate. Humans alone could reason. Humans alone could love. But scientific studies of everything from chimpanzees to moss have dispelled this myth. *Homo sapiens* are high functioning, no doubt. We can write long treatises, like this one, exploring the nature of God. But we don't have a monopoly on God. We are not somehow granted elite access to the kingdom while the plants that generate the very air we breathe are shut out.

All is connected, and all is included. If God is within us humans, then God is within all other creations as well, from a hippopotamus to a poppy to a pebble. And if God is *within* all creation, then God must also be *throughout* all creation. This is what we mean when we claim God's omnipresence. "The true doctrine of omnipresence is, that God reappears with all his parts in every moss and cobweb," writes Ralph Waldo Emerson. Throughout means throughout.

GROUNDSWELL

I stopped teaching middle and high school students well over a decade ago, but I haven't loosened my grip on this imperative of Parker Palmer's: of seeing and being in truthful ways. Maybe that's because so many forces conspire against any kind of intentional living. There are the extravagantly efficient and wickedly insidious devices that we have strapped to our wrists and glued to our faces. And on these devices are platforms that facilitate endless croaking without the possibility of conversing or even listening. There are the platforms that prey on our desire to belong and be praised, reducing legions of people into mere poses of themselves—and filtered ones at that. There are also the platforms that prey on our desire to be right, reducing authentic dialogue into soapbox sound bites.

Nearly 150 years ago, Emily Dickinson nailed contemporary culture with her line: "How public—like a Frog—To tell one's name—the livelong June—To an admiring Bog!" How public like a frog, indeed. And how bog-like, our image- and opinion-obsessed society. It is sucking us under. The consequences of our disconnected, disenchanted culture have been amply documented. Anxiety and depression at all-time highs. Staggering numbers of young people attempting to take their own lives. Mass shootings—in *elementary schools*. The culture wars subsume us. The political divide embattles us. The tides of mass desperation, mass desecration, mass rage, mass exhaustion, mass burnout, mass everything are sucking us into a quagmire of our own making.

The fact that we are not enchanted by our lives goes without saying.

And yet.

And yet hope is a groundswell we couldn't stop if we tried. Humankind is not only resilient but ebullient. That's one of the best things we have going. We are perennially seeking better: for ourselves, for our communities, for our future. Mindfulness is a common term, goal, and practice. The happiness project has matured into a gratitude movement. Whereas tolerance was the prized virtue when I was growing up, DEI replaced it as the social ambition of the age.

Diversity, equity, and inclusion are more than buzzwords; they are the applied science of love. Under siege as they may be, these qualities are the very nature of God. They have to be if God is throughout.

The goal of all our truest efforts is not to be "woke" but to be wise. To be able to look out from different eyes, wiser eyes, eyes capable of seeing in truthful ways and being in truthful ways.

But what does that mean?

How are you? is a common question. *Good. Busy.* seems to be our go-to answer. It feels honest enough. We go about our hectic days, making ourselves busy with daily commutes and errands, kids' drop-offs and pick-ups, grocery and toilet paper and present purchases, meeting prep and meetings themselves, follow-ups and punch lists, phone calls and texts and emails and social updates, on and on and on. And when all that is done, our engines are still turning, so we piddle around the house, busying ourselves with nothing, or we lie in bed, busying ourselves with all that was left undone. All this busyness, American culture has been telling us, is what enables us to say that we are "good." It's the backbone of the country, the stuff of its dream. A busy life is the only way to go.

I have relished being busy, considering efficiency one of my superpowers. And the productivity it yields I have worn as a badge of honor. I have been one of those people who adds things to my to-do list that I have already done, just so that I can cross them off and be pleased with myself. I have listened to the voices that say the opposite of busy is lazy. Or unproductive. Or useless. People who aren't busy might look in the mirror and find their lives hollow, empty, meaningless. But I know from personal experience that people who are only that—busy—also look in the mirror and find that their lives are hollow, empty, meaningless. Behind all that activity might be a frightening void of purpose, so that if we stop, we might discover that we aren't so good after all. We are sad or lost. We are closed off from ourselves. We are closed off from God. This sense of disconnection is the plight of humanity and the force against which hope pushes.

Thousands of years ago, in the region of Decapolis near the Sea of Galilee, there lived a man who suffered from deafness and from what the Greeks called *mogilalos*, or trouble speaking. He was well cared for by the community, but nevertheless he suffered. He could not hear the wind sweeping across the surface of the bay, nor the soft voice of his wife. Enclosed in a chamber of soundlessness and unable to express fully his thoughts and feelings, the man's one fervent prayer was for healing. Those who loved him prayed for the same, and so when a young rabbi reputed to be capable of performing miracles arrived in their city, the people brought the man to the rabbi and beseeched him to lay his hands on their friend for healing.

The man who was deaf, who suffered from *mogilalos*, was a real person. His life is documented. He is also a character in the story told in Mark 7:31–37. He is a character to whom we as readers can relate. We share in his inability to hear and to speak truthfully.

Ever compassionate, the young rabbi took the man aside, away from the crowds. He wanted to give the ailing man his undivided attention, and he wanted no audience for the miracle he was to perform. Placing his fingers into the man's ears and placing his own spittle on the man's tongue, the rabbi Jesus breathes one beautiful word over the man, and in that instant, the man finds that he can hear and that he can speak plainly. The word that Jesus prays over the man is *Ephphatha*, which means be opened.

EPHPHATHA

Ephphatha: Years ago, I started a short-lived blog by that title and still return to it as an occasional mantra when I am meditating. It is, like YHWH, more breath than word, more whisper than enunciation. Appearing to have a jumble of letters and sounds, it's pronounced with only three syllables: eh / fa/ tha. What appears complex is in actuality simple: a lesson we might do well to receive on repeat.

If we want to be healed of our common illnesses of malcontent, anxiety, fear, and mistrust, and if we want to hear, or see, or taste, or touch, or feel the things around us, the people around us, the God we profess to believe in, the life we have, then we have to be opened. Not just open but *opened*. The difference between the two is subtle but significant. Open is temporary; opened is ongoing. Open is physical; opened is spiritual, mental, emotional. Open is two-dimensional; opened is multidimensional, very much like the Divine.

The healing that Jesus offers and the invitation he extends are to be opened. That is how we begin to put ourselves in touch with the pervasiveness of the Divine. That is how we position ourselves to see as God sees, with eyes that recognize the image of God everywhere. It happens organically, born out of our genuine desire for discovery and our deepening capacity for awareness.

Sometimes, the experience is one of awe. Awe happens to us in moments of stunning beauty, of gushing love, of arresting shock, of searing pain coupled with surrender. Awe comes unbidden and stuns us. It can also happen to us when we encounter the ordinary, the unthrilling, the familiar. It all has to do with the eyes that we look out from. As Rabbi Abraham Heschel conveys, "Awe is a sense for the transcendence," no matter the subject matter.

What often follows awe is tenderness. Tenderness is our truest reaction to the realization that God exists throughout all creation. There is no thing we see, we touch, we hear, we taste, we smell that is not infused by God. God floods all, and when we recognize this truth, we in turn are flooded. Our hearts expand and soften. What this amounts to is love.

Not at first, though. At first, it is a mist. And then a drizzle. A light rain. And then steadying, maybe a downpour. God floods all creation—not as a means of wiping everything away but as a means of seeping into and saturating and slaking all things. Everything is drenched in the Divine.

Developing more truthful ways of seeing and being in the world is to see this God-soaked land and to see this God-soaked people, and to be wetted through with awe and with tenderness and with love. "The universe is full of magical things patiently waiting for our wits to grow sharper," writes English dramatist and poet Eden Phillpotts. Are we up to the task of sharpening our wits? Are we committed to more truthful ways of seeing and being in the world?

I cherish snapshots and children's artwork; I just don't like them on the refrigerator. Instead, I paste them on the inside of the pantry doors. Reaching for the bag of granola, I can smile at the portrait my daughter made of me, the one with the enlarged head and the stick body, the huge grin and the round eyes. Grabbing a can of beans, I can smile at the photo of my daughters and their cousin all dressed as Disney princesses for Halloween.

On the refrigerator, though, I prefer an uncluttered look. Two magnets and two magnets only have earned a place in common view. They sit, side-by-side squares, bearing their important announcements for our family:

FIND JOY IN EACH DAY. *Saint Philip Neri*	The aim of life is to live, and to live means to be aware: joyously, drunkenly, serenely, divinely aware. *Henry Miller*

When God is throughout, there is joy to be found in each day. We find it by becoming aware—"joyously, drunkenly, serenely, divinely aware"—that all things are drenched in the Divine. The ordinary becomes a liturgy, as the title of one of Tish Harrison Warren's books suggests. The stranger becomes a child of God. The trees and streams become companions. So too all creatures. We call the sun Brother and the moon Sister, as Saint Francis did. Suffering becomes an opportunity for growth. Death becomes a threshold for new life. Synchronicities and signs become increasingly evident and increasingly prevalent. The universe communicates with us. God communicates with us, through and in and throughout all things. She begs us to see her. She coaxes us to notice. Having allotted our time on this earth and our place, she desires us, impels us, emboldens us to feel after her and find her (Acts 17:26). Accessing

God Throughout is not a search of the logical. It is a probing of sensation and intuition. It is a heartfirst endeavor.

When we feel into God and find her, our revelation is that everything is connected and everything is beautiful and everything belongs because everything is infused with the sacred Divine. This is the process of developing more truthful ways of seeing and being in the world. This is the process of coming to know a God who is not at all, in any way, too small.

The opportunity awaiting us—or, more accurately, the divine invitation extended to us—can be summed up in the lovely, succinct line of Taoist master Li Ching-Yuen, a Chinese herbalist who is purported to have lived well beyond the normal range of human life expectancy. The wisdom he shares is simply this: "Miss no opportunity to savor the ineffable."

God hides Godself, and simultaneously God reveals Godself in all things. That distinct combination of revealing and hiding, of manifestation and mystery, quickens the heart. Going about one's day as if on a scavenger hunt for the stealthy but accessible God is a delightful way to walk in faith. When we greet the stranger, we are also greeting God. When we pick wildflowers or find feathers or collect stones, we are also collecting God. When we draw in a deep and calming breath, it is God entering our bloodstream.

As French writer Marcel Proust professes, "The real voyage of discovery consists not in seeking new landscapes but in having new eyes." Those new eyes belong to God. Looking for God, we learn to look as God looks. The view is at once panoramic and intimate. The vision is at once sharp and soft. The gaze is at once knowing and mysterious.

A PRAYER TO GOD THROUGHOUT

Wild Divine,

you are holy, unique, and manifold.

You are subtle, mobile, and clear.

There is no place where you are not dwelling.
There is no thing in which you are not hidden.
There is no creature in which you are not manifest.

Help us develop truthful ways of seeing this—your—world.
Help us develop truthful ways of being in this—your—world.

Help us be aware.
Help us find joy.

Lead us in the path of awe.

In your name we pray,

Amen.

CHAPTER TWELVE

Among

For the Lord your God is living among you.
He is a mighty savior.
He will take delight in you with gladness.
With his love, he will calm all your fears.
He will rejoice over you with joyful songs.

Zephaniah 3:17 NLT

That which makes of God a human being
makes gods of men and women.
And dwelt among us, that is,
he took possession of our nature
so that he might make us participators in his own nature.

John Scotus Eriugena

One of the things a spirituality of prepositions illuminates for us is the nondualism at the heart of God. God is both this and that. God is both here and there. The preposition *throughout* emphasizes and elucidates this omnipresence. The natural next preposition—if God is indeed throughout—is that God has to also be *among.*

With this new preposition, the abstract pervasiveness of the Divine assumes a new specificity and invites a new orientation.

Whereas *within* focuses on the self and *throughout* focuses on all creation, *among* focuses on the other. God exists as a member of our community, living among us.

Christians learn of God Among through the physical personhood of Jesus: "God's love was revealed among us in this way: God sent his only Son into the world so that we might live through him" (1 John 4:9). It is not a terribly surprising concept to us, now that we have the benefit of two-plus millennia of entrenched thinking on the matter. But this assertion—that God dwells not only on high but also among us piddly, fragile, less-than-heroic human beings—is hardly self-explanatory.

Indeed, why would the Creator and Ruler of all things materialize as a small Jewish boy from the remote town of Nazareth, hemmed in by hills and inaccessible by roadway? Why in that place? Why at that moment in time? Why as *him*? Why at all? It's preposterous. It belies the grandeur of God and defies any sort of logic. Plenty of folks have ruled out Christianity for the sheer ludicrousness of its premise. I can't say that I blame them.

And yet faith is the realm of the far-fetched, the land of "things hoped for" and "things not seen," as Hebrews 11:1 puts it. Logic isn't the rule of law here. Love is. And that's what drives all these relationalities, all these prepositions. For God to be among is a profound act of humility and empathy. It is the antithesis of a God of anger and retribution.

PLUMB LINE

I don't like to think about God being mad. The God that I experience, love, and trust is not an angry one. Yet when God talks to Amos, an Israelite who had been a simple shepherd and arborist before he responded to the call to prophesy, God is mad. Really mad.

God has had it with the pride of the Hebrew people. He detests their fortresses and their gluttony. "Woe to you who are complacent!" he warns (Amos 6:1 NIV). I can hear God's voice rising, his nerves inching toward their edge. God is so worked up that Amos feels the need to talk him down, beseeching him not to send swarms of locusts and devastating wildfires.

God takes in a long, slow breath, centers down, and acquiesces. He leans back against a wall and thinks. The wall, God notices, is well built. It does not buckle or lean. God considers this. And then, after some time, he takes up an object in his hand. Whether he pulls it out of his pocket or picks it up from the ground or makes it appear by magic, we do not know. It is of no matter. "What do you see, Amos?" God asks (Amos 7:8 NIV).

Amos looks. In God's hand is a string with a weight on the end of it. It hangs perfectly straight, pointing toward the ground. It seems like a trick question, but Amos answers with the obvious. "A plumb line," he responds.

God nods. He is not angry anymore. He is not threatening to send swarms of locusts or fires. He has a different plan now. "I am setting a plumb line among my people," God tells Amos, nodding some more. "I will spare them no longer," he adds.

It is Amos's turn to nod. Maybe he thinks God is a little off his rocker. A plumb line is an odd choice for a tool of destruction, especially for someone with all conceivable methods of calamity at their disposal. God has made himself clear, though: He is no longer going to spare the folks who are failing to live by his standards, by the Law he had given to Moses. Nope. He's done with them. It's time for the plumb line.

A plumb line is a definitive means of determining the center of gravity and thereby of measuring whether a line is perfectly straight. It is the exact vertical axis. It connects what is *above* to what is *among*. No plagues needed to make this point, just a plumb line: something to connect God to his people in a more straightforward way. Something that will really hit home—a weighty solution, if you will.

The story is a Hebrew one, recorded in the Old Testament, and the plumb line is, for people of Christian faith, Jesus. He is the begotten-not-made, one-off amalgam of human and divine, the only Son of God. He—his physical being, his personhood, his impossible possibility, his life, and too his death and resurrection—is the great solution to the problem of our sinful proclivities. God drops a line straight down into our midst, giving us an example to follow, a measuring stick by which to self-evaluate, a direct line to the Divine. No locusts. No fires. Just Jesus: the embodied version of the Godhead. A sentient, speaking, eating, sleeping, bleeding *being*. An actual person who could talk to us and touch us and share with us in the joys and challenges of this mortal life.

Living with teenagers often means hearing the refrain *You just don't get it*. It's a common weapon in the arsenal of those who feel misunderstood and alienated. When my daughters say this to me, what they mean is that I, as a middle-aged woman, cannot and do not understand what they, as teenage girls, are feeling. I am too far removed to get it, much less to be of any help. I am as good as useless.

A God who sits on a throne in heaven is, similarly, as good as useless. He definitely can't identify with the trials of a fourteen-year-old girl, nor with the trials of a middle-aged man. Job proves that. But a God who has been human? A God who grew up dealing with parents and elders who were teaching all the wrong stuff? A God who was a revolutionary and also loved animals, who fished with his buddies and got so mad he turned over some tables? *This* is a God we can relate to. More importantly, this is a God who can relate to *us*.

Jesus's life reveals the powerful truth that God is not only almighty; God also accepts vulnerability. This is a critical claim of Christian theology: the balance of God's transcendence with God's immanence. God isn't just somewhere out there, being big, powerful, omniscient God. God also isn't just somewhere near, hovering in the wild just out of reach. God isn't just with us, a source of unseen support and companionship. Because of his willingness to come into creation, to exist within each of us and throughout all creation, God is also tangibly here, among us, interacting with us in myriad, proximal ways, inviting us into acts of compassion, mercy, and kindness.

LEAST OF THESE

Thanksgiving in our family is a robust affair. We gather at the farm where I grew up, and when I say "we," I mean a lot of us. Usually thirty-five people or so, but sometimes upwards of forty-five kinfolk. Brothers and sisters, aunts and uncles, grands and greats, cousins by blood and cousins by marriage, in-laws and in-laws' parents: It's a full house. My mother, who is an octogenarian though no one would believe it, prepares most of the food that lines the buffet, a dish to suit everyone's pleasure: from a fried wild turkey to a roasted store-bought one, from macaroni and cheese to arugula salad, with everything in between, including at least three kinds of potatoes. Before we get our plates, all of us circle up and join hands. Someone locates the remote and mutes the football game. Someone locates the stray relative who missed the memo. Someone hushes a little one. The fire crackles in the background and my mother begins to speak. She gives instructions about who should sit where, and then we bow our heads to pray, and then she gives thanks—often for doctors and teachers—and always, every year, she closes her prayer by asking God to help us remember that everyone who crosses our path is at least as important to God as we are, if not more.

Her prayer is an invitation to seek and serve Christ in others. It is to get out of our heads and our egos and to behold the Divine among us in the faces of strangers, *all* strangers.

That is just really hard for most of us to live out. We want God among us, but on our own terms. We want to claim God here but not over there, in this group but not in that one. Jesus adamantly and repeatedly refuted this brand of spiritual elitism. His purpose—*to be among*—was and could only be universal. By among, he meant fully, inclusively among. Among tax collectors and prostitutes. Lepers and beggars. Children and elders. Samaritans and Romans. Believers and nonbelievers.

And further inverting our understanding of what God is and can be, Jesus claimed that not only was he *among* these who were the lowest and the least; in some way he *was* the lowest and the least. In the parable of the sheep and the goats, Jesus explains that whatever we have done for one of the least of our brothers and sisters, we have done for him: "I was hungry and you gave me food, I was thirsty and you gave me something to drink, I was a stranger and you welcomed me, I was naked and you gave me clothing, I was sick and you took care of me, I was in prison and you visited me" (Matthew 25:35–36).

Not surprisingly, the disciples don't understand what he means. They can't recall when Jesus was hungry or naked or sick. They rack their brains but can't seem to remember. "When did we do that?" they ask. Jesus answers them, but not by repeating himself. Instead, he inverts his original message, making its opposite also true: "Truly I tell you, just as you did not do it to one of the least of these, you did not do it to me" (Matthew 25:45).

With this declaration, Jesus adds a further layer of irony to the point he is making. Yes, God is among us, and no, he's not the one with the most power. God among us may be the Son of Man, sent to redeem the world, but God among us may also be the man huddled in a stairwell with no home to return to come end of the day. God among us may be the woman on the corner sold into slavery. The child whose face is dirty, whose stomach is empty, whose head teems with lice. *Whatever you do for the least of these, you do for me. Because I am them. Whatever you don't do for them, you don't do for me. Because I am them.*

Christ is not just one human; Christ is all humans. Christ is not just one creature; Christ is all creatures. That is why Father Rohr so frankly reminds us that Christ is not Jesus's last name; Christ is universal.

Though the notion of God Among is comforting to us theologically, it nevertheless—in real time—proves discomforting. We don't want to see God in the guy in the checkout line. We don't have time for that. And we definitely don't want to see God in folks with dirty faces, whether literally or figuratively. Over and over again, we reject the invitation to seek the face of God in the man sleeping on the sidewalk, his smell thick. We deny the invitation to seek the face of God in the know-it-all colleague who got the promotion that was clearly intended for us. We deny the invitation to seek the face of God in the little-miss-perfect mom who looks put together all the time and volunteers in the classroom every day and sends kale chips for lunch. Or in the emo teenager who has multiple piercings and purple hair. Or in the immigrant whose name is difficult to pronounce. Or in the person shouting epithets. The person shooting up. The person seeking an abortion. No. No. No. No. We are content to find comfort in the belief that God came among us in the person of Jesus, but we are not content to heed Jesus's well-documented claim that when we serve the persons most in need, most alienated, most forsaken, only then are we serving Jesus and in turn serving God. We would rather postpone kingdom living until after death because it's way too much work to cultivate in the here and now.

But kingdom living is the abiding reality and the abiding opportunity of God's aliveness among us right now. If we want to discover God, we will find him among us. He will be in the faces of those we love most as well as in the faces of strangers, at this very moment.

RESURRECTION

A biblical account of this very type of occurrence—when God is among us in people we perceive as strangers—involves Cleopas and his buddy on the road to Emmaus. It is three days after Jesus died on the cross, and these two men—disciples of Jesus's, no less—are walking along the dirt road. They've got about seven miles to go, and they are chatting animatedly. Reports had come in that the women had been to the tomb and found it empty. Angels had appeared. What could it mean? I can imagine their state of sorrow, befuddlement, exhaustion, and hope.

As they are hashing it out, along comes a stranger—passing, perhaps conveniently, in the other direction. He hears them confabulating and asks them what's going on. Clearly something big is happening. What is it? That's when they proceed to tell Jesus the story of Jesus.

Have you ever done this? Taken with the thrill of a story, do you find yourself recounting it to the actual person it happened to? Or the one whose life was affected? It's embarrassing. The drama gets the best of us. This kind of telling and rehashing is not inherently bad, but it stands in direct contrast to Mary the Mother of God, who simply took things in and pondered them in her heart. These disciples aren't pondering so much as jabbering. Jesus tells them outright that they are foolish. They didn't pay attention to the details of the story ahead of time, and they don't have eyes to see: He, Jesus, is standing right in front of them!

This story, as it is told in Luke 24, takes us right up to the next "among" moment, the big one. Cleopas and his friend have returned to Jerusalem and met up with the other disciples. Once again, they are deep into rehashing recent events, telling all about what happened on the road and asking themselves, "Were not our hearts burning within us while he was talking to us on the road?"

And then, Jesus does it again. "While they were talking about this, Jesus himself stood among them" (Luke 24:32–36). There he is, the risen Christ!

The disciples thought they were seeing a ghost. They were "startled and terrified." Jesus kindly asks them why. I mean, this God—God Among—was the whole point all along. God chose to pour Godself into creation and to assume his own humanity. He came as a baby born among the animals in the manger. He came as a prophet teaching and healing among the crowds. And he came as the resurrected body appearing among his devotees. In this moment of return, the risen Christ proves that death has no hold on us. Death is no obstacle to the Divine among. It is for this reason that Scripture tells us to keep awake, our belts fastened and our lanterns burning (Luke 12:35).

STEWARDSHIP

Indeed, we should remain on alert for God Among, but it can be with joyful, watchful expectation rather than with cowering or furtive fear.

God is not on a witch hunt. What makes God want to return does not seem to be the thrill of a slammed gavel. On the contrary, what makes God want to return is a gathering in his name. We know the verse from Matthew that says, "where two or three are gathered in my name, I am there among them" (Matthew 18:20). God doesn't want to catch us acting badly; God wants to join the party. This is because God relishes community.

Counterintuitively, God Almighty prefers to be God Among because this amongness is what provides God the sense of connection he so clearly values and craves. When I think about it from this angle, I realize that for God to have come among us is the most ironic and yet also the most natural cosmic occurrence of all. Why *wouldn't* God desire to come among his creations, his children? What would it say about a God who opted *not* to do so, who chose to remain separated? The God we believe we know is one who wills to come and dwell herein. This is because there is no more optimal place to know a people and to love a people than to live among them.

Scripture suggests that God was doing just that well before Jesus came onto the scene. While Christians tend to think of Jesus as being the primary instance of God Among, the Old Testament repeatedly suggests otherwise. In Numbers and in Deuteronomy, in Isaiah and in Jeremiah, in Ezekiel and Hosea and Haggai, references to the Lord God being "among" the people are prevalent. "You shall not defile the land in which you live, in which I also dwell, for I the Lord dwell among the Israelites" (Numbers 35:34). "Do not be terrified by them, for the Lord your God, who is among you, is a great and awesome God" (Deuteronomy 7:21 NIV). "I will not carry out my fierce anger, nor will I devastate Ephraim again. For I am God, and not a man—the Holy One among you. I will not come against their cities" (Hosea 11:9 NIV). Talk about prepositions showing up all over the place!

This last one strikes me as particularly salient. God emphasizes God's amongness not as a man but as a deity. God *as God* (not man) was among us in Eden and in the Exodus. God as God was among the Israelites, generating spontaneous signs, speaking commands, reprimanding behavior, and calling attention to God's own cohabitative existence.

God's preferred style of authority seems to be less heavy on dominion and more focused on stewardship. In Old English, the word *steward* or *stigweard* meant the guardian of the house, the one in charge of keeping it. Keeping the house meant overseeing the affairs of those living in it and ensuring things were running smoothly. Those dwelling therein needed to be kept safe, they needed to receive proper meals, and they needed to be cared for. All this was the job of the steward who, though he was above the others in rank and ability, nevertheless lived right there in the house among his charges. This makes total sense. How could he do the job of keeping the house if he were not indeed in and at the house? How could he help those under his charge manage their affairs if he were not there to show and teach them? The steward viewed his authority as a summons to live and dwell among his subjects, ensuring their upbringing and well-being. It is the same with God.

Rather than being enthroned in a cloud-high castle, God is a keeper who takes up residence in our very homes. "Don't you realize that all of you together are the house of God, and that the Spirit of God lives among you in his house?" (1 Corinthians 3:16 TLB). The emphasis is not on hierarchy (who has the most power) so much as it is on community (being in it together). God opts to play the role of steward as much as he plays the role of ruler, and he expects the same of us.

When God placed—and places—us in positions of authority, God expects us to follow his lead. Journalist and author Krista Tippett conducted an interview with theologian Ellen Davis of Duke Divinity School for her podcast *On Being*. In it, Davis discusses the creation story and the impact of the word *dominion* as it is translated in the King James version of Genesis 1:28. The verse reads: "Be fruitful and multiply, and fill the earth and subdue it and have dominion over the fish of the sea and over the birds of the air and over every living thing that moves upon the earth." Davis suggests that a more accurate translation of the Hebrew word *radah* would be to "exercise skilled mastery *amongst* the creatures." The call to humans—in their position of power and privilege—has more to do with the craft or art of caretaking than with the imposition of authority, Davis suggests.

Her understanding of the word *radah* shifts the relationship of human and earth from a position *above* to a position *among*. The role to which we humans are called, in our position of leadership and in our position of faith, is never dominion but rather stewardship. We weren't given "dominion" over our children to be tyrants. We were called to be their stewards, to live among them and ensure their safekeeping and well-being. We weren't given "dominion" over the plants. We were called to be their stewards, to live among them and ensure their safekeeping and well-being. Likewise with the animals.

Restoring that one word to its proper interpretation has radical implications. It instructs us that being in community is more divinely inspired than being in power and that being a steward is more effective than being a dictator. This is the model that God establishes, and this is the demand that faith makes of us. In her book *The Unbearable Wholeness of Being: God, Evolution and the Power of Love*, Ilia Delio beseeches us to "have faith, to believe that the reign of God is among us."

We reinforce "the reign of God among us" every time we recite the phrase *thy Kingdom come* in the Lord's Prayer. Every time we pray these words, we are bringing God down from the mountaintops and the heavens, we are bringing God up from the depths and out of the shadows, and we are locating God right here among us where God already is. In doing so, we are responding to an invitation that God has already disseminated, which is an invitation into connection, into community, into stewardship, and into caring.

Jesus also assured us that God shows no partiality. No one of us is more precious to God or more an expression of God than another. If so, if true, then our guiding questions might ever be: Where is God Among us right now? Do I feel my heart burning?

A PRAYER TO GOD AMONG

Holiest One,
Creator and Ruler of All,
whose will it is to come among us,
to dwell in our homes
and help us manage our affairs,
whose will it is to be in community with us
despite how exclusive we can be,
despite how poorly we care,
have mercy on us.

Holiest One,
Creator and Ruler of All,
in the form of your Son, Jesus Christ,
you came among us most humanly,
a flesh and blood baby,
a thinking, feeling man
who understands our woes directly,
who invites us into understanding,
who beseeches us to care,
we praise You.

Holiest One,
Creator and Ruler of All,
you remain among us yet,
in the faces of our beloveds
and also in the faces of those we most fear,
those we most ostracize,
those we most revile.
Give us the courage to look for you.
Bestow on us the bold compassion
that you so unfailingly possess.

May we love as you love.

Amen.

CHAPTER THIRTEEN

Between

As for the matter about which you and I have spoken,
the Lord be between you and me forever.

1 Samuel 20:23

I may never have full rest nor very bliss: that is to say,
till I be so fastened to Him,
that there is right nought that is made betwixt my God and me.

Julian of Norwich

Having explored the preposition *among*, I really thought we had made it to the home stretch. I thought we had reached what I knew would be the penultimate preposition: *around*, the last stop before the inevitable *beyond*. But it turns out there was one last preposition to discover, hiding in plain sight even more than all the rest of them. It was so hidden, in fact, that I almost missed it, because to be hidden is its very nature. Noticing it requires not just focus but *refocus*, the skill of seeing what is not there but is very much there.

At some point you may have been shown a drawing with a white object against a black background and asked what you see. The majority of us will say that we see a white vase. The ones who see the trick question coming, or who have hyper right-brain sensitivities, might instead say that they see two faces. The faces exist in the black space surrounding the white vase. They are nose-to-nose, nearly kissing.

This inquiry is an exercise in learning about positive space and negative space. We are hardwired to see the positive space: the primary object, the area of interest. It is the thing we are *supposed* to see. But it is not the only thing. Between the objects (and also around them) is what we call negative space. It is what enables the positive space to exist, establishing its boundaries and also its relationships. To see it, we have to look where we aren't used to looking: *between*.

The word *between* is derivative of the Old English word *betwēonum*, which is composed of *be* and *two*. We have presumed that being "two" means being separate. Indeed, most definitions of the word *between* use the word *separate*. *Between* is defined as "at, into, or across the space *separating* (two objects or regions)." It is "in the period *separating* (two points in time)." It is what keeps this over here and that over there.

But the nature of this relationality need not, by default, be one of separation. A slight adjustment of perspective, as with bringing negative space into focus, reveals that the nature of this relationality is also—and perhaps more critically—one of connection. Science would support this altered perception, as betweenness is always, without exception, characterized by gravitational *pull*. There is no such thing as gravitational push.

The same could be said for spiritual betweenness, as betweenness is the "inescapable network of mutuality" in which all exist, as Martin Luther King Jr. describes it. That which impacts one person directly impacts all indirectly. We are not the isolated, separate selves we think we are.

As in art, reality also comprises positive space and negative space. If God is indeed *throughout*, then God inhabits not only positive space but also negative space as well. Not only molecules but intermolecular space, not only form but formlessness, not only presence but absence, not only text but context. God dwells not just in bodies but also in the space between bodies, not only in what already exists but also in the potential to exist. Negative space is as ripe a dwelling place for the Divine as positive space.

If we think of all that seems to be separating us instead as a sacred and inevitable connection, then we are all united. God is the network of our mutuality, the gravitational pull of our souls, the negative space that interrelates us.

The British idiom "mind the gap" pragmatically teaches us to be wary of the gap between the platform and the train. But existentially, minding the gap also means looking at the in-between spaces for important, life-saving knowledge. There may be something right before our very eyes that we miss, something hidden in plain sight with critical wisdom to impart, like a preposition ready to illuminate God.

INTERSTITIUM

Anatomists recently made an astonishing discovery that gives evidence for this theory. It had seemed, until not that long ago, that they had it all nailed down. How could they not? Experts have been studying anatomy for millennia, and what they have discovered about the body is remarkable in its detail and accuracy.

But then, a mere decade ago, scientists looked at all they had been looking at for decades, centuries even, with altered vision. They noticed, for the very first time, what isn't there but is very much there: spaces, gaps, holes in our tissue. What they had believed to be walls were in fact not walls at all but fluid-filled vacancies—a kind of negative space network that is not only functional but also essential. They had eyes to see, for the first time in the history of medicine, the highly functional, highly significant spaces *between*. And the function of this anatomical *between*, which scientists discovered exists all throughout the body, is—not surprisingly—to connect. The name they gave this pervasive web of betweening is *interstitium*.

The interstitium has been likened to a highway and to a shock absorber. Its presence bespeaks a heretofore hidden *interstitial space*—like intergalactic space but inside us. According to the National Library of Medicine, the interstitium is composed "mainly of collagen types I, III, and V, elastin, and glycosaminoglycans . . . which are mechanically entangled and cross-linked to form a gel-like reticulum reminiscent of a brush-pile in terms of its three-dimensional organization." What that amounts to is that the interstitial space opens channels of gel, of flow, of qi, which may account for the efficacy of Eastern medicines like acupuncture. Yielding significant insight into the flow of cells and maybe even into the flow of God, it illuminates how we get sick and how we might heal. The network of mutuality that Martin Luther King pronounced integral to interpersonal space is now evidenced in our very own interstitial space.

What's more, we never saw it. That something was entirely visible and yet somehow invisible to countless experts over countless hours of inspection is deeply heartening. What else is right here, under our noses, that we are nevertheless overlooking? What gap might we be wise to mind? What intractable force might be mobilizing? What or who might we be magnetizing?

BRIDGE

Who knows what attracts one person to another? Who knows why there is so obviously something between two people? That's where all erotic love starts: in the super-charged space *between*. Between is the force field of all procreation, the frontier of all fruition. It is where love begins and likewise where love is carried. God is there as surely as God is anywhere.

Between is a force field of another kind as well: not only *eros* but also *philia* (friends' love), *pragma* (companionate love), and *storge* (family love). It is what ties friend to friend, sister to sister, spouse to spouse. It is that which abides between two people, sustaining, guiding, and grounding them. Between is what connects souls across the dinner table or across oceans and even across the lines of death. When words fall short of relaying the truth and the magnitude of our feelings, we often refer to this powerful connection as "what we have between us." What we have between us exceeds our capacity to characterize because it is the heart of the Divine.

"What has come between us," however, carries an altogether different meaning. When something *comes between* people, the situation is one of discord. Our differing views on religion, on politics, on anything and everything drive a wedge between us. This kind of between does not feel like God at all. It feels like mistrust, hatred, suspicion, wounding. But this is when we need God Between more than ever.

When Jesus insists that people love their enemies and pray for them, he is demanding that we bring God to the space between (Matthew 5:44). Rather than loathing, we are called to loving, which often begins by building bridges. Just as we are called to seek and serve Christ among us, we are also called to cultivate relationships between us, especially ones that are interfaith, interracial, and intercultural. The prefix *inter*, of the word *interstitium* reappears in this context, pointing us again toward the spaces between.

When we form friendships between disparate groups, bridging perceived gaps and finding common ground, we are inviting God to occupy the space between us rather than letting our own fears or opinions create greater division. History offers us inspiring examples of relationships forged across religious and political divides, like those between Christian civil rights leader Martin Luther King Jr. and Rabbi Abraham Heschel and also between King and Buddhist monk Thich Nhat Hanh. These spiritual leaders viewed the differences between them as an opportunity for coming together rather than staying apart. By doing so, they were able to effect social change and deepen our collective humanity.

So often, though, our relationships with those who differ from us, who are our "enemies," are not fruitful so much as fraught. How hard it is to love and not to loathe in these scenarios!

A minor case in point: A couple of years ago, I spent several months working on a communications piece for my church. It consumed hundreds of hours of my time as I finessed the project into what was, for me, perfection enough. The first person to see it outside my committee was an employee of the church who let me know in an email that she was—"not to be disrespectful," she assured me— "frankly underwhelmed." Suffice to say, I did not have Christian thoughts. I let her comment gnaw at my insides like a rat. I turned it over in my head at two in the morning. I obsessed over it while my daughter was trying to tell me about her day at school. My ego was hijacking any possible work of the Holy Spirit, and I knew it, and yet . . . yet . . . it was so darn hard to release. There was nothing between this woman and me but hostility (and we were working on behalf of the *church*!).

What would happen if we invited God into the tense spaces in our relationships? What if, in arguments with our spouse, we asked God to come between us, filling and illuminating that space? What if, in conflicts with our colleagues, we asked God to enter the fray? What if, in disputes with our kids, we asked God to do the work of betweening? Surely our anger and self-righteousness would diffuse and our edges soften. Surely we might learn to listen better, empathize more, speak carefully.

This kind of mediation, from the Latin word *mediare*, meaning placed in the middle or placed between, was clearly part of Jesus's calling and daily work. He is the living evidence of God's own commitment to connection, the bridge between what is seen and unseen, between what is divine and manifest. "For there is one God, and one mediator also between God and humankind, Christ Jesus, himself human" (1 Timothy 2:5). Jesus embodied theologically what he undertook pragmatically every day: an effort toward reconciliation. In various accounts of Jesus's life, we see him—the Prince of Peace—mediating and advocating for mediation emphatically. "Settle matters quickly with your adversary," he advises. "Blessed are the peacemakers," he proclaims (Matthew 5:9). "And forgive us our debts, as we also have forgiven our debtors," Jesus insisted (Matthew 6:12). When he looked around, Jesus saw the same kind of egoism and strife that we see today. He taught a different way, demonstrated a different way, begged for a different way, and died for a different way. Jesus's mission was to bring respect, understanding, and healing to the in-between places that had been tainted.

The collaboration between my colleague and me was never exactly smooth, and I admit that I never fully released the color of my impressions. But maybe perfect harmony is not the ultimate or only expression of God Between. Perhaps what Christ insists upon, and helps engender when invited in as a mediator, is some basic form of connection: a mutually recognized dignity. Looking with dignity upon our enemies is often an ego check because our egos are eager to judge. That's how they feel better about themselves. What the call for mediation does instead is ask us to forego being right and instead to embrace being merciful.

In fourth grade, my youngest daughter had a slip of paper in her school binder that read: *Instead of being right, be kind.* It was a note the teacher had given all her students at the start of the year to establish a culture of dignity and connection in her classroom. Counter to centuries of "Christian" dealings and counter to so many contemporary "Christian" claims, this theology of connection—of being merciful and kind rather than right—is central to what it means to be a follower of Christ. Mediating—which is, in effect, to make *between* a place of connection rather than separation—is the way of God.

MIZPAH

The story of Jacob and Laban from the Old Testament—dramatic as it is—bequeaths to us the Hebrew word *mizpah*, which describes the sacred bond between two people who are apart from one another. This term and the story behind it elucidate for us more about the loving nature of God Between.

The story begins with Jacob becoming enamored of Laban's daughter Rachel and agreeing to seven years of indentured servitude in order to win her hand in marriage. On the wedding night, however, Laban switches Rachel for his oldest daughter, Leah. What follows is an elaborate story of selective breeding for both sheep and humans, as well as mounting conflicts between father-in-law and son-in-law over who owns and who is owed what.

One night, Jacob decides he is finished: He is leaving. He packs up his wives and his mottled herds and escapes to the hill country of Gilead, where Laban pursues him. The confrontation could be explosive, but God appears to Laban in a dream before he overtakes Jacob and advises him "not to say anything to Jacob, either good or bad" (Genesis 31:24). God's counsel in this moment reflects God's wisdom and his nature. Again, he leans not toward judgment but toward understanding. God cautions Laban against being reactive and advocates instead for patient and active listening.

What ensues is a heated but honest and productive conversation between the two men. They share their perspectives, each speaking and listening, until Laban suggests they come to an agreement and commemorate it with a pile of stones. The agreement becomes more than heap of stones, however. "It was also called Mizpah," which in Hebrew means watchtower. "May the Lord keep watch between you and me when we are absent one from the other," Laban prays. "Remember that God is a witness between you and me," he tells Jacob (Genesis 31:49).

What a beautiful truth. When two people are apart from one another, God keeps watch over them and also *between* them, spanning the distance and transforming it from one of separation to one of connection. This is true across scenarios, major and minor: children who go off to camp or to college; husbands or wives who go off to war or to work; close friends who move across the country. Even when loved ones pass from this world into another: God keeps watch between us even then—after death. Especially then. Utterly then.

When we are away from each other, God is our tether, our unbreakable betweening. "I have set my bow in the clouds," God told Noah and his family, "and it will be the sign of the covenant between me and the earth" (Genesis 9:13). The rainbow is inherently beautiful, but its symbolism is paramount. As the ultimate and lasting Between,

God not only mediates, God bridges, connects, and illuminates. With God Between, a tactical agreement transfigures into something more poignant and lasting: a genuine connection, a *covenant.*

COVENANT

God underscores the importance of covenants from the very outset of Scripture. In Genesis, he establishes a covenant between himself and Abraham and Abraham's descendants, saying, "I will establish my covenant between me and you and your offspring after you throughout their generations, for an everlasting covenant, to be God to you and to your offspring after you" (Genesis 17:7). God assures Abraham that his children and grandchildren and great-grandchildren, on and on, would be cared for, protected, and in some way saved.

I cannot think of a single more important thing for someone confronting his or her own mortality to hear. Death will come, but God will keep watch over all those you love in perpetuity. *All will be well when you are gone*, God says. *All will be well forever with your loved ones.* This vow to Abraham was localized and also representative. God was speaking to Abraham about Abraham, and to Abraham about all of us. Scripture states explicitly that the covenant was formed with the people of Israel. And yet, in Genesis 9:12, when God gives the rainbow to Noah as an abiding symbol of his love, of his identity, and of our very destiny, he also makes this proclamation:

> This is the sign of the covenant which I make between Me and you, and every living creature that is with you, for perpetual generations: I set My rainbow in the cloud, and it shall be for the sign of the covenant between Me and the earth. It shall be, when I bring a cloud over the earth, that the rainbow shall be seen in the cloud; and I will remember My covenant which is between Me and you and every living creature of all flesh; the waters shall never again become a flood to destroy all flesh. The

> rainbow shall be in the cloud, and I will look on it to remember the everlasting covenant between God and every living creature of all flesh that is on the earth. (Genesis 9:12-16 NKJV)

Three times, God repeats the refrain: between me and you and every living creature forever. The "old covenant" is neither exclusive, designed only for the Hebrew people, nor outdated, stamped with an expiration date. It is the ultimate and impermeable connection of God to every living creature in perpetuity.

And Jesus, as the "new covenant," preaches, models, and himself embodies this sacred truth. As the Between, Jesus calls for universal *betweening*. He calls for us to cross the aisle, touch the unclean, offer a hand. He instructs us to love the self, love the neighbor, love the enemy. He invites us—over and over again—to be the rainbow.

On December 25, 1914, five months into a world war that would last four years, something sacred happened on battlefields across the Western Front: what you might call a rainbow moment. It's an event that still tethers us to hope well over one hundred years later, and we refer to it as the Christmas truce or Weihnachtsfrieden or Trêve de Noël. That morning, war-weary soldiers—exhausted and muddied, cold and heartsick—returned to being men and came out to greet one another. Longing for loved ones, for warmth, for cheer, out they came. A German man crawled out of the wretched trench where he had been hiding. A British man strode courageously into the open. A French man put down a gun and held out a hand, greeting another with a gravelly, cheery, teary *Joyeux Noel*. There were games and gifts. There was singing. In this moment, the vast and hostile space between—between trenches, between warring nations, between ideologies and staunch convictions—was infilled by a force sublime, generous, amiable, and life-giving. Rather than sullied, the space between became instantaneously sacred.

This happened the moment God was summoned into the very place he had already long been and promised to be. God Between was realized, and in turn hostility transformed instantly into joviality. Fear transformed into fraternity. Separation transformed into connection. Permitting God to come between us, where he always is and seeks to be, is the truest triumph. It is a victory that doesn't involve flags. It is a truce that requires no further bloodshed.

God is waiting for this. God is waiting for our consciousness to catch up with his presence because he is already there: between all things. He tethers us to one another whether we know it, see it, like it, or care. He connects us to one another whether or not we pray him into existence or imagine him or seek him or not. For God, it is not a question of *whether* he exists between. It is only a matter of whether we abide in the divine relationality that is available to us—an abiding that asks us to be patient and to be opened and to wait, often uncomfortably, for glory to reveal itself. This waiting is a kind of liminal space, and God is in that too.

THRESHOLD

Deities have presided over liminal space across cultures and centuries. A "threshold guardian," as they are sometimes called, dwells in the in-between spaces, be it a river or a gate or a crossroads, with the purpose of ushering mortals safely across the divide. Many of these deities are psychopomps: beings whose duty it is to escort souls from death into the afterlife. Charon, in Greek mythology, is one such psychopomp who ferries souls across the River Styx and the River Acheron. In Roman mythology, Janus, who gives his name to the month of January, is the two-faced god who looks to both past and future. He is associated with doorways and gates, which symbolize passage and transition. In Hinduism, this role is filled by Ganesha. In Chinese mythology, the threshold guardians are called *menshens*, and they oversee the comings and goings of spirits. Across all these peoples, a common understanding arises of the reality and importance of the between. It is a liminal space presided over by God.

Liminal refers to any period or space of unknowing and waiting. It is a gap, a gray area, a gestation. The word *liminal* derives from the Latin word *limin*, which means threshold: a point just past departure but just before arrival. Liminal spaces confront and beckon us all the time, no matter how much we might resist and deny them. And resist and deny them we do. Liminal space is not a place we tend to like because it lacks certitude and forward motion. As a society that prizes decisiveness and action, determination and achievement, we do not know how to embrace liminality. We associate states of liminality—losing a job, going through a divorce, undergoing treatment—with fear or shame. Those who abide in a state of unknowing are deemed unproductive, even failures. Even mid-life liminality is cast as a crisis when, in fact, it is the soul doing the good hard work of souling.

Though resisted, liminal space is the antidote to all the output that society requires of us. It invites us to abide in the sacred space between breaths, between tasks, between jobs, between selves, even. Abide in unknowing long enough, and its awesome power begins to reveal itself. The name of that power is possibility, which is fueled by an even more awesome power: hope. In liminal space, which is the house of God, all things are possible (Matthew 19:26). With enough patience on our part, anything might unfold. In this way, liminality invites us to trust the process of Life itself. It invites us to, as Parker Palmer articulates, "let your life speak." We cannot hurry it. We cannot control it. We must wait, actively and wakefully, for what is yet to arrive.

Between what we have done and what we will do, between what we have been and what we will be is a pause, exceedingly sacred. Nature knows this. I think of all the boughs of all the maples and the oaks as they endure winter, waiting for their green to come. I think of the aged bear, all stored up with fat, hibernating. I think of the slow waking of bodies and of the pause between each inbreath and each outbreath. These are passages of waiting, which occur throughout creation and throughout lives and throughout our very days. They need not be feared, though our experience of them may well be agonizing.

Weathering the desert, the pilgrimage, the pit, and even the grave are examples of liminal space repeated throughout Scripture, not the least of which is the forty days Jesus spends in the wilderness. During this time, he battles egoic temptations and clings to fervent prayer. He also sits and waits. Vying for a higher, deeper way as he lives alone in the desert wilds, he is not what he was and yet he is not quite ready to be what he will become.

Betweening often creates such a crucible. In it, we are forged anew. Contemporary theologian Thomas Rundel asserts a truth many of us unwittingly come to know: "God can again use liminality to transform his people and prepare them for mission." The church reinforces the fruitfulness of such liminality in its liturgical calendar, which celebrates Advent and Lent as periods of active waiting and reflection, while God mirrors it for us unequivocally in the creation story. For six full and fruitful days God created, and on the seventh day God chose to rest. He took a break. He portioned out a sacred time and space between what had been and what was yet to be.

In this way, God was work and God was rest. God was action and God was contemplation. God was certitude and God was liminality. We like to think of God as the One with the plan, the One who makes things happen, which God is. But God also presents himself as the One who withdraws, the One who waits. Denying the between—refusing to hold space for uncertainty, for reflection, for liminality—inhibits spiritual maturation. "Evangelical theology and practice actively discourage those in liminal space. As a result, Christian maturity is frustrated," Rundel asserts. Propositional truth—pronouncing this to be right and that to be wrong with no understanding of what might lie between—is an aberration of the nature and behavior of God as conveyed through prepositional truth.

How like God to consecrate emptiness. To occupy not only form but formlessness: no gap left bereft, no span uninhabited.

Cocking our heads and looking at the negative space of eternity rather than the positive space of the current moment, we see a new contour to our very existence. We recognize that life itself is, as Carl Jung writes, "a short episode between two great mysteries, which are yet one." This life is itself an interlude, beautifully liminal yet eternally tethered. A blessed between.

A PRAYER TO GOD BETWEEN

Holy One,

you abide in negative space,
inviting us to behold anew.
Help us to shift our focus.

Holy One,
you abide in gaps,
inviting us to mind the connections.
Help us to build bridges.

Holy One,
you abide in liminal spaces,
inviting us to let our lives speak.
Help us to embrace the pause.

Holy One,
you abide in absences,
tethering souls across even the greatest of distances.
Help us to cross the divide,
which is no divide at all
but rather the sweet arc of you.

Amen.

CHAPTER FOURTEEN

Around

In him we live and move and have our being.

Acts 17:28

This entire universe is enveloped by My unmanifested form.
All beings exist within Me, yet I am not confined within them.

Bhagavad Gita 9:4

Who is God? What is God? Where is God? These questions, as we now know, can be answered ever so powerfully with prepositions. We have covered thirteen already, a lucky number. What could possibly be left? At least two important prepositions remain, including one so self-evident that my nine-year-old identified it with ease.

It was a summer morning, and she and I were sitting at the breakfast table. I asked if I could pose a somewhat random question to her, and she agreed.

"Do you feel like God is somehow inside you?" I asked.

"Yes," she said confidently. "God made me, and so God's magic is in me. Why?" she inquired: a bright and direct question.

I told her about this book and asked if she knew what a preposition was. We did a quick lesson on prepositions using my coffee mug and a candle and the table, and then I asked her which preposition she thinks best describes God.

She didn't skip a beat before answering. "Around. God is all around," she asserted matter-of-factly.

I nodded, taking this in.

"Like *throughout*?" I suggested.

She frowned a bit. "Like *around*," she insisted, waving her spoon in the air before taking another bite of Honey Nut Cheerios.

MAGICAL

This conversation with my daughter got me thinking. What is the difference between *throughout* and *around*? Do we need both?

In one sense, we use *around* and *throughout* interchangeably. I might say that God is throughout everything and is thus everywhere. To convey the same meaning, I could just as easily say that God is *all around*. Both prepositions connote pervasiveness; both invite holy looking.

But *around* has a different feel to it. Whereas *throughout* suggests God permeating everything or manifesting in everything almost in a flat way, across an endless breadth, *around* has an encompassing effect. It bends space back onto itself and holds it tight. It is like God Before: uniting Beginning and End, as with Alpha and Omega.

Adding the word *all* in front of *around* gives it an even different bent. The idea of God *all around* has a dose of twinkle and enigma. It is God Throughout and also God Among, Between, and Near. This God frolics and suffuses. It inhabits positive space and negative space, matter and energy, the manifest and the hidden, the real and the imaginal—or what some, like my child, call the *magical*.

In third grade, I learned the word *expedition* from my teacher, Ms. ElAmri, and I was delighted at how aptly it described my favorite pastime. Friends would come to spend the night, and we would go on "expeditions" into the woods, up the river, among the haystacks, through the fields, all around the farm. There was magic in the natural world and in the expedition as well. Venturing out with an attitude of seeking always opens us to the possibility of magic. It is the practice of *prospecting.*

In architecture, particularly landscape design, a theory about what humans crave spatially was posited in the 1970s and continues to prove salient. It's called the *prospect-refuge theory*, and it determines that humans are drawn to spaces that allow them to scan their environment for opportunities (prospect) while also being tucked into a hidden nook that keeps them safe (refuge). The argument is that this dynamic need—of being able to see widely while being safely enclosed—is rooted in our evolutionary processes. As predators, we needed to be able to see without being seen.

Might this particular dynamic of prospect and refuge be deeply rooted in our spiritual processes as well? An innate quality of being human seems to involve prospecting: to go searching for something more, something elusive, something deeper, something out of reach yet somehow attainable. We prospect for God, scanning our environments, our relationships, our stories—living, historical, and mythical—for signs of God. We look for opportunities to witness God's work or do God's work. We scan landscapes—actual, inner, cultural—for vestiges of the Divine or for direction from the Divine. Any glimpse. Any assurance. Any crumb trails. Anything. From a place of our deepest yearning, we seek God. Curiosity impels us, as does hope and some innate conviction that there is, in fact, something to seek.

This propensity to seek is itself, I believe, evidence of the Divine. To be made in the image of God is to know of God on some level, conscious or unconscious. We intuit, as my daughter did, that the Divine is somewhere around, and so we go looking for it. "Seek and ye shall find" is a commonly quoted verse. I find this verse equal parts comforting and maddening. How many of us have felt like we have been doing nothing but searching—for days, months, years—and have found nothing? We are no closer to work that fulfills us. We are no closer to finding a partner. We are no closer to understanding or believing in God.

This verse, which holds so much promise, can feel pithy, and yet it declares the full nature of God. Seeking will prove its own finding. Prospecting will ultimately lead us back to knowing. What goes *around* comes *around*. That's why it feels so hard and yet reveals itself to be so simple. It is a full-circle endeavor, but we can't grasp it until we have taken the full journey around.

FULLNESS

The apostle Paul was a fan of this idea of fullness. In his letters to the churches in Ephesia and Colossae, Paul extols the "fullness of God," characterizing it as a multidimensional expansion of space. He prays that the holy people to whom he writes may grasp how wide and long and high and deep it is (Ephesians 3:18). He prays that they can comprehend just how *around* God is.

By definition, *around* means on every side of. We don't simply mean width, height, and depth, nor do we mean north, south, east, and west, or even the additions of northeast, southeast, northwest, and southwest. Eight sides can be broken into more sides. Within the concept of fullness, the word *sides* no longer applies, and we start using the word *degrees*. Count every degree around something until you return to the point of origin, and you cover 360 degrees. Count those in a sphere, and you encounter 41,253 degrees, more or less. Get more detailed than that, and you start to talk arcmins. An arcmin strikes me as an aptly named unit of measurement for the overarching Divine. It's reminiscent of an archangel. And yet even *it* fails to get granular enough. No unit of measurement can quantify wholeness.

The three points of a triangle certainly cannot, and yet, for the most part, Christians think of God as a triangle and the world as a pyramid. "Many of us, consciously or unconsciously, have pictured God and reality as a pyramid-shaped universe. We placed a male God at the top of the triangle and everything else beneath," writes Father Rohr in one of his daily meditations for the Center for Action and

Contemplation. What we miss, what we lose, and what we distort by heralding the symbol of the triangle exclusively is the dynamism at the heart of its very meaning. True trinitarian thinking, writes Rohr, "is more spiral, circle, and flow than pyramid."

This is a truth my young daughter grasped with ease as she whirled her spoon in confident circles. When we move from an image of God with sharp edges and pronounced vertices into one that is fluid, organic, and dynamic, our understanding of the nature and behavior of the Divine shifts seismically. We understand the Divine, and by extension all reality, not as a top-down pyramid but as a sphere, not as a triangle but as a circle, with a comprehensive wholeness.

This conceptual shift is hardly new. Celtic crosses, as one example, are distinct for the way they incorporate the circle into the icon of Jesus's crucifixion. The origin stories of how the circle came to be are various. The circle was an engineering solution, added to fortify the structural integrity of the cross beams. The circle was a holdover from pagan culture, which idolized the sun and likewise the moon at its fullest. The circle incorporates the four relations of north, south, east, and west and also the four elements of earth, air, water, and fire. The circle signifies the womb. It echoes the medicine wheel. These diverse explanations underscore the universality of the circle as a symbol. It is the all-in-one, far more so than a triangle. The circle or sphere expresses the full fluidity and inclusivity of God. The Circle, when truly Divine, is never static; nor is it finite; nor is it exclusive. Its infinite energies circulate pervasively, and its infinite boundaries encapsulate fully.

The first time I encountered the idea of God as a sphere in which we each and all exist—God Around—was not in church but in a high school English class. We had learned about the Great Chain of Being my sophomore year, and now as juniors, we were tackling subject matter a bit (or a lot) more esoteric and intellectually challenging: transcendentalism.

Reading Ralph Waldo Emerson is not easy, but I have to say: Transcendentalism blew my mind. I mean, a transparent eyeball? I was and continue to be an absolute sucker for it. In his essay "Nature,"

Emerson bemoans the fact that adults can no longer *see*. He too longed for more truthful ways of seeing and being in the world. When light hits our eyes, our photoreceptors make quick work of turning that light into electrical signals and sending them off to our brain, but our hearts are not involved. We are not absorbing all that Divine that is awaiting intake, all those magical things awaiting sharper wits, all that ineffability awaiting savoring. To *see*, to achieve mystical union, we must become transparent somehow, dissolving our sense of self and one-ing with the universe. We must become, as Emerson writes, a transparent eyeball. "Standing on the bare ground,—my head bathed by the blithe air, and uplifted into infinite spaces,—all mean egotism vanishes," he writes. "I become a transparent eye-ball; I am nothing; I see all; the currents of the Universal Being circulate through me; I am part or particle of God. . . . I am the lover of uncontained and immortal beauty."

Emerson describes a mystic experience of absolute self-dissolution, which enables him to see all. It is the exact moment novelist Alice Walker's character, Shug, describes in *The Color Purple* when she says: "I believe God is everything. . . . Everything that is or ever was or ever will be. And when you feel that, and be happy to feel that, you've found It."

God is no longer a fixed point on high but a sphere of which we are part and a current of which we are particle. In this way, God becomes that which is *all around us* and also that which is *around us all*. God is at once circulating and encircling. The discovery—what we become able to see—is that we are already in God. God's got us.

REFUGE

The same daughter who asserted that God is primarily *around* likes to be tucked into her bed tightly. By tight, I mean compacted. She crawls into the sheets, lies on her back, and then begins meticulously tucking her comforter into both sides of her mattress with as little movement of her torso as possible. Once snug, she smooths out the top and then pulls her arms in last, giving her eyes a long restful blink. I can feel her relax. Yet the whole ordeal seems kind of excessive, and so I ask her one night, as she lies pinned in to her liking, why, "Why do you tuck yourself in so thoroughly?"

Her answer: "I like feeling my sheets around me. It makes me feel cozy. And safe."

The word she uses is *around*. And the experience she is describing is that of refuge. Just as we thrill going on expeditions for prospecting, we also deeply crave being hidden. This is evolutionary, in the sense that it enhances our capabilities as predators—to see and not be seen—but it is more elemental than that. We can survive three weeks without food and three days without water, but we cannot survive five hours without shade from the heat or warmth in the cold. Biologically, we need to be able to hole up; shelter is critical.

Emotionally, we need to be able to hole up too; shelter is critical. We find refuge in the arms of people we love and trust. We find refuge in blankets and in our beds. Young children, when upset, hide. They tuck themselves into small places and wait out storms or arguments or consequences. They crawl into laps. At a cellular level, we all need embracing. When my oldest daughters were a mere two years into this world, they had learned to express their needs in a few key short phrases. "Hold you, Mama," was one such phrase. "Hold you, Mama," they would say, lifting their arms to me, beseeching me with their wide eyes. "Hold you," they would repeat.

Spiritually, we need to be able to hole up too; shelter is critical. The notion of God as refuge is illuminated in Scripture. One psalmist writes, "God is our refuge and strength, a very present help in trouble" (Psalm 46:1). Another writes, "I will say of the Lord, 'My refuge and my fortress, my God, in whom I trust'" (Psalm 91:2). Under God's wings, we take refuge, asserts Ruth (Ruth 2:12). God is our safe place, and *Hold you* is one of our most basic prayers. This is our primal cry to the God that mothers us and fathers us: to be held by God—to experience God *arounding* us—is to know love.

The image of God the Father, at its most precious, at its most tender, is the promise of this deeply desired refuge. God the Father builds a house where all have rooms. God the Father regards us all as his children. God the Father envelopes us in his loving arms and holds us in the palm of his gentle, capable hands. When ones we love are in danger, we ask God to surround them with angels. When someone is suffering, we ask God to hold them and keep them. God the Father, and equally God the Mother, is a God Around. Theirs is a lap we yearn to crawl into, an embrace we melt into for eternity. In this way, God becomes our sanctuary. It is the one truly safe place. Knowing this love, which otherwise surpasses knowledge, we "may be filled up to all the fullness of God" (Ephesians 3:19). This is what God Around provides for us—refuge, comfort, and safety—also fullness and wholeness. An infinity that nevertheless encloses. This is the intuition of a child and the epiphany of the seeker.

IMAGINAL

One symbol used to articulate this infinite yet enclosing *Universal Being* is the bubble. Bubbles are both innocuous and extraordinary. They manage to blur otherwise distinct forms of matter, appearing at once to be a gas, a liquid, and a solid. They are fragile and yet can withstand a surprising amount of poking. A plaything of a toddler, the bubble is nevertheless an ancient and abiding archetype of the Divine, as noted in the treasurable tome *The Book of Symbols*. "Like the circle or sphere, the globular roundness of the bubble connotes oneness, wholeness, totality, completion, and spiritual perfection." As the entry further notes, "it constitutes an invisible reality imaged by mystics throughout the ages, a round nothingness that is paradoxically the primordial source of all."

The metaphor of the bubble captures the dynamism at the heart of the true meaning of the Trinity. It also echoes the dualities that Emerson sought to articulate: the *nothing* and the *all*. This "round nothingness that is paradoxically the primordial source of all" returns us to the womb of our origin. God Around becomes synonymous with God Before. Space and time curve back upon one another and become one, ceasing to be and yet sourcing all that is. Emptiness and generativity coexist.

It all begins to seem too heady, but our minds aren't the right tools for grasping this sacred wholeness. We need some other way to engage this Holy Mystery, this realm that scholars call the *imaginal*.

The term *imaginal space* was coined by a friend of Carl Jung's named Henri Corbin, a twentieth-century theologian and professor whose specialty was Islamic mysticism. The imaginal, as opposed to the imaginary, is a reality accessed by radical self-emptying, by the vanishing of what Emerson calls "mean egotism." In this place, one has no knowledge, no power, no ability to stand whatsoever. Dynamism is its defining characteristic. It is the vibrational field where the singular heart and the universal Divine cooperate: the overlapping dimension of reality as we know it and eternity as we conceive it. It is *not* an idea. It is, as Magdalene scholar Cynthia Bourgeault writes, "a realm that objectively exists." To help us conceptualize it, she suggests "we think of it as an enveloping matrix of meaning *around* our own space-time dimension" (emphasis mine).

The imaginal is that which encases us: an enveloping matrix of meaning, a God Around. What this means is absolute inclusion. The organizational shift in perspective—in how we see—goes from hierarchy to *holarchy*: a system in which the individual parts are themselves whole and self-contained but are also integral to the larger network. God is no longer the top of the pyramid; God is the sphere that contains, holds, supports, and empowers all self-contained things. We are indeed part and particle of this all-encompassing God. Sue Monk Kidd summarizes it beautifully when she writes: "What we need to remember is that we are carried in God's womb, in God's divine heart, even when we don't know it, even when God seems far away. That's been my growing awareness," she shares. "First God was only 'up there.' Then God was 'all around.' Next I begin to see that God was also 'within me.' And now, most shocking of all, I was finding that I am and always was 'within God.'"

This has been the revelation of countless mystics, saints, clergy, and layfolk who have come before us, and it is our revelation now too.

As Rabbi Levi Yitzchak penned, and Rabbi Rami Shapiro collected for us in his anthology of perennial wisdom:

> Where can I find You,
> And where can I not find you?
> Above—only You;
> Below—only You;
> To the east—only You;
> To the west—only You;
> To the south—only You;
> To the north—only You;
> If it is good—it is You;
> If it is not—also You;
> It is You; It is only You.

ULTIMATE REALITY

Growing up, I heard my mother use the phrase *heart of hearts*. "You will know in your heart of hearts," she might say. Or "In her heart of hearts, she's not a bad person," she would remind us. The heart of hearts was the source of one's deepest knowing. It was the seat of integrity and the fount of wisdom.

In the Old Testament, the Greek word used to denote the heart of hearts was *nous*. The *nous* is what links our will to God's. When "strong and clear, [the nous] creates a synchronous resonance between the realms," writes Bourgeault. In order to be strong and clear, it has learned to practice nonduality and nonattachment. It does not rush to claim this over that, nor does it cling to this or that, because it understands that all is integrated. It holds the tension of opposites peaceably, rendering itself immune to the swings of moods and emotions. It understands that its purpose is to engender the interconnection that already exists.

Developing eyes to see is an exercise of the heart of the hearts. It is what moves us beyond the duality of self and other, including God, and enables us to experience firsthand that "uncontained and immortal beauty" that Emerson evokes.

Those who are called mystics make this move with admirable frequency. Those of us who are slowly, fitfully, developing eyes to see might catch a glimpse. We access it, if at all, only briefly. In visions. Intuitions. Revelations. Dreams. Deep meditative journeys. Supercharged flashes. Summit vistas. Thin places. Rock bottoms. Synchronicities. Sacrifices. Signs. Wrenching prayers. Near-deaths. Transparent eyeballness. Nonattachment. We access it by vesseling. Virgining. Prospecting. And bathing in the air ever so blithe.

There are so many portals to the imaginal. The actual direction we go to enter this realm is impossible to name. I have heard it described as sinking beneath our thoughts, which it is. I have heard it described as rising above our false self, which it is. I have heard it described as expanding outward, like water thinning on a flat surface, which it is. I have heard it described as an opening, which it is, and a distilling, which it is. It is all directions, as we now have language to fathom, to map, to encounter together.

We have explored myriad relationalities that characterize God's nature and behavior. We can fathom that God is above and beneath. We can intuit that God is near and with and alongside. We can believe that God is before and that God is for and that God is through, into, and within. We can discover that God is throughout and thereby also among and between. And ultimately, yes, we can come to recognize, and effectually *realize*, that God is around. We can grasp what Paul preaches to the Athenians when he says, in what I believe to be one of the most revealing and reassuring passages in all of Scripture:

> The God who made the world and everything in it, he who is Lord of heaven and earth, does not live in shrines made by human hands, nor is he served by human hands, as though he needed anything, since he himself gives to all mortals life and breath and all things. From one ancestor he made all peoples to inhabit the whole earth, and he allotted the times of their existence and the boundaries of the places where they would live, so that they would search for God and perhaps fumble about for him and find him—though indeed he is not far from each

> one of us. For 'In him we live and move and have our being'; as even some of your own poets have said. (Acts 17:24–28)

We seek God. We fumble around for God, only to discover that God is not far. God is, in fact, all around.

The revelation, and by extension the *invitation*, is for us to experience continuous union with God, which is already and always that in which we exist. An imaginal reality has become visible to us, and the result is that our heart of hearts has been activated. With it as our guide, we can come to know with assurance that the fullness of God is a state of unitive being available to us in the here and now.

Not merely *possibly* but *undeniably* and *essentially.* Not merely *peripherally* but *directly* and *actively.*

What is the takeaway of all of this revelation? What is it I need to remember?

Bourgeault tells us outright, and I thank her for it: "The point to keep uppermost in mind is that it designates [the imaginal] as a sphere that is not less real but *more* real than our so-called objective reality and whose generative energy can change the course of events in the world." In other words, the enveloping matrix of meaning—the multifaceted dynamism that we call "God"—is very much real. And not only that, it truly does interact with reality as we know it. It does interact with us, and we can in turn interact with it.

As Brother Carlo Carretto writes in his book *Letters from the Desert*: "What is our life on earth, if not discovering, becoming conscious of, penetrating, contemplating, accepting, loving this mystery of God's, the unique reality which surrounds us, and in which we are immersed like meteorites in space?"

We go about this discovering by using our heart of hearts, which is our God radar. Bourgeault calls it our "organ of spiritual perception"—our guide toward more truthful ways of seeing and being in the world. Hearkening to it, we live in the fullness of God. We find ourselves precisely where we have always been and will always be—within Ultimate Reality: the all-around, around-all I AM.

A PRAYER TO GOD AROUND

Holy Life-Giving and Sustaining Divine,
you are all around.
If we seek you, we will surely find you,
God, grant us eyes that see.

Holy Life-Giving and Sustaining Divine,
you are around all.
Your circle includes us.
Your arms embrace us.
Your being contains us.
God, help us grow our heart of hearts,
that we may know you as Home.

Amen.

CHAPTER FIFTEEN

Beyond

How great is God—beyond our understanding!

Job 36:26 NIV

Beyond the senses is the brain.
Beyond the brain is the intellect.
Beyond the intellect is the Great Atman.
Beyond the Great Atman is the Unmanifest Brahman.
Beyond the Unmanifest Brahman is the I,
all-pervading Subject impossible to objectify.

Katha Upanishad 2.3.7–8

We were, in some exquisite way, doomed to fail in this endeavor, this attempt to know God through a series of overlooked words. The exploring we have done in these pages has been illuminating. A preposition revolution may well be afoot!

And yet, in the end, prepositions—as revelatory as they are—also prove inadequate. This is because the tools we have used—words and thoughts, language and reason—prove unsuitable to the task. The Divine cannot be accessed in these modalities or any modalities. I am reminded of a verse by Rumi: "Define and narrow me, you starve yourself of yourself. Nail me down in a box of cold words, that box is your coffin."

God remains what God is: a Holy Mystery. A Beyond Almighty. And the only paths that can draw us near it are deep welling, patient abiding, sacramental living, grounding, bridge-building, vesseling, prospecting, homing—all the pursuits of the heart of hearts. The only guides that can take us there are faith and hope and love.

I first learned about these things—faith and hope and love—not from Jesus but from Dorothy. All in all, *The Wizard of Oz* terrified me. The ease with which a house could be lifted off the ground and battered about. The shoes shriveling grotesquely. The green face of that witch with her nasty cackle and her awful *I'll get you, my pretty*. Not to mention the flying monkeys. They are the stuff of nightmares. They *were* the stuff of nightmares. Why would I sit through such horror? The answer is Dorothy. I would sit through it for Dorothy.

The picture of innocence, Dorothy is nevertheless the bravest of them all. She stands down lions and witches and those creepy flying monkeys. She is the kindest of them all, agreeing to help others even though they slow her down with their fears and their trauma. And she proves the wisest of them all, pulling back the curtain on false idols and coming back to the core knowledge that of course there is no place like home, the very ground of our being, the very sphere enveloping us.

Throughout all these trials, Dorothy maintains the core things needed to survive and to prevail: faith and hope and love. She believes in some *Thing*, some *Place*, some *Force* that is beyond the pain and despair of this life. She doesn't find it in the Emerald City, epicenter of wealth, though countless people told her to look there. She doesn't find it in a projected image of God, booming insults and commands, though countless others mistake that smokescreen for truth. She doesn't even find it in quelling the enemy, though she had to do that in order to free all who were captive. Where she finds it is in a tune so spellbinding that she was compelled to follow it, a lullaby so endearing she knew it to be real and true from the very beginning. It might be what you sensed to be real and true from the beginning too, before you got lost on winding roads, mistaking the Emerald

City and the booming voice and assorted victories for the Divine. That lullaby speaks of a paradise, a God-place, that is—as we all know—somewhere over the rainbow, somewhere way up high, where dreams come true and troubles melt. It is somewhere high above the chimney tops, where the clouds are far behind. It is a haven of fulfillment, security, and peace: what many call heaven, what some call God's kingdom, what a scholarly few call imaginal space.

In Dorothy's song, God is not just *in* the land she dares to dream of; God *is* the land she dares to dream of. God is the Beyond: a vast and beautiful hopescape we intuit but cannot—on our own, with our typical tools of wayfinding—reach or in any way obtain. We recognize it as real only by our deep yearning for it. Sometimes the yearning feels like despair. Other times like hope. No matter the flavor, yearning is the click in the lock of the human condition. We sense that we are not whole, and yet we fathom that wholeness exists. In this knowledge, we despair and we hope. We toil and we tire. God Beyond both entices and eludes us. This is the only way. As Saint Augustine wrote: *Si comprehendus, non est Deus*. If you understand, it is not God.

For some spiritual seekers, the unknowability of God is the ultimate roadblock. For others, it is the proof in the pudding. Our nonunderstanding is not a sign that we are missing the point but rather a sign that we are quite on point. Encountering that which is unknowable and unnamable, we find ourselves treading lightly in the Divine.

To get at God, here now and always, we are asked to do that which is counterintuitive. We are asked to call off the search.

MYSTERY

I first heard that phrase, *Call off the search*, at a spiritual retreat I attended in Sewanee, Tennessee, in early March 2020, held by the One River Wisdom School. It was the suggestion of our ever-wise, ever-gentle leader, Gordon Peerman, whose work has helped illuminate the vivid intersections of Christianity and Buddhism and whose teaching has brought many seekers closer to their own souls.

It was midmorning, and our group of some forty-odd attendees was seated in a room with large glass windows that looked out over a valley we could not see because our eyes were closed. Our muscles were struggling to submit to gravity, our minds were struggling to lay to rest their compulsive efforts, our wills were struggling to allow their own banishment. So much hidden struggle in this room of otherwise quiet, still, closed-eyed people.

Gordon's voice is soft always, but when leading meditation, it is like dew. The words he spoke, once he had given us time to acclimate to a posture of meditation, were droplets of wisdom, beguilingly tender and simple.

Call off the search, he invited us. And then he extended us the gift of a long pause.

It is, after all, a mystery.

When I speak about the nature of my faith—which tends to eschew doctrine and adore the enigmatic; when I posit the notion of a multi-dimensional God that can be experienced directly and drenchingly; when I insist on the real possibility that we can all be "lay mystics"—people often point me in the direction of Buddhism. *Have you looked into Buddhism?* they'll ask, as if the God I am describing isn't the one I have built my faith on to date. It seems to some that I am barking up the wrong tree of enlightenment.

But when I look at Jesus, I see someone who is not so different than what I find when I look at Siddhartha. Each is en*light*ened, and each is en*live*ned. This, by saturation in Holy Mystery, for both of them.

If we are disciples of anything, it must be Mystery. This, because God is, inevitably and rightfully, beyond.

I attend church, yes. I attend church because the Holy Spirit inhabits the place inexorably. She swirls within the chalice of wine. She saturates the windows that centuries ago were stained to tell precious old stories of healing and welcome and resurrection. She weaves among the words of the liturgy and among the vibrations of the organ's pipes and among the voices of people, ages two to ninety-two, who sing hymns, their voices rising up from the generations past and the generations yet to come. It is a place steeped in Holy Mystery. One that reveres and honors God Beyond, even as it emphasizes God Among and Near and With.

There are aspects of church that do not resonate with me—even that flat offend me. Sometimes I find that I still cannot say certain words. There is one line, however, that I always say, a line that accompanies the preparation of the sacraments of bread and wine. I can hear the assembly of voices declaring it boldly and humbly, in unison, right now:

We proclaim the mystery of faith.

The church proclaims a lot. Especially these days, the "church" proclaims a lot. It holds Jesus captive and puts words in his mouth and in God's. It twists and manipulates—sometimes willfully, sometimes despite itself. It likes to proclaim what God does and doesn't like and *who* God does and doesn't like, regardless of the abundant evidence that *liking* is not the operating system of the Divine. Liking and disliking are what we do, not what God does. The *mystery of faith* is not convincingly, consistently at the core of many Christian proclamations.

And yet here it is, unabashedly: *We proclaim the mystery of faith.*

All of that yearning and searching, all of that prospecting and praying, all of that looking and pondering links up to form the outlines of faith that needs and has no defense of itself. Faith is less about holding fast to conviction and more about abiding in mystery. It is to hold out hope for that which is beyond our capacity to know, prove, or in any way control. *Christian* faith, in particular, invites us to abide in the mystery of Christ: an Incarnate God who lived and died and yet lived again and lives always. For us, the resurrection is, in the words of French theologian Jean-Yves LeLoup, "not merely an event of the past . . . but the imaginal, transhistorical symbol of all love." This is the *Christ* at the heart of hearts of our faiths: a self-perpetuating love lived out across directions and dimensions.

How it is real or possible is beyond us, which is the entire point. The truthful ways of seeing and being in the world that we have sought to learn reveal themselves to be channels of faith. Not a faith characterized by righteousness, clarity, or even conviction. Not a faith bound up in doctrine and creeds. But one characterized by and impelled by Holy Mystery.

UNBINDING

We are invited to call off the search. We are invited to wipe clean all our preconceived notions of who or what "God" is. We are invited to unbind ourselves from the word "God" itself. We are invited to unbind altogether.

Siddhartha left home questing "aging-less, illness-less, deathless, sorrow-less, undefiled, unexcelled rest [from] the yoke," as Thanissaro Bhikkhu's translation of the *Ariyapariyesana Sutta: The Noble Search* tells us. He undergoes an experience of profound and thorough *unbinding*. His enlightenment is the fullest expression of this unbinding.

Jesus calls this experience dying to live.

Any enlightenment that I or you may come to experience is a death, an unbinding, a way opening for rebirth, regardless of the teachings and religious systems that usher us here.

There is another lovely verse of Rumi's that I turn over in my mind like a smooth stone in my palm. It is this: *Out beyond ideas of wrongdoing and rightdoing, There is a field. I'll meet you there. When the soul lies down in that grass, The world is too full to talk about.* The field of which Rumi speaks—akin to the kingdom of which Christ speaks, akin to the land of which Dorothy sings—is beyond any idea of wrongdoing or rightdoing, beyond any notion of good or bad. It is beyond any notion of a him or a her, or of a you or a me. It is far beyond the word "or," being beyond opposites. It is beyond form itself, beyond constructs of any kind, beyond comprehension. It is a place of true nonduality, a place where no one thing is distinct but rather all is integrated. This field, this clearing, is divine oneness. The body cannot lie there, only the soul. And when it does, *the world is too full to talk about*. All that is: *is*. And God: God is not "a being but being in and beyond all beings," as the inestimable rabbi and mystic Abraham Joshua Heschel expresses.

Or, you might say, God is not so much a noun as a whole host of prepositions.

A PRAYER TO GOD BEYOND

Bless us, Almighty Mystery,
As we yearn for you.

Abide with us, Almighty Mystery,
as we call off the search.

Beyond all that we know is you.

Beyond all that is is you.

May we lie down, soul-bare, in the blithe air,
and unbind into the mystery of faith,
into that which is,
here,
and beyond.

Amen.

Epilogue

When I taught high school kids how to write essays, the closing paragraphs were always the hardest. The point had been made. The ideas had been exhausted. What more was needed?

"The conclusion is the place we offer a takeaway," I encouraged them. "It's where we answer the question 'So what?' or 'Now what'"?

Here we are, with those very questions in our laps.

So what? Now what?

The promise of these pages has been to illuminate God through overlooked words. Stealthy little things these prepositions have proven to be, and so adept at detailing God's indefatigable dynamism and fullness. They do their revealing in a subtle but thorough way. Prepositions are the most effective portals to the ineffable that I have found.

Journeying through fifteen of them, letting their mysteries and meanings become known to us, we can see a kind of blueprint of God's DNA: a detailed sketch of the very real and living workings of the Divine. And what we have discovered—what prepositional truth reveals for us—is the deep connection that God has with us, and the opportunity that we have in all times and in all places to activate that connection.

That is what this book is all about: being able to encounter the Divine more fully and more frequently.

As we cultivate an awareness of the Divine—whom we now know to be manifold, subtle, and agile, also keen, beneficent, and humane (Wisdom 7:22)—new dimensions of understanding open for us. I have found these new understandings to be so powerful as to be entirely faith-reorienting. At any given time, we might pause to consider where we intuit God to be. Drawing near to us in the quiet of the morning? Or watching over us from above? Or walking alongside us through a difficult passage? At any given time, we might ask God to assume a certain relationality that we feel like we need, or that someone else needs. Maybe we ask God to occupy the space between us and our spouse. Or we ask God to wrap arms around someone who is grieving.

When reading Scripture or holy texts of any kind, we might train ourselves to look between the primary words to the seemingly trivial ones that prove revealing: those little prepositions hiding in plain sight. Likewise, in our own theological reflections, we might shuffle through prepositions, like a kaleidoscope, noting how they change the colors and angles of things. The prayers that close each chapter are another beautiful way to begin to animate this awareness and experience of God.

To engage with the material more deeply, you can access a resource guide available online at www.varinabuntinwillse.com. For visual learners, the guide includes simple diagrams that illustrate the direction God is moving with each preposition. It also features key takeaways and a handful of questions for each chapter. You can use these questions as prompts for prayer, for journaling, or for contemplation as you drive to work or wander the vegetable aisle. You can use them as prompts for discussion, whether with a friend on a walk or in a Bible study or class or cohort of some kind. This is a wonderful book to bring into conversation with a group. We learn so much from listening, both to ourselves and to others.

Your answers to these questions may change over time or after listening to the stories and insights of other people. If this book has anything to reveal, it is that nothing is static. As I said in the introduction, my hope is that *Beneath and Between* might be evergreen, a place you can return to over and over again, one that offers up something new at each visit. In different seasons of our spiritual lives, one preposition about God may mean more to us than another.

Find what resonates today and also dip back in every now and then for fresh spiritual fodder and sustenance.

It is important to note, though, that the vision of God, as presented through the lens of these fifteen prepositions, is purposefully composite and whole. It is likely true that different denominations or churchly traditions or families or even personalities might lean into a particular preposition to the detriment of others. This proclivity merits our attention. If we *always* talk about God Above, what aspects of God's loving proximity do we miss? Or if I *only* relate to God Within, is it possible that I end up in a solipsistic faith? Reflecting on which prepositions resonate more for us than others might reveal something helpful about our faith tradition or our current stage in life. Likewise, taking into consideration the prepositions that don't click for us or that we actively resist might have valuable insights to yield also. My advice is to receive what arises on any given day while holding loosely to the whole.

So much of this experience for me was about becoming watchful. I learned to attend to God in new and generative ways. Discovering these prepositions, allowing each one to offer up their revelations and challenges, has revolutionized my faith. I know God to be electric and profound, persistent and so relentlessly loving.

There is a very real and present dimension awaiting us, a fullness begging to be experienced. Prepositions—those overlooked little words, so functional and stealthy—prove an invaluable resource for tapping into that dimension. And the way they just keep coming, popping up everywhere, more and more, with their singular wisdom?

Call it a frequency illusion if you like, but I think it's the Holy Spirit doing what she does best.

Acknowledgments

I have to start by acknowledging the Holy Spirit, which came through me on plenty of days when I myself had nothing to say—not to mention all the magic sprinkled, all the synchronicities orchestrated, all the guidance provided, all the comfort, joy, awe, mystery, and love bestowed. Thank you, Wild Divine. I'll do my best to keep my window, and my heart, ever open.

Before I get to all the beloved people who helped bring this book to fruition, I want to acknowledge the places that have shaped me from the outside in. These are places that have not only touched my soul but molded it: the farm, where all of it began and continues; the nave at Christ Church, with its dapple-colored splendor; the lake in CVX, source of decades of rejuvenation; Clifton, home to our holy and hot mess stage of life; and Sherwood, where my soul unfurls. May I also put in a word for trees, who are for me both balm and mentor. Thank you for all the oxygen and inspiration, old friends.

I am so profoundly grateful for my team, beginning with Don of Pape Commons. Thank you for seeing me as I most aspire to be: a slice of fresh bread. Being found by you was lottery-winning. Valerie, my world changed when you believed in this book. Your attentive eye, thoughtful criticism, and hard-won wisdom have elevated everything about this project. Thank you. To the entire team at Broadleaf, thank you for all your efforts to spread the prepositions near and far. It is an honor to be on your author roster. Ami and Shannon, I would not have had a proposal if it weren't for you. And Julian, you set this whole thing in motion. I am forever indebted.

To my spiritual teachers—Timothy, Lissa, Madeline, Betsy, Gordon—and the entire community at Christ Church Cathedral, worshiping with you has opened so many pathways. To my writing teachers throughout the decades, some of whom are now reading all the books they want in paradise: Beverly Roberts, Margaret Burnett, Margaret Renkl, Diann Shoaf, Joel Williamson, Hermione Lee, Myra McLarey, and John Edgerton. And to the giants on whose shoulders I stand: poets, prophets, mystics, seers, and writers through the ages. You know who you are because you are quoted throughout this book. Thank you for informing the faith of so many, me included. A special thanks to Rabbi Rami Shapiro for his much-cited anthology of sacred teachings.

Tribe, my heart swells when I think of you (in absolutely no particular order): Liz, Lena, Eva, Mary, Molly, Tiffany, Kemp, Rory, Mary, Laura, Caroline, Blaire, Holly, Lettie, Kim, Caroline, Devereux, MC and those I fear I am forgetting—thank you for listening, reading, encouraging, supporting, loving. You are a power *for* posse. Your friendship carries me.

To Frazer and Jeffrey, we share so many layers of story, of meaning, of life and death, that it overwhelms me. Suffice to say: "I like you; I love you."

Pop Pop. I told you, in that sacred time, that I would miss you when I went on book tour, even though I had no book deal, no agent, no reason to believe all this might happen. Perhaps you have been pulling strings? I do—miss you—acutely, even while I know you are here, in the audience, cheering me on, as you always did. I also know that you are walking the fields and woods, resolved back, fully unbound, at peace and free. Thank you, for everything.

Readers, you have met my mom often in these pages. She is even more incredible in person. VV, I have biggest loves for you.

My girls: Mary Varina, Pierson, and Campbell. Being your mom has transformed my understanding of what God is and what God does and what God feels, and how God loves, which is to say: Being your mom has transformed everything. Your lives are blessings beyond words. Your lights, they shine.

Walker: this loving of ours, it makes everything possible. Thank you for taking all those dirty plates to the kitchen. Thank you for bringing all those feathers home. Thank you for believing in me, as I believe in you.

To anyone reading: you and I, we share an uncommon intimacy. We are strangers, letting each other in. Let's keep doing more of that in this world. Thank you for coming alongside me.

Permissions

Notes

INTRODUCTION

6 ***"Western Christian patriarchal boxes":*** Sue Monk Kidd, *The Dance of the Dissident Daughter: A Woman's Journey from Christian Tradition to the Sacred Feminine* (HarperOne, 2016), p. 113.

10 ***"heartbroken Christians":*** Cynthia Bourgeault, *The Meaning of Mary Magdalene: Discovering the Woman at the Heart of Christianity* (Shambhala, 2010), p. 188.

10 ***our language about Jesus:*** Diana Butler Bass, *Freeing Jesus: Rediscovering Jesus as Friend, Teacher, Savior, Lord, Way, and Presence* (HarperOne, 2021), p. XXI.

12 ***God* for *us, God* alongside *us:*** Richard Rohr, "A Trinitarian Universe." Center for Action and Contemplation, December 15, 2022. https://cac.org/daily-meditations/a-trinitarian-universe-2022-12-15.

CHAPTER ONE: ABOVE

19 ***"He is Allah":*** "Surah Al-Hashr-23." Quran.com, 2025. https://quran.com/al-hashr/23.

22 ***As American professor of mythology Joseph Campbell notes:*** Joseph Campbell, *Goddesses: Mysteries of the Feminine Divine*, ed. Safron Rossi (New World Library, 2013), p. 60.

22 ***The Divine, whether Greek:*** Campbell, *Goddesses*, pp. 60, 34.

25 ***"The Holy Ghost over the bent":*** Gerard Manley Hopkins, "God's Grandeur," in *Gerard Manley Hopkins: Poems and Prose* (Penguin Classics, 1985), p. 27.

CHAPTER TWO: BENEATH

33 ***"Gaia / mother of all":*** Andrew Harvey, ed., *The Essential Mystics: Selections from the World's Great Wisdom Traditions* (HarperSanFrancisco, 1996), pp. 112–13.

37 ***"Please help me to get down under":*** Flannery O'Connor, *A Prayer Journal* (Farrar, Straus and Giroux, 2013), p. 4.

38 ***"there lives the dearest freshness":*** Hopkins, "God's Grandeur," p. 27.

39 ***"From the great heaven":*** *The ETCSL Project*, Faculty of Oriental Studies, University of Oxford, Updated December 12, 2006 by JE. https://etcsl.orinst.ox.ac.uk/cgi-bin/etcsl.cgi?text=t.1.4.1# August 2027.

40 ***"[God] is [the] Ground":*** Julian of Norwich, *Revelations of Divine Love*, trans. Grace Warrack (Christian Classics Ethereal Library, 2009), p. 134.

40 ***"All the ways you imagine us":*** Richard Powers, *The Overstory: A Novel* (W. W. Norton, 2019), pp. 3–4.

41 ***"If one has the root stock":*** Clarissa Pinkola Estes, *Women Who Run with the Wolves: Myths and Stories of the Wild Woman Archetype* (Ballantine, Books, 1995), p. 32.

41 ***We tune in:*** Estes, *Women Who Run with the Wolves*, p. 4.

42 ***"If your mind were only a slightly greener thing":*** Powers, *The Overstory*, pp. 3–4.

43 ***Their message, when received:*** Mary Oliver, *Devotions: The Selected Poems of Mary Oliver* (Generic, 2017), p. 86.

43 ***"She had once believed":*** Lauren Groff, *The Vaster Wilds* (Riverhead Books, 2023), p. 244.

44 ***"Jesus is not far away in the sky, but here":*** Bass, *Freeing Jesus*, pp. 249–51.

44 ***Tillich resisted the notion of God:*** Paul Tillich, *Ground of Being: Neglected Essays of Paul Tillich*, ed. Robert M. Price (Mindvendor, 2015).

45 ***"The sublime, inner essences":*** Harvey, *The Essential Mystics*, p. 102–3.

46 ***"ordinariness, heaviness, weightiness, and soberness":*** Robert Bly, *Iron John: A Book About Men* (Hachette Books, 2020), p. 73.

46 ***It is what deepens our ability to understand:*** Bly, *Iron John*, p. 96.

47 ***"down there . . . which is holding me in":*** O'Connor, *Prayer Journal*, p. 15.

47 ***"where the dark wound, and the most powerful yearnings live":*** David Brooks, *The Second Mountain: The Quest for a Moral Life* (Random House, 2019), p. xii.

48 ***"To put it another way":*** Cynthia Bourgeault, *The Wisdom Jesus: Transforming Heart and Mind—a New Perspective on Christ and His Message* (Shambhala, 2008), p. 64.

CHAPTER THREE: NEAR

51 ***"I have a capacity in my soul":*** Meister Eckhart, "The Nearness of the Kingdom." *Meister Eckhart's Sermons*, ed. Johannes Eckhart. Christian Classics Ethereal Library, June 10, 2025. https://ccel.org/ccel/eckhart/sermons/sermons.

51 ***"the nearness of you":*** "The Nearness of You," by Hoagy Carmichael and Ned Washington, 1937; track 14 of *Come Away with Me*, 2002, by Norah Jones, produced by Blue Note Records.

57 ***"the weight of your aloneness":*** David Whyte, *Essentials* (Many Rivers Press, 2020), p. 84.

58 ***"exactly what a prayer is":*** Oliver, *Devotions*, p. 316.

58 ***when the world is too much with me:*** William Wordsworth, "The World Is Too Much with Us." Poetry Foundation, August 1, 2024. www.poetryfoundation.org/poems/45564/the-world-is-too-much-with-us.

CHAPTER FOUR: WITH

67 ***"We call upon all":*** Harvey, *The Essential Mystics*, p. 5.

75 ***"God dwelling with the world":*** Bass, *Freeing Jesus*, p. 223.

76 ***"God is with me":*** Howard Thurman, *Meditations of the Heart* (Beacon Press, 2022), pp. 27–8.

79 ***"The ultimate touchstone of friendship":*** David Whyte, *Consolations: The Solace, Nourishment and Underlying Meaning of Everyday Words* (Many Rivers Press, 2021), p. 54.

CHAPTER FIVE: ALONGSIDE

89 ***"How did we ever get the idea":*** Sue Monk Kidd, *When the Heart Waits: Spiritual Direction for Life's Sacred Questions* (HarperOne, 2006), p. 28.

90 ***"I understand Jesus as God alongside us":*** Rohr, "A Trinitarian Universe."

92 ***"Every temptation that comes to us He has felt":*** *S.D. Gordon, "Quiet Talks on Service," May 2023.* https://biblehub.com/library/gordon/quiet_talks_on_service/yoked_service.htm.

CHAPTER SIX: BEFORE

97 ***"Before time—I am":*** Rami Shapiro, ed., *The Divine Feminine in Biblical Wisdom Literature: Selections Annotated & Explained* (Skylight Paths, 2014), p. 3.

97 ***"born before heaven and earth":*** Harvey, *The Essential Mystics*, p. 22.

98 ***"God is the beginninglessly pre-eternal":*** Al-Ghazali, *Ghazali on the Principles of Islamic Spirituality: Selections from the Forty Foundations of Religion.* Quoted in Rami Shapiro, ed., *Perennial Wisdom for the Spiritually Independent: Sacred Teachings—Annotated & Explained* (Skylight Paths, 2013), p. 89.

98 ***"I sit at the moon-filled window":*** Harvey, *The Essential Mystics*, p. 85.

100 ***"So deep! It seems to be the source of all things":*** Shapiro, *Perennial Wisdom*, p. 79.

100 ***"Know that my Superior Nature is the very Life":*** Shapiro, *Perennial Wisdom*, p. 63.

103 ***"having been is the surest kind of being":*** Victor E. Frankl, *Man's Search for Meaning* (Beacon Press, 2006), p. 121.

CHAPTER SEVEN: FOR

111 ***"Everything is laid out for you":*** Harvey, *The Essential Mystics*, p. 6.
113 ***"God, like a good father, is for us":*** Rohr, "Trinitarian Universe."

CHAPTER EIGHT: THROUGH

125 ***"Christ has no body now but yours":*** Harvey, *The Essential Mystics*, p. 206.
126 ***"are always and forever merely seconding the motion":*** Richard Rohr, *The Naked Now: Learning to See as the Mystics See* (Crossroad, 2009), p. 23.
127 ***"We do not pray to Christ":*** Rohr, *Naked Now*, p. 23.
127 ***"Those who are free from selfish attachments":*** Harvey, *The Essential Mystics*, p. 43.
131 ***"recognize religious concepts as symbolic":*** Esther Harding, *Woman's Mysteries Ancient and Modern* (Longmans, Green, 1935), pp. 77–79.
135 ***"the pain we encounter in confronting our lives honestly":*** Kidd, *The Heart Waits*, p. 167.
136 ***"The universe is a procession":*** Walt Whitman, "I Sing the Body Electric." *Poetry Foundation*. www.poetryfoundation.org/poems/45472/i-sing-the-body-electric June 11, 2025.
136 ***"Let it do with you and lead you as it will":*** *The Cloud of Unknowing*. The Classics of Western Spirituality, edited by James Walsh (Paulist Press, 1981), p. 185.

CHAPTER NINE: INTO

139 ***"Out of himself he brought forth the cosmos":*** Harvey, *The Essential Mystics*, p. 39.
142 ***Scientists have extrapolated:*** Alice Harvey and Charles Q. Choi, "Our Expanding Universe: Age, History & Other Facts." *Space.com*, March 15, 2022.
142 ***"Everything that exists in material form":*** Richard Rohr, "The First Incarnation." *Center for Contemplation and Action*, December 18, 2022. https://cac.org/daily-meditations/the-first-incarnation-2022-12-18.
144 ***"a portrait of a patient God":*** Kidd, *The Heart Waits*, p. 30.
144 ***a God that "somehow poured itself into":*** Adapted from Richard Rohr, *The Universal Christ: How a Forgotten Reality Can Change Everything We See, Hope for, and Believe* (Convergent, 2019), pp. 12–13.

145 ***"God loves things by becoming them":*** Rohr, *The Universal Christ*, pp. 16.

145 ***Delio argues against seeing God:*** Ilia Delio, *The Unbearable Wholeness of Being: God, Evolution, and the Power of Love* (Orbis Books, 2013), pp. 74–7.

148 ***The word* baptism *derives from:*** Richard Rohr, "You Must Start with Something Positive." *Center for Contemplation and Action*, January 11, 2015, https://cac.org/podcasts/feast-of-the-baptism-of-jesusyou-must-start-with-something-positive.

CHAPTER TEN: WITHIN

153 ***"I know the Immovable comes down":*** Harvey, *The Essential Mystics*, p. 190.

154 ***notion of sin as somehow original:*** Daniel Patte, "Original Sin," in Daniel Patte, ed., *The Cambridge Dictionary of Christianity, Two Volume Set* (Wipf and Stock, 2019), p. 83.

156 ***"All of nature with its forms":*** Bourgeault, *The Meaning of Mary Magdalene*, p. 46.

157 ***"It is for this very reason that the Good has come":*** Bourgeault, *The Meaning of Mary Magdalene*, p. 46.

157 ***"important integrative work":*** Bourgeault, *The Meaning of Mary Magdalene*, p. 49.

158 ***"It is for this reason," Jesus continues:*** Bourgeault, *The Meaning of Mary Magdalene*, p. 46.

159 ***"I, a frail, small mortal in the world":*** Harvey, *The Essential Mystics*, p. 190.

159 ***"there is something in the soul that is so akin to God":*** Meister Eckhart, *Meister Eckhart: An Introduction to the Study of His Works, with an Anthology of His Sermons* (Thompson, Nelson & Sons, 1957).

159 ***"deep within us all there is an amazing inner sanctuary":*** Thomas R. Kelly, *A Testament of Devotion* (Harper & Brothers, 1941), p. 29.

159 ***"There is a spirit in every human":*** Joy Harjo, *Crazy Brave: A Memoir* (W. W. Norton, 2012), p. 59.

159 ***"The Divine Indwelling is central":*** Rohr, "A Trinitarian Universe."

159 ***"He who begins by seeking God within himself":*** Benjamin B. Warfield, "Mysticism and Christianity." *The Works of Benjamin B. Warfield, vol. 9* (Baker Book House, 1991), pp. 649–66.

161 ***"for Him to come and dwell in [us]":*** Thurman, *Meditations of the Heart*, p. 8.

162 ***"We are all mothers of the Buddha":*** Thich Nhat Hanh, *Living Buddha, Living Christ* (Riverhead Books, 2007), p. 40.

163 ***"the fluid area of consent":*** Thurman, *Meditations of the Heart*, p. 2.

163 ***"I found god in myself":*** Ntozake Shange, *Colored Girls Who Have Considered Suicide When the Rainbow Is Enuf* (Bantam Books, 1980), p. 63.

CHAPTER ELEVEN: THROUGHOUT

165 ***"O Almighty God! I see in You the powers of Nature":*** Shapiro, *Perennial Wisdom*, p. 69.

166 ***"more truthful ways of seeing and being in the world":*** Parker J. Palmer, *The Courage to Teach: Exploring the Inner Landscape of a Teacher's Life* (Jossey Bass, 1998), p. 6.

169 ***"God is one, hidden in all beings":*** Shapiro, *Perennial Wisdom*, p. 105.

169 ***"Let it observe how the Soul flows":*** Harvey, *The Essential Mystics*, p. 133.

169 ***"To Allah belong the East and the West":*** Harvey, *The Essential Mystics*, p. 139.

169 ***"The whole world is pervaded by Me":*** Shapiro, *Perennial Wisdom*, p. 65.

170 ***"God co-inheres and interpenetrates everything":*** Cynthia Bourgeault, "Oneness: The Secret Embrace," in *Thomas Keating's The Secret Embrace* (2020). www.spiritualityandpractice.com/ecourses/course/view/10274/thomas-keatings-the-secret-embrace.

171 ***"The true doctrine of omnipresence":*** Ralph Waldo Emerson, "Compensation," in *Essays: First Series* (1841).

172 ***"How public—like a Frog":*** Ralph W. Franklin, ed., *The Poems of Emily Dickinson* (Belknap Press of Harvard University Press, 1998), Poem #260.

175 ***"Awe is a sense for the transcendence":*** Abraham Joshua Heschel, *I Asked for Wonder: A Spiritual Anthology*, ed. Samuel H. Dresner (Crossroad, 1992), p. 3.

176 ***The ordinary becomes a liturgy:*** Tish Warren Harrison, *The Liturgy of the Ordinary* (InterVarsity Press, 2019).

177 ***"savor the ineffable":*** Harvey, *The Essential Mystics*, p. 32.

177 ***"The real voyage of discovery consists":*** Marcel Proust, "Remembrance of Things Past," in *La Prisonniere* (1923).

CHAPTER TWELVE: AMONG

179 ***"That which makes of God a human being":*** Shapiro, *Perennial Wisdom*, p. 239.

189 ***"that the reign of God is among us":*** Delio, *Unbearable Wholeness of Being*, pp. 83–4.

CHAPTER THIRTEEN: BETWEEN

191 ***"I may never have full rest":*** Julian of Norwich, *Revelations of Divine Love*, p. 5.

192 ***"the period* separating *(two points in time)":*** "Between," bab.la (IDM 2025), https://en.bab.la/dictionary/english/between#google_vignette.

192 ***"inescapable network of mutuality":*** Martin Luther King Jr., "Letter from Birmingham Jail" (Penguin Classics, 2018), pp. 85–6.
194 ***"a gel-like reticulum":*** Virginia Huxley, Ronald Korthuis, and Joshua Scallan, "The Interstitium." *Capillary Fluid Exchange: Regulation, Functions, and Pathology.* National Library of Medicine (Morgan & Claypool Life Sciences, 2010). www.ncbi.nlm.nih.gov/books/NBK53447.
202 ***"let your life speak":*** Parker J. Palmer, *Let Your Life Speak* (Jossey-Bass, 2000), p. 2.
203 ***"God can again use liminality to transform":*** Thomas J. Rundel, "Liminal Spaces: A Narrative Spirituality of the Bible" (2015). *Doctor of Ministry.* 109. https://digitalcommons.georgefox.edu/dmin/109.
203 ***"two great mysteries, which are yet one":*** Carl Jung, *Selected Letters, 1909–1961*, ed. Gerhard Adler (Princeton University Press, 1984), p. 77.

CHAPTER FOURTEEN: AROUND

205 ***"This entire universe is enveloped":*** https://www.bhagavadgitaforall.com/verses/9-4 (Faith Tech Labs 2025).
209 ***"more spiral, circle, and flow than pyramid":*** CAC. https://cac.org/daily-meditations/the-circle-dance-of-god-2022-03-16.
210 ***"the currents of the Universal Being circulate through me":*** Ralph Waldo Emerson, "Nature," in *The Complete Works of Ralph Waldo Emerson: Nature Addresses and Lectures*, vol. 1, p. 10.
210 ***"God is everything":*** Alice Walker, *The Color Purple* (Penguin Book, 2019), p. 194.
212 ***"a round nothingness":*** Kathleen Martin, ed., *The Book of Symbols: Reflections on Archetypal Images* (Taschen, 2010), p. 52.
213 ***"First God was only 'up there'":*** Kidd, *The Heart Waits*, pp. 149–150.
214 ***"It is only You":*** Shapiro, *Perennial Wisdom*, p. 107.
214 ***"[the nous] creates a synchronous resonance between the realms":*** Bourgeault, *The Meaning of Mary Magdalene*, p. 51.
216 ***"whose generative energy can change the course of events":*** Bourgeault, *The Meaning of Mary Magdalene*, p. 166.
216 ***"What is our life on earth, if not discovering":*** Carlo Carretto, *Letters from the Desert* (Orbis Books, 2002), pp. 127–8.
216 ***"organ of spiritual perception":*** Bourgeault, *The Meaning of Mary Magdalene*, p. 51.

CHAPTER FIFTEEN: BEYOND

219 ***"Beyond the senses is the brain":*** Shapiro, *Perennial Wisdom*, p. 53.
219 ***"that box is your coffin":*** Harvey, *The Essential Mystics*, p. 155.

221 ***If you understand, it is not God:*** St Augustine, "Sermon 117." *Patrologia Latina* (PL), vol. 38, pp. 661–71.
223 ***"imaginal, transhistorical symbol of all love":*** Jean-Yves LeLoup, *The Gospel of Mary Magdalene* (Inner Traditions, 2002), pp. 128–9.
224 ***profound and thorough* unbinding:** Thanissaro Bhikkhu, trans., *Ariyapariyesana Sutta: The Noble Search, Translated from the Pali* (Creative Commons, 2004). www.accesstoinsight.org/tipitaka/mn/mn.026.than.html, August 2025.
224 ***"Out beyond ideas of wrongdoing":*** Coleman Barks and John Moyne, trans., *The Essential Rumi* (HarperCollins, 1995), p. 36.
225 ***"being in and beyond all beings":*** Heschel, *I Asked for Wonder*, p. 8.